A Curriculum of

REPRESSION

Studies in the
Postmodern Theory of Education

Joe L. Kincheloe and Shirley R. Steinberg
General Editors

Vol. 208

PETER LANG
New York • Washington, D.C./Baltimore • Bern
Frankfurt am Main • Berlin • Brussels • Vienna • Oxford

HAROON KHAREM

A Curriculum of

REPRESSION

A Pedagogy of Racial History in the United States

PETER LANG
New York • Washington, D.C./Baltimore • Bern
Frankfurt am Main • Berlin • Brussels • Vienna • Oxford

Library of Congress Cataloging-in-Publication Data

Kharem, Haroon.
A curriculum of repression: a pedagogy of racial history
in the United States / Haroon Kharem.
p. cm. — (Counterpoints: studies in the postmodern theory of education; v. 208)
Includes bibliographical references and index.
1. African Americans—Education—History. 2. Discrimination in
education—United States. 3. United States—Race relations. 4. Whites—
Race identity—United States. I. Title. II. Series:
Counterpoints (New York, N.Y.); v. 208.
LC2741.K53   375'.006—dc22   2005002296
ISBN 0-8204-5663-2
ISSN 1058-1634

Bibliographic information published by **Die Deutsche Bibliothek**.
Die Deutsche Bibliothek lists this publication in the "Deutsche
Nationalbibliografie"; detailed bibliographic data is available
on the Internet at http://dnb.ddb.de/.

Cover design by Lisa Barfield

The paper in this book meets the guidelines for permanence and durability
of the Committee on Production Guidelines for Book Longevity
of the Council of Library Resources.

© 2006 Peter Lang Publishing, Inc., New York
29 Broadway, New York, NY 10006
www.peterlang.com

Printed in the United States of America

CONTENTS

ACKNOWLEDGEMENTS

Like any subject matter, this book has been the outcome of studying the struggles and history of Black people in America. My mother use to always ask why do White people eschew Black people and think we are inferior to them. My Dad taught me at a young age to question what was being taught to me. As a child this constant cause to inquire proved vexing for my teachers and annoyed my friends. When I entered the wider world of academics and life, my parent's training served me well. The writings of Malcolm X, John Henrik Clarke, Vincent Harding and a series of other scholars gave me the clarity that set me on a lifelong journey to seek out the answers. I am grateful to those who have journeyed before me and provided the signs for me to follow in my quest to find truth.

First I would like to thank my mother for teaching me about life and my father who taught me as a child to never give allegiance to those who have historically oppressed your people. I am grateful to Wilson Moses who mentored me in the study of history, Joe Kincheloe and Shirley Steinberg for mentoring, letting me write "what I like," reading everything I wrote and encouraged me to continue to press the envelope. I want to thank Frances Rains and Lourdes Diaz Soto also for their advice during my graduate studies at the Pennsylvania State University. I thank my children for their patience and Audrey who encouraged me when this project was just a faint idea over 10 years ago. I want to thank the African and African American Studies Department at the Pennsylvania State University for giving me the opportunity to teach and the students who took my classes. I am forever grateful to the librarians at the Pennsylvania State University for their assistance during my research. I appreciate the continual support and encouragement you give Theresa and for reading my manuscript. I want to thank all the others whose names are too numerous to list for all the assistance, advise and encouragement you gave.

I give thanks to all the Black people who survived the Middle Passage, who prayed and looked ahead for a time when there would be no more chains. I am the result of those prayers and I owe my freedom and this book to them. I am indebted to my ancestor's resistance.

CHAPTER ONE

INTRODUCTION

The most formidable of all the ills which threaten the future existence of the Union arises from the presence of a black population upon its territory; and in contemplating the cause of the present embarrassments or of the future dangers of the United States, the observer is invariably led to consider this a primary fact.

Alexis de Tocqueville, 1835

The Civil Rights Movement was not a struggle by blacks just to achieve full voting rights, to have the same social and economic opportunities as white people; it was a fight against white supremacy and its ideological and physical system of apartheid ingrained and interwoven in American society since the Jamestown colony and the landing at Plymouth Rock. White supremacy involves much more than a few hooded men riding around in the dark terrorizing black people or some fringe right wing group promoting the purity of the Anglo/Nordic race marketing hate and exclusion. Rather, it is a social and legal construction, a discourse and system of ideas that denigrates and exploits the people it relegates to the margins of society. White supremacy is also a "way of seeing" espoused by the intelligentsia and spurious intellectuals—their theories, in turn, are transformed into public policy with the help of their political and civil service sympathizers. It affirms white people as being genetically superior and privileged, thus inheriting the right to claim the lion's share of the world's resources and to dehumanize others within a system of economic domination and exploitation. This ideology creates social distinctions based on physical characteristics and ancestry, finding evidence of congenital inferiority in what are, in fact, the debilitative consequences of the historical disfranchisement of citizenship imposed by the dominant culture. In sum, white supremacy underlies the socioeconomic foundations of the United States benefiting the dominant white population. It rationalizes racial segregation, poverty, unemployment and even homelessness through supposed genetic superiority, capitalism, and the cultural institutions of Anglo-Protestantism and its work ethic, which epitomizes its values and virtues (Higginbotham, 1978; Zinn, 1995; Haney Lopez, 1996; Munford, 1996; Wilson, 1996; Joshi, 1999; Smedley, 1999).

The agenda of white supremacy in the United States has never changed. Rather than disappearing as some claim it is doing, it altered its strategy, hiding itself in neoconservatism and liberalism, encouraging many to believe racism and inequality have been reduced to just class conflicts or to some extreme right wing organizations. More importantly, while it no longer requires overt physical force (although it still resorts to violence on occasion, as in the lynching of James Bryd Jr. near Jasper, Texas, in 1998) as it did in the past as recorded in Ida B. Wells Barnett's *On Lynching* (1892), Ralph Ginsberg's *One Hundred Years of Lynching* (1962), Donald Nieman's *Black Freedom/White Violence, 1865–1900* (1994), James Allen's *Without Sanctuary* (2000), and Philip Dray's *At the Hands of Person's Unknown: The Lynching of Black America* (2002) to manifest its presence (Klinker, 1999; Omi and Winant, 1994). Today, white supremacy has rearticulated itself by consolidating its power through an elaborate system of cultural beliefs, ideas, and practices upon society through the academy, the media, religion, traditional myths, the political system, and public education (Ani, 1994; Macedo, 1994 & 1999; Munford, 1996; Wilson, 1996; Yeo, 1997).

Southern whites were not the only ones maintaining white supremacist attitudes and public policies, as some want to believe; most Northern whites (where Jim Crow practices first originated under the name of Black Codes) exhibited their abhorrence of black people more than Southern whites. While Northern slavery was not the same as in the South, the same strict slave codes were passed for the purpose of social control. Northern white hostility toward black slaves had very little to do with the hatred of the institution of slavery; the hostility came from the physical differences, inferiority beliefs, presented a social danger if allowed to integrate with whites (Jordan, 1968; Litwack, 1961). Slave owners hiring out their slaves as skilled or unskilled laborers threaten the employment of white laborers. Many whites refused to work alongside enslaved or free blacks and rioted to impose their will (Greene, 1942; Roediger, 1991). Northern whites argued and believed that blacks were savages, inferior, unclean, and prone to criminal activity, violent, sexual deviants incapable of self control, therefore were a threat to society. When slavery ended in the North, whites became even more apprehensive of their jobs, integration and miscegenation and forced black people into dilapidated segregated communities, segregated blacks in public spaces and schools if education was available. Blacks were forced to sit in segregated church pews and endured other numerous Black Codes (Berwanger, 1967; Fredrickson, 1971; Litwack, 1961; McIntyre, 1984; Ratner, 1968). Many Northern states enacted laws that required black people to leave the state once emancipated. Race riots were also a problem in Northern urban centers as whites expressed their dislike for blacks and their fear of miscegenation and these beliefs still exist today (Berwanger, 1967; Lipsitz, 1998; Litwack, 1961; Reider, 1985; Richards, 1970).

Northern whites also resorted to violence to maintain their white spaces (Klinker, 1999; Litwack, 1961; Massey & Denton, 1993). Since the existence of the English colony of Virginia in the 1600s to the Civil Rights Movement of the 1960s, non-white people have been blatantly excluded from political participation in many parts of this nation (Berry, 1971; Higginbotham, 1978; Klinker, 1999; Litwack, 1961; Logan, 1954). White supremacy supports a specific power structure ensuring its socioeconomic privilege, the norms for distribution of material wealth, educational, and employment opportunities, and societal benefits (Ani, 1994; Munford, 1996). The ideology projects its dominance through media perceptions and cultural images of morality and rationality, while portraying people of color as immoral, lazy, undeserving, sensual, oversexed, irrational, prone to crime, and not worth educating (Carspecken, 1996; Gray, 1995; Hall, 1997; Jewell, 1993; King, 1996; Quadagno, 1994; Semali, 1996).

Educational institutions historically have been used and still are employed by advocates of white supremacist ideology to transmit their culture of dominance by turning schools into agents of white supremacist culture to preserve their ideological hegemony. The dominant white culture uses education as a vehicle to determine and influence what values and social patterns society will follow. Mwalimu J. Shujaa clearly states in his essay "Education and Schooling: You Can Have One without the "other" (1994) that:

> [t]he maintenance of the social order depends upon the development of this pattern of thinking among some of society's members. It is one of schooling's functions to facilitate the "selection" of individuals to occupy low-status, but necessary, roles in the society. What better way to accomplish this selection process than to imbue some members with the idea that they (or their group) are unworthy or unprepared for the quality of life they see enjoyed by others (pp. 19–20).

Schools and other cultural institutions select, preserve, and distribute ideas of the dominant white elite as seen in their quest to control knowledge and true transformation in our society. The dominant society constructs opinions that make nonwhite people feel there is something wrong with them. Shujaa argues instead of educational programs focusing upon ways to "de-legitimize" the existing social order which maintains the racial, social and economic inequities, educational support programs for nonwhites are created and focused to "fix the things that are" allegedly "wrong with us" as people who are purportedly intellectually deficient to make us "internalize" the typical labels placed upon us, such as "at-risk" and accept our supposed lack of achievement skills (p. 20). Instead of changing the social, economic and educational inequities as the problems in our society, society continue to label black and other nonwhite students as deficient in intellectual abilities and provide funding for educational support programs at the college level that address alleged deficient academic skills of black and other nonwhite students.

Historically, the cultural images of nonwhites as savages, prone to violence and crime, animalistic, subhuman, hypersexual, and of inferior intelligence have confirmed in the minds of many whites they have the right to treat nonwhites as the "other" (Bates, 1975; Kozol, 1991; Macedo, 1994; Miller, 1996; Pieterse, 1992; Pinar, 1995; Shujaa, 1994; Spring, 1997). Cultural images created from the seventeenth into the twentieth century have done so much damage that some teachers still believe these demeaning cultural images, which illustrates to us how much white supremacist ideology still influence our society (Kozol, 1991; Macedo, 1994 & 1999; Ferguson, 2000;

Feagin and O'Brien, 2003). Also, social studies textbooks are worded in ways to cultivate the mind with a false consciousness so they cannot recognize social injustice (Freire, 1985). Textbook knowledge is homogenized and provides teachers with questions for students that functions to intellectually suppress students from critically examining the text, which in turn provide society with dependable citizens from subjugated groups. It is very important for the dominant society to continue structuring schools and the curriculum to domesticate the mind and make it a blank space to receive only predetermined knowledge that is chosen by those who benefit from the status quo (Freire, 1985; Loewen, 1995; Macedo, 1994; Spring, 1994). Teachers, educators, and curriculum developers thus need to begin to question not only the contents of the school curriculum, but also public policies and the latent factors that maintain the dominant culture in schools. Teachers can question curricula which do not allow them to teach in ways where students can have access to knowledge that frees them to question the inequalities in society and encourages them to engage in critical reflection. More importantly, they will understand and act upon the pervasiveness of the curriculum as a servant of conservative interests to homogenize society (Apple, 1988 & 1990).

We need to examine the pedagogy of white supremacy in the United States. Specifically, we need to investigate the origins of white supremacy in America, why it was formulated into an ideology to preserve white Anglo Protestant culture and how it was taught to American society. We also need to examine the aims and the objectives of several white supremacist movements. This study will look at the ideological foundations and perspectives of the first white supremacist organization in the United States, the American Colonization Society, and its supporters. Related issues such as the eugenics movement and the way it promoted and influenced educational and congressional public policies to benefit white supremacy. More importantly, this work will show how public schools operate as an agency of white supremacy. White supremacist ideology has historically used education to instill children with the idea Americans are on a sacred mission to evangelize the world and economically control its resources, as the heirs of the ancient Israelites' role as God's chosen people. This racial superiority is firmly entrenched in the minds of some white Americans who have been imbued to believe the Judeo-Christian God has instilled in them special capabilities for liberty (Bercovitch, 1975; Horseman, 1981).

This study hopefully will show not only how the white elite founded and used the American Colonization Society, supported the eugenic movement and the theory of psychometrics to uphold white supremacy, and established a system of racial apartheid, but also how it maintains its cultural, political, and socioeconomic power through school curricula. Schools have always been pedagogical sites to teach the American public an ideology of white supremacy and the idea black people represented an inferior race whose savage ancestral African culture made them unsuitable to participate as citizens in the United States, and protect their Anglo Protestant culture. The ruling elite hid behind American business interests and believed black people were a problem to American society. They declined to address or attack the dilapidating social conditions their avarice produced within American society. The ruling elite along with America's public's racial attitudes forced blacks into the lowest level of society while at the same time called free blacks nefarious (Bodo, 1954; Fredrickson, 1971 & 1988). Instead, they cited the oppressive system of slavery, political disfranchisement, social proscriptions, and social vices in the United States and attributed these problems to black people's allegedly potential depravity. Hiding behind the label "reformers," these racists imbued the public mind that blacks posed a danger to the social order and security of the United States. They argued blacks displayed perfect behavior when enslaved and freedom caused them to become depraved and nefarious. Therefore, these reformers suggested the removal of all blacks (especially free blacks) from the United States, while others argued to deport only free blacks, while others debated black people would die out and give way to the superior white Anglo-Saxon population.

Prominent government, religious, intellectual, and other important public figures made systematic and conscious efforts to make race and color a qualification for citizenship within American society. They also used their influence to ensure the domination of Anglo Protestant American culture in schools and promoted a theory that whites were genetically superior to blacks throughout this nation's history to support specific political and social agendas. Eminent public figures and clergymen clearly used white supremacy to advance their dogma of differentiation of race to justify a *Herrenvok* society, a homogeneous "master race." Where black people have been consistently treated as undesirables no matter how hard they try to assimilate Anglo-Protestant culture (Fredrickson, 1981).

In addition, we need to understand how white supremacist ideologues influence education, how they have historically affected and still affect the performance and opportunities of black and other nonwhite students. This ideology has taught not only whites into believing blacks are lazy, inherently inferior, prone to crime, have no history or culture, but also indoctrinated some blacks to believe that Eurocentric culture and society is superior. It has imbued society to believe black people have no history outside of enslavement, come from a savage culture, and God allowed us to be enslaved for our own benefit, that it was "God's will." These beliefs have influenced many teachers, both black and white, whether unconsciously or consciously, and other educators in various positions into believing that Anglo Protestant American culture is superior and universal, black students do not possess the ability to think abstractly or perform on an equal level with whites. Moreover, until educators in general adequately examine and act upon the historical, social, economic, and political role race has played and continues to play in the United States, children of color will continue to face the prospect of failure in schools that suffer from public policy, societal beliefs, and the desire to keep power within certain quarters.

Race has always been a necessary construction to the identity of the United States and during the 1980s we witnessed a resurgence of white supremacy and the need to degenerate black people to protect the alleged loss of white privilege (Apple, 1996b; Lipsitz, 1998; Omi & Winant, 1983). This "white privilege" represents a particular social order and historical formations that are consistently reproduced through specific discursive and material processes and circuits of greed and power. Thus, white privilege was deliberately calculated as a measure of social control and maintained to ensure black subjugation (Allen, 1994; Munford, 1996). This idea of white supremacy and black inferiority has already been studied and documented in numerous studies such as Thomas Gossett's *Race: The History of an Idea in America* (1965), George M. Fredrickson's *The Black Image in the White Mind: The Debate on Afro-American Character and Destiny, 1817–1914* (1971) and *White Supremacy: A Comparative Study in American and South African History* (1981), Ronald Takaki's *Iron Cages: Race and Culture in 19th-Century America* (1979), Allen Chase's *The Legacy of Malthus* (1980), and Stephen Jay Gould's *The Mismeasure of Man* (1981). More recently there have been Elazar Barkan's *The Retreat of Scientific Racism* (1992), Marimba Ani's *Yurgugu: An African-Centered Critique of European Cultural Thought and Behavior* (1994), Ivan Hannaford's *Race: The History of an Idea in the West* (1996), Carter A. Wilson's *Racism: From Slavery to Advanced Capitalism* (1996), Clarence J. Munford's *Race and Reparations: A Black Perspective for the 21st Century* (1996), and Audrey Smedley's *Race in North America: Origin and Evolution of a Worldview* (1999). The notion evolved during the Renaissance that blacks are depraved and nefarious has remained (whether unconsciously and consciously) in the psyche of whites to this present day. Scholars like Charles Murray, the late Richard Herrnstein, and Philip Rushton have continued to publish and promote white supremacy and racial differences in American society.

Murray, Herrnstein, Ruston and other spurious scholars have contributed tremendously to the field of white supremacy and its pedagogical influence upon the American public. While many have chronologically examined the historical evolution of the ideological beliefs of white supremacy, I have chosen to historically examine how white supremacy pedagogically ensured its influence upon the American public and how it continues to influence education. While there is a wealth of scholarly works on white supremacy and how it has historically influenced the American public to believe in black inferiority, these studies have not focused upon the men who governed and framed this nation's laws formulated white supremacist ideology, made it the law, and taught the American public blacks were not only inferior, but also a threat to this nation's well-being. Furthermore, the plan to remove all black people from American society, keeping them in utter poverty, and the insidious eugenics movement that eventually led to the rise of Nazi ideology and the resurgence of social Darwinism in the form of statistical measurements of intelligence are also a part of maintaining white supremacy in the United States. These movements have not been some fragmented strategies by demented minds, but the workings of highly educated public figures and the intelligentsia intent on making sure they maintain their white privilege over people of color.

This study will hopefully not only shed new light on the fact that these old beliefs are still with us, but will begin to show us that white supremacy is so intertwined with the economic wealth of this nation, what kind of education students of color receive and white privilege is maintained at the cost of degenerating blacks. The degeneration of black people forces all other ethnic groups and even some blacks, as described in F. James Davis' *Who is Black? One Nation's Definition* (1991) and bell hooks' *Where We Stand: Class Matters* (2000) to align themselves with whiteness. Hopefully, this will cause new debates concerning this insidious ideology, educate the American public forthrightly about what is actually white supremacy. Begin to implement and enforce public policies to bring about a more equitable and emancipatory educational system in our society. It is also important to understand how white supremacy historically evolved into a pedagogy that matured into a subtle and powerful educational tool to maintain power and status of the white elite, which continually oppresses nonwhite people.

This study is not only significant for scholars, but for teachers who interact with students every day, in understanding why most urban schools remain in poverty and why most urban students are always playing catch up with white students in better suburban schools (Apple, 1996; Noguera, 2003; Orfield & Lee, 2005; Spring, 2005). School administrators need a working knowledge of white supremacy and how they consent to white supremacist public policy set in place by government officials. They need to understand how the American public is persuaded to vote for certain politicians who steer our nation and educational system in certain directions (Herman & Chomsky, 1988; Chomsky, 2000; Spring, 2005). This is important because certain elite members, government and other public figures pedagogically articulated ideas and beliefs have caused massive harm to black children, and the American public consented to these beliefs that blacks are inferior and deserve no civil or political rights in the United States. They gained the support of so-called empirical scientific research in the nineteenth century, which by the beginning of the 1900s turned into a social Darwinist ideology and eugenics movement.

This pseudoscience has now become a phenomenon whereby the intellectual and moral ambience of the twenty-first century is crucial and apocalyptic as testing and standardization consistently strips teachers of the creative art of teaching (McNeil & Valenzuela, 2001; Ohanian, 1999). Students receive only factoids that relate to the policy of standards and nonwhite children are forced to learn only what the dominant culture views as necessary (Apple, 1996; Ohanian, 1999). In nonwhite neighborhood schools, the push for state standards takes away from teachers real classroom instruction and curriculum development has dire consequences as they focus on test prep and discipline that replicate prisons (Davis, 2003; Johnson, Boydon & Pittz, 2001; McNeil, & Valenzuela, 2001).

Instead of spending more time on useful lessons, teachers are required to spend more class time on memorization strategies for tests and severely handicap substantive education. Tests have become the only way to demonstrate performance, which punish schools that do poorly and reward those who do well. Schools that historically do poor resort to test taking prep rallies that concentrate on methods rather than content knowledge. This standardization causes inequities to widen between what kind of education is provided in predominately black schools verses what is provided in predominately white schools (McNeil, 2000; McNeil & Valenzuela 2001; Freire, 1985). As schools in predominately nonwhite areas are financially punished when they fail to meet these standards, they become targets for those who support psychometric measurements and those who want to privatize education. This theory and debate about the inferior intelligence of certain groups of people has persuaded some public officials and educators and many voters to believe that blacks are genetically inferior and it is wasteful and useless to spend public tax dollars to educate them, thus leaving masses of people of color to squalor in utter poverty.

It is also important to understand how white supremacy has maintain segregation in housing through unfair housing, renegotiation of antidiscriminatory laws in construction contracts and hiring practices to protect white privilege against Affirmative Action, and the refusal to desegregate schools (Harris, 1993; Lipsitz, 1998; Massy & Denton, 1993; Orfield, 1993). While whites resisted antidiscrimination laws, corporate America blamed schools for not providing a workforce qualified to make America number one in the global market. Corporate leaders joined with conservatives and liberals for a standardized curriculum, who wanted a curriculum that advocated for an obedient submissive workforce, a curriculum that promoted the dominance of Western culture and history. Corporate leaders fought against higher tax laws and suggested state wide low cost standardized exams to make students learn. When the economy began to falter, corporate leaders began to pack up and move to more lucrative regions around the world, which left thousands of workers unemployed and were quick to blame schools for producing unqualified workers. They refuse to acknowledge the real reason for a sluggish economy has been the growth of technology in industry, the streamlining of production and workers, and the growing reliance on cheap foreign labor.

Along with the economic decisions of the Reagan and Bush era, the flight of corporate America and the dismantling of unions left thousands of middle, working class, and poor whites angry who blamed their economic problems on blacks and other nonwhites. Instead of holding both Republican and Democratic bureaucrats, corporate conglomerates, and the elite ruling class responsible for the economic decline, middle and working-class whites in fear of losing their economic status are moving more and more to the Right (Aronowitz & DiFazio, 1993; Bluestone & Harrison, 1982; Kincheloe, 1995; Omi & Winant, 1983; Reich, 1991).

As society and the economy changes, the intellectual apparatuses in education and politicians articulate public editorial opinions, publish textbooks, and use the media to promote the dominant society's perspective. Eurocentric intelligentsia arbitrates what passes for scholarship, how research is conducted and validated, and who will speak for the academy. Historically, theoretical research in education and the social sciences has always been explained and practiced from a European worldview. This worldview defines itself through a scientific paradigm that maintains a cultural power structure, which continually supports a white supremacist ideology. European historical methodology or historiography has and "still offends the deepest senses of" nonwhite people's humanity (Smith, 1999, p. 1). Proclaiming Cartesian ideas as the standard of research and scholarship from the eighteenth to the twentieth century, today the academy continues to support and uphold a Eurocentric theoretical paradigm that historically created and maintained colonialism, neocolonialism, and imperialism, which is now renamed globalization. African, Asian and Native American cultural systems and their way of thinking are consistently disregarded and prejudged as uncivilized. Nor were indigenous nonwhite people considered humans according to European standards (Memmi, 1991; Bederman, 1995). Consequently, Eurocentric theoretical research and methodologies are promoted as universal (Ani, 1994; Apple, 1990; Asante, 1991; Smith, 1999; Spring, 1997).

The academy instructs students, especially history students, to maintain an objective role of impartiality or the disposition of a disinterested judge, never degenerating into that of an advocate or, even worse, propagandist for any certain cause. Within this Eurocentric paradigm, the intellect must be separated from the emotions. It is only through this separation, this denial of who we are and our relationship with the cosmos that we achieve "objectification." The academy hopes to detach a person from his or her emotions or control them by placing "reason" in control of emotions. Yet, the ultimate goal is to cause disorder or a self-hate in the nonwhite student, disconnecting him or her from his or her histories, spaces, language, culture, cognition, emotions, and way of interaction with others.

The assumption is the historian's conclusion should be objective, displaying standard judicial qualities of balance and evenhandedness so he or she is not influenced by social justice, politics, or by the individual's investment in arriving at a conclusion (Zinn, 2005). Linda Tuhiwai Smith (1999) states, the nonwhite student "[h]aving been immersed in the Western academy which claims theory as thoroughly

Western, which has constructed all the rules by which the indigenous world has been theorized, indigenous voices have been overwhelmingly silenced" (p. 29). Eurocentric historians continue to write history from their own cultural bias, uplifting their own culture at the expense of the colonized and conquered, they have required colonized and conquered scholars do the same and not analyze the colonizer or conqueror. In other words, the academy only tolerates nonwhite educated scholars when they have been redescribed into whiteness, thus protecting white supremacy.

Today, under the umbrella of globalization, which in reality is the new term for neocolonial economic control of nonwhites, there is greater support of the idea of objectivity, of trained historians completely purging themselves of all emotional values, resulting in a tendency to hypothetically let the facts speak for themselves. There is a greater emphasis on the interpretation being verified by the facts; there is no forum for any other kind of paradigm such as an African-centered hermeneutical approach, which emphasizes the primacy of the person as an individual that seeks the collective harmony of the community. An African-centered hermeneutical paradigm is the process of interpretation that brings out multiple meanings, which uncovers various layers of experience and textual facts (Asante, 1987; Cone, 1986; Wilmore and Cone, 1976; Wilmore, 1996). Nonwhite scholars are only recognized if their methodologies or ideas have originated from Western paradigms; if the methodologies are indigenous, they are dismissed as primitive or inconsequential. Linda Tuhiwai Smith (1999) asserts:

> Imperialism still hurts, still destroys and is reforming itself constantly...Many critiques of research have centered around the theory of knowledge known as empiricism and the scientific paradigm of positivism which is derived from empiricism (pp. 18, 42).

Empiricism hurts when nonwhite students and scholars are required to look and study how Western nations raped, pillaged, and oppressed their people with supposed evenhandedness so as not to be influenced by social justice or politics. To not become emotionally involved is not only wrong, but impossible. History is written from positivistic ahistorical and apolitical points of view, led by scholars who undermine potential research that will critique Europe's conquest, pillage and rape of nonwhite regions of the world, and Eurocentric research methodologies that enforce positivistic perspectives of rationality as objective and universal.

When I was a graduate history major with an emphasis in African American history, I was always told I was too passionate in my writings. However, how can I, as a person of African descent, not exhibit passionate emotions when studying the story of my people's past, our struggles and our present challenges? As one professor once explained to me, as a black man she understood why I would be emotionally touched and angered at studying the history of African Americans. Although the anger has dissipated, how can I withhold from raising passionate questions about the oppression of blacks and other people of color and provide some interpretation based not only on factual data, but also incorporating a hermeneutical interpretation from the lens of the marginalized and the so-called other? Thus the foundational methodology used in this study is a historical contextual analysis that is grounded in the cultural foundations of an African-centered hermeneutical analysis. I chose to investigate white supremacy from the lens of those who have suffered from the influence and consequences of white supremacy. The development of this qualitative study is derived from a critical theoretical approach of non-Western paradigms. This work was gathered from studying primary and secondary historical sources, philosophical sources and documents such as the papers of the American Colonization Society, the *African Repository*, *The Colored American,* and *Freedom's Journal* to critique and analyze the cultural origins and dynamics of white supremacy as it pertains to the social, educational, political, and economic struggle blacks and other nonwhites have endured in America since its beginnings.

The success of white supremacy in America is not its military superiority but its continual support of itself through the weapon of culture. Culture gives people group identification and builds on shared experiences, creating a collective personality. It represents the values that are created by the group out of shared knowledge as a methodical set of ideas into a single coherent affirmation. It includes history, language, literature, poetry, art, music, religion, law, philosophy, customs, and values. Therefore, culture provides the foundation for obligation, priority, and preference that gives direction to the development and behavior of the group. Culture is the basis for informing the world as to whom a people are; it also serves to inform the people themselves about how they look at the world. The epistemology of a culture constructs knowledge, inquiry, and the way research is accomplished (Ani, 1994; Carruthers, 1994).

It is important to understand that the dominant class constructs a white supremacist culture by generating their discourse about subjugated oppressed nonwhite groups. They disseminate their ideas through politics, education, and the media; thus the images of blacks and other people of color center on sexual promiscuity, laziness, criminal activity, and an unwillingness to conform to the dominant group, thus presenting the public with ideas that the oppressed groups are to blame for all the problems in society and therefore need to be controlled. White supremacy maintains its grip upon people of color through cultural hegemony, which allows the oppressed groups to volunteer their allegiance and pacify their will to resist outright. Hegemonic white supremacist institutions within the United States have convinced many that the Civil Rights Movement was a success and racism has been resolved. Hegemony does not ignore the demands of the oppressed groups—instead under public pressure white supremacy made concessions to the demands of the movement and has allowed the emergence of a black middle class that has a vested interest in supporting the dominant social structure (Artz & Murphy, 2000; hooks 2000). Certain parts of black culture have become acceptable to the dominant white culture until dominant forces feel threatened; at the same time, white supremacists will always guard and protect their political dominance in the United States and hinder or marginalize any attempt by blacks to form any independent political coalitions. Although the black middle class continuously gets frustrated with marginalization and racism, they will always consent to the status quo of the dominant white society (Feagin, 1991; hooks, 2000; Scott, 1990; West, 1993). White supremacy will always support conservative blacks because, as bell hooks states, "the miseducation of underprivileged blacks" will always strengthen "the class power of the unprogressive black elite" (p. 97).

While the method of research used is a historical contextual analysis, it utilizes an African-centered philosophy and epistemology as a theoretical basis. This theoretical foundation allows for an understanding of how white supremacy uses culture as a distinctive product that develops into a political ideology. Because epistemology is based upon cultural constructs, culture becomes the lens of the people and it communicates the structure that defines a people. Analyzing white supremacy through Afrocentric cultural constructs—rather than through Eurocentric theoretical paradigms that will only be fragmented—one begins to see the elements of white supremacist philosophy and behavior in an integral fashion.

While historians interpret the facts through empirical frameworks, there is little if any investigation of the ideological hegemonic forces that shape history and culture or why such events dominate others. Western empirical frameworks only recognize the exclusive validity of efficiency models and calculating the manipulation of variables. In modern discourse, measurement and accounting came to be the only legitimate ways to establish what is important, significant, and true. Everything else is idle chitchat, essentially unverifiable and of little value. When history is viewed through Newtonian/Cartesian lens it becomes easy for Eurocentric historiography to see itself as universally applicable (Brickman, 1982). Oswald Spengler (1928, p. 3) defends Euro-American ideology by calling it the only culture that has achieved any sense of fulfillment. Thus, the knowledge of oppressed groups and their hermeneutic interpretations of history and culture are not remembered or valued within a Newtonian/Cartesian society. The idea there are other interpretations, that African-centered and other cultures necessitate different methodologies from Eurocentric paradigms as crucial to the development of educational historiography is not accepted as a way of interpreting history. The incorporation of African, Native American, or other indigenous ways of hermeneutical theoretical research will make us more competent and more conscious of generating a more sophisticated representation of the history of education and the ideological relationships involved (Asante, 1987).

African-centered and other non Eurocentric theories of education, otherwise known as indigenous knowledge, can be functional, emancipating, and empowers students to critique and produce their own interpretation of historical periods and events. Indigenous ways of knowledge are service-oriented and communal to the needs of people. This communal way of knowing the world is in direct conflict with Eurocentric notions of knowledge. Thus, Eurocentric domination of research is maintained through ideological management and cultural hegemony over all people of color (Ani, 1994; Smith, 1999; Spring 1997). In other words, the cultural hegemony of Eurocentric forms of research in the academy consistently refuses to legitimatize the empowering research methodologies, inquiries and strategies of people of color. Therefore, Afrocentric and other forms of non Western theoretical research methodologies concerning culture and education have been kept out of the mainstream of academic discourse.

Eurocentric historiography is more than just research that is located in a positivist tradition. Eurocentric research brings to bear its cultural orientation, its values, its own conceptualization of knowledge, language, time and space, and its structures of power and ideology. Such historiography serves to not only exclude African American history from the curriculum, but also perpetuates the colonization of people's minds. Writing history from a Eurocentric academic methodological framework theorizes people of color from a white supremacist perception and overwhelmingly silences any voice that brings any other interpretation. Even as some well-meaning white liberals are intent on saving the minds of African American youth, the continual colonization of the minds of black youth serves the economic needs and ideologies of Eurocentric legitimization (Apple, 1990; Yeo, 1997). In addition, potential teachers are also being colonized as they study positivist scholarship and methodologies of the historiography of education. The globalization of Eurocentric knowledge and culture reaffirms itself as the center of legitimate knowledge and what is defined as the source of all knowledge. This form of historiography repositions other non Western forms of historiography on the "outside" to continually legitimatize colonial rule in education.

In opposition, the postmodern paradigm shift brings a change allowing many forms of genres and expressions that seek to transform the ravages of modernity through new forms of language and power. This paradigm shift forces Eurocentric historiography to no longer assume it is superior to other forms of knowledge. This has immense implications for education—particularly the way curriculum is rationalized when Afrocentric and other non Eurocentric forms of hermeneutic interpretations are incorporated to understand the different forms of knowledge that nonwhite people bring to scholarship. Hermeneutic interpretation provides various options for understanding curriculum in light of historical and contemporary social and political events. Hermeneutics also recognizes the necessity of incorporating a new consciousness that transcends Eurocentric categories of metaphysics, epistemology, and axiology.

This struggle to reconceptualize the historiography of history and the curriculum emerged in the midst of the social and political upheaval of the 1960s and 1970s. The rise of radical black and white scholars whose vision was based on racial equality challenged the aristocratic paradise of Eurocentric historiography that was based on racial caste systems. Young black scholars such as Vincent Harding, Julius Lester, Sterling Stuckey, A Leon Higginbotham, and others along with leftist white scholars such as Staughton Lynd, Eric Foner, Howard Zinn, Leon F. Litwack, and others pushed the envelope of scholarship and acknowledged identification with those at the bottom of society.

Some endorsed the strategic doctrine of the Italian communist Antonio Gramsci, who argued that social transformations would not be won through swift wars, but now would be accomplished on the cultural fronts of society. At issue here was the relationship between the demands of civic responsibility and scholarship—the "neutrality" of not just the work of scholarship, but of the institution of scholarship itself. They, along with black scholars, adopted the attitude of challenging and attacking the institutions of hierarchical positivist organizations. They agreed with Barrington Moore's (1966) observation: "In any society the dominant groups are the ones with the most to hide about the way society works" (p. 522). The reconceptualization of knowledge was to make room for the narratives of oppressed people alongside those of the dominant society. For example, the narratives of slaveowners and their points of view would be placed alongside the narratives of enslaved blacks, thus bringing balance to the historiography of slavery.

Historiographers can begin to uncover in their methodologies the kind of scholarship that will allow others to examine the multiple meanings emerging from a non Eurocentric hermeneutical analysis. Black historiographers can begin to free themselves from Eurocentric methodologies that do not allow the inner self to participate in the hermeneutic process and reap whatever benefits from being black in a white world. One of the most important benefits to incorporate into the hermeneutical process is what W. E. B. Du Bois called the gift of "double consciousness" the sense of always living in two worlds, one white (American) and the other black (African). According to Du Bois, whiteness always measured "one's soul" by the parameters "of a world that looks at on in contempt and pity" to make one feel inferior (Du Bois, 1997, pp. 38-39). Living in the white man's world but never allowed to be a part of it because being black is unacceptable to white America. On the other side, being black allows one to see himself as others see him which forces him to struggle to see himself as an American and as one of African descent. He refuses to bleach his black skin because he believes as a black man he brings a message to white America. Inside this black man or woman is the gift to share with America six thousand years of African genius through the eyes and mind of an African way of thinking, yet America rejects the gift Africa brings to it (p. 39). It is here that one can begin to see and understand the sensitive paradoxes and ironies that dominate American society.

We can begin to reveal how whites conceived of and responded to those they relegated to the margins of society, whether they were poor, immigrant, female, or black. Through this process we can uncover the nonsense and anguish that is embedded in the propensity of the early white invaders in America to create categories and containers in which they stuffed human beings.

Historiographers can discard their Puritan ideas of work and labor to find new ways of seeing how our society has always obliged itself because the "worthy poor" retain their self-respect and only ask for aid reluctantly and infrequently, while the "unworthy poor" too often and too willingly demand aid as their right. This kind of analysis can cause us to grasp the possibility that those who were most in need of aid were deemed the least "worthy," and that charitable reformers never thought the poor might have a unique insight into their own circumstances. Eurocentric capitalist forms of knowledge never will consult the poor as to how to solve poverty; like schoolchildren, they are the last to be consulted about their own interests. Thus historiography will always continue to exclude the voices of people of color, the working class, and the poor and believe that they need to be "guided," told what to do, reproached for being poor, cajoled, pushed, punished, and even treated as irresponsible little children.

Hermeneutical interpretations of history can bring to the forefront of scholarship not only the paradoxical behavior of the rich and middle class reformers, but also the collisions of cultures, involving a culture they could never perceive, which separated them from those they claim they were attempting to help. It is through this hermeneutic process that we can observe the voices of the poor, who break through the rigorous records of empirical data so we can sense them as human beings, fellow human creatures to be contended with. The minds of the historiographers who have stepped within the critical hermeneutical paradigm will no longer see methodological assumptions as neutral activities; they will begin to attempt to reinterpret their own lives within schooling and produce their own knowledge (Kincheloe, 1993). Teachers will no longer simply teach history as facts to be memorized because they allow students to bring their autobiographical histories into the classroom. Thus, allowing history to become "our story," instead of the usual master narratives of Eurocentric male dominated wars or hierarchical discourses (Asante, 1987).

This kind of historiography allows us see how conservative reformers refuse to see the simple truth that the poor just have no money. The implication of this kind of insight is more radical when one include race to show how reformers separated themselves and formulated ideas about blacks and the poor. Also it becomes insightful for scholarship that the wealthy reformers will never consider distributing society's wealth so that humanity would not have to suffer with inequities. With this understanding, educational scholarship can begin to formulate solutions to the problems of racism, poverty, and inequality. We can begin to uncover this nation's refusal or inability to perceive blacks, other nonwhites, and the poor as adults with lives and culture worthy of not only academic study but the right as human beings to be included in society economically as well as socially. One can begin to understand the importance of the American Colonization Society and the eugenics movement in the maintenance of white supremacy, their influence on American culture, how their pedagogy taught white citizens Africans and people of African descent were supposedly inferior and have no right to live within the borders of the United States, and how this racist epistemology has continuously been taught, supported, and upheld in American culture and education.

This study, divided into six sections, follows both a historical and thematic arrangement. This first chapter introduces certain concepts and definitions of white supremacy, its ideas and the specific ways white supremacist thought maintains its control in America. It includes the purpose of the study, the background to the problem, methodologies that explain how this study will view white supremacy through the knowledge of oppressed groups and their hermeneutic interpretations of history and culture, and the significance of the study.

Chapter 2 describes white supremacy and its manipulative influence upon the American people and its control of the public school system in the United States It examines the curriculum of internal colonial education and the curriculum of "Americanization" that reinforces passive obedience, the continual celebration of Anglo Protestant American culture, events and mythical heroes used to indoctrinate children. It investigates the cultural values, patriotic nationalism, political and economic systems along with the language, and religion that reflect Anglo Protestant Americanism. Chapter 3 discusses white supremacy and its maintenance through the curriculum of repression and exclusion. It analyzes Anglo Protestant culture as it seeks to Americanize children through education. How American education has excluded African American history and culture from the curriculum that would critically inform African American students that they are the descendants of a continuous historic struggle against racism and white supremacy.

Chapter 4 investigates the American Colonization Society, the foundations of white supremacist ideology, and how white government and public figures articulated a theory that black people were inferior and a threat to the nation's security. Chapter 5 concentrates on how white supremacy turned to scientific determinism to validate racism from the colonial period to the eugenics movement in the United States in the twentieth century. How it incorporated an ideology of black inferiority and set out to influence public policy concerning education and crime. Chapter 5 also addresses how white supremacy continues to manipulate public policy that causes inequity and disparity within American society. Chapter 6 explores the debate of I.Q. and its claim that African Americans are less intelligent than whites. While individual wealth plays a part in the opportunities of education, public policy shapes the lives of those who have and those who have not and the widening destructive disparity of economic resources. Racial inequality has nothing to do with the myth of innate racial inferior genes but it is the unequal rewards of capitalism and the scholarship of white supremacist academicians.

CHAPTER TWO

INTERNAL COLONIALISM: WHITE SUPREMACY AND EDUCATION

When we send our children to school, they learn nothing about us other than we used to be cotton pickers. Why your grandfather was Nat Turner, your grandfather was Toussaint L'Ouverture, your grandfather was Hannibal. It was your grandfather's hands who forged civilization and it was your grandfather's hands who rocked the cradle of civilization. But the textbooks tell our children nothing.

Malcolm X, June 28, 1964

We see our present with little understanding as we view our past because aspects of the past which could illumine the present has been concealed from us. This concealment has been effected by a systemic process of mis-education characterized by a thoroughgoing inculation of colonial values and attitudes—a process which could not have been so effective had we not been denied access to the truth... As a consequence we have become a people without a sense of history.

Renato Constantino, 1978

Our lack of understanding regarding the colonial legacy that informs and shapes the cruel and often violent racist reality which characterizes our democratic society is mainly due to a colonial ideology.

Donaldo Macedo, 1999

The inequalities of education children of color and the poor have to live with are institutional, socioeconomic, and ideological expressions of a white supremacist capitalist society. Public schooling in the United States requires the internalization of ideology and discipline, which produces workers to be obedient to capitalist interests (Apple, 1990). Public schools have always been agents of capitalist social control as an antidote for social unrest, so there would be no need to maintain a standing army to control the urban masses, a site to imbue the poor and working class with the moral values of the elite (Katz, 1971, p. 141; Mohl, 1970).

This philosophy of white supremacy and its influence upon the American people and public schools has been and still is used to indoctrinate children with the cultural values, patriotic nationalism, political and economic system, language, and religion that reflect Anglo Protestant American norms. This curriculum of "Americanization" or as Donaldo Macedo (1994) calls it "Literacy for Stupidification" reinforces passive obedience and the continual celebration of Anglo Protestant American culture, events, and mythical heroes. For colonized African Americans, the poor and other nonwhite children, school is no more than mindless drills for standardized multiple choice exams that "comb" away anything in the mind that would lead to a true learning experience. This schooling does not encourage critical thinking or any sense of community among students. Instead it promotes a passive nature of obedience, indoctrinating nonwhites, working class and poor students not to inquire why events happen or how those events affect and shape society, but to accept and memorize certain predetermined facts and the dates of events. Public education officials, politicians, and other public figures argue that raising standards will provide a better economy. Yet, for children of color, they claim raising standards lift students of color from their inferior "backwardness" and the poverty of their culture. Conclusions are made that subjugated and colonized groups are not ready to manage themselves and education becomes extremely mechanistic based on standardized tests that are supposed to measure and fix deficiencies, and prepare students to fit perfectly a technocratic society (Carlson, 1975; Carspecken, 1996; Macedo, 1994; Ohanian, 1999; Shujaa, 1994; Spring, 1997).

While students in middle and upper middle class suburbs and private schools are encouraged to critically examine the literature, reflect, and compete with each other, enhancing their odds for individual achievement and success. Whereas, inner city schools are mostly occupied by predominately nonwhite children who through public policies like tracking and standardized testing are taught isolated skills that lead only to low level or menial employment and often left on the margins of society (Apple, 1990: 61, 65). Teachers in predominately nonwhite schools focus upon classroom management, discipline and teach to test (Johnson, Boydon, Pittz, 2001; McNeil & Valenzuela, 2001). Reward systems include candy as if the children are horses to be fed sugar cubes for completing a trick correctly. Administrators, teachers, parents, and students all advocate letter grades and technocratic evaluations to assess children's intellect; social inclusion or exclusion forces the individual student to draw conclusions about the quality of life based upon this empirical format. Schools have become sites of instruction for knowledge that does not encourage higher order thinking (Haberman, 1995; Kincheloe, 1999; Kozol, 1991; Shujaa, 1994).

White supremacy is interwoven in documents and speeches by various public and governmental figures that have been included and supported in many textbooks pertaining to the building of the United States for and by white men only (Adams & Sanders, 2003; Joshi, 1999; Loewen, 1995). White supremacy oppresses not only people of color, but also segments of its own white population. The concept that North America belongs to the white man was used the by Puritan fathers, who argued God had favored and chosen them, that the indigenous Native Americans had not subdued and utilized the land correctly according to Puritan standards based on their interpretation of biblical principles (Adams & Sanders, 2003; Friedman, 1975; Jennings, 1975; Springs, 1997; Wood, 1990). This idea that America was a white man's land also led them to formulate a pedagogy of Manifest Destiny, which almost exterminated Native Americans and a pedagogy preaching blacks were inferior, degraded, disturbed the social order, and posed a danger to the nation's security. Thus American leaders conceived a plan to deport and colonize all free black people from the United States while at the same time maintaining perpetual enslavement in the South (Bodo, 1954; Frederickson, 1971; Staudenraus, 1961). The question to ask is: Why has this knowledge been excluded from the textbooks and kept just among academic scholars just for the purpose of intellectual debate? This exclusion of certain knowledge from textbooks allows the dominant culture to maintain control of society and its resources and causes oppressed people into believing they are accepted as a part of the dominant culture. This exclusion of knowledge purges textbook writers of wrong doing, eradicates cultural differences within society and reshapes it around a common culture that is Anglo Protestant. This allows a hierarchy that sees white as the civilizing agent and demeans the colonized and subjugated groups as "others," "ethnics," "aliens," thereby promoting that the "other" is bringing down the nation's social order. In so doing, white supremacy is able to hide the hegemonic foundations of the United States behind a veil of deceit (Bennett, 1969; Zinn, 1995) and claim "outsiders" such as people of color are threatening the social fabric of the United States. Education becomes the tool of the dominant culture to indoctrinate colonized and subjugated students with obedience and selective knowledge and lead them to blindly pledge allegiance to a nationalism that consistently demeans them. White supremacist rhetoric employs a "poisonous pedagogy" (Macedo, 1994, p. 66) clearly promoting an idea of black inferiority, which articulates black people threaten the social order and have no place in American society.

While African American Studies departments along with some other college courses expose and present a critical perspective on white supremacy, the majority of college courses offer very little public discussion in the classroom concerning white supremacist ideology in the United States. In classrooms that address race and white supremacy, professors and students are often force to abandon traditional methods to openly discuss race and the issues that confront society. Both nonwhite and white students are able to struggle through their colonized education and examine white supremacy and its grip upon society. Students alongside teachers and instructors can begin to incorporate strategies that promote emancipating discussions and students are encouraged to create and invent new strategies to resist white supremacist ideology (Castenell & Pinar, 1993; Harding, 1991; hooks, 1994; Howard, 1999; Kincheloe & Steinberg, 1997; Loewen, 1995; Shujaa, 1994).

Academicians, politicians, religious leaders, and other public figures influence public opinion and public policy pedagogically communicating the idea America is an Anglo Protestant nation whose God-given destiny is to lead the world. This meant Native Americans were to be deculturalized, assimilated, or exterminated; Mexicans and other Hispanics were to be also deculturalized and subdued. Blacks were first enslaved, those who gained freedom were deported or were predicted to disappear altogether—when that failed, they regulated masses of black people to suffer under the exclusionary laws of Jim Crow, and utter poverty. The idea of removing black people was supported by the belief that blacks were inferior and savage, which, in the latter part of the nineteenth century, led to scientific racism and the eugenics movement of the early part of the twentieth century. Today, in response to multicultural initiatives, white supremacy has evolved into a subliminal political agenda of neoconservatives and conservatives who demand that education focus upon the Western canon as the only legitimate knowledge worth knowing and maintain utter poverty for masses of Hispanics and people of African descent (Apple, 2001; Kozol, 1991; Spring, 1994 & 1996).

Alongside this idea of Manifest Destiny, some white scholars created a pseudoscientific intellectual agenda in which certain children were considered genetically inferior and therefore unworthy of education or the financial support that would enhance their opportunities to succeed (Mauer, 1999; Selden, 1999; Smedley, 1999). We must uncover and discuss this pervasive ideology publicly to enable parents, students, teachers, educators, professors, and administrators to understand and initiate discussions about how white supremacy has governed and influenced our society since colonial times and to seek and implement sincere solutions to the racial problems in the United States. Possibilities to openly talk about how schools have historically been institutions of social control for the elite whose hegemonic curricula and pedagogy endangers the ethics of the thousands of students who have and still attend them.

The struggle by African Americans to gain access to public facilities coupled with the struggle for an equal education has caused us to fall in line with hegemonic white supremacist ideology. As blacks fought to integrate schools during the Civil Rights Movement, we ignored that integration would cost black teachers their jobs. We did not consider ths lost of a large number of excellent black teachers when our children were sent to predominately white schools. According to Lisa Delpit, the hiring process for black teachers still suffers within the black communities across the country (Foster, 1997, pp. ix–x). Integration was harmful to black children when they were bussed to predominately white schools. Black children were treated as if they were dysfunctional with low I.Q. and in need of constant discipline. Integration also insured black students would receive an education that deculturalized them to maintain a social order conducive to the needs of the dominant white society (Dempsey & Noblit, 1996; Spring, 2004; Zweigenhaft & Domhoff, 1991). This maintenance depends on the development of people of color that will think and facilitate the continuing domination of a Eurocentric/Cartesian worldview. Thus hegemony is accomplished by imbuing a select few with the mores and ideas that will continue a Eurocentric-dominated epistemology (Ani, 1994; Ratteray, 1994; Shujaa, 1994; Woodson, 1933). Hegemonic forces elevates a few African Americans and other nonwhites into political and other societal positions due to their relationships with white leaders and whose interest is not only maintaining the social order, but also protecting the business interests of the elite and the white middle class (Artz & Murphy, 2000; Marable, 1978; Spring, 2004; Zweigenhalft & Demhoff, 1991).

In the 1930s, about the same time Antonio Gramsci articulated the concept of hegemony, Carter G. Woodson, in his work *The Miseducation of the Negro* (1933), eloquently laid out in layman's terms how hegemony has been consistently used on black people. Whether or not Woodson was familiar with Gramsci or his ideas, he obviously understood the concept of hegemony as the necessary condition of the white elite in the United States to continue consolidating their control and influence over black people. The concept of hegemony explains the dominant elite ability to maintain their position despite grassroots opposition. Martin Carnoy, in his work *The State and Political Theory* (1984), summarizes Gramsci's concept of hegemony:

> In his doctrine of "hegemony," Gramsci saw that the dominant class did not have to rely solely on the coercive power of the state or even its direct economic power to rule; rather through its hegemony, expressed in the civil society and the state, the ruled could be persuaded to accept the system of beliefs of the ruling class and to share its social, cultural, and moral values.(p. 87).

In other words, control of the masses can be obtained by force, but it cannot be secured and maintained, especially today, without the consent of the people. The ruling elite obtains this consent by means of propaganda and other subliminal concepts through mass media, academics, moral values, and culture to promote their beliefs and practices (Gramsci, 1971, p. 182; Hall, 1977; Herman & Chomsky, 1988; Sassoon, 1987). This hegemonic racist ideology is worked out through the accepted leadership of the oppressed, who adhere to the politically dominant cultural alignment. These accepted leaders impose the ideas, cultural values, and skills of the white elite upon their own people through society and the school curricula (Burman, 1995; Spring, 1997; Woodson, 1933).

Woodson critically argues education is not neutral or apolitical, but education in the United States attempts to produce people who are prepared to contribute to society in ways consistent with the dominant culture. He asserts African American children are educated not only to embrace a Eurocentric worldview, but also a pedagogy that disparages their own African American culture. African American heritage is either erased or disparaged, black children are given a curriculum on the preeminence of European culture and history. Woodson believes that American education not only colonizes but corrupts the minds and hearts of black children. He is not alone in this assessment of the education of black children: Michele Foster, in her edited work *Black Teachers on Teaching* (1997), and Mwalimu J. Shujaa's Too Much Schooling Too Little Education (1994), agree with Woodson that black children were and are still abused psychologically and intellectually by a system that truly believes blacks are inferior. Woodson understood the curriculum is a "racial text" promoting an Anglo Protestant national identity. While not rejecting Euro-American history or culture, he suggests there is a need for African Americans to establish a curriculum for their own children to undo the miseducation inculcated by the dominant system.

In Foster's work, she records an interview documented in Ellen Lawsen and Marlene D. Merrill's book *The Three Sarahs: Documents of Antebellum College Women* (1984), conducted in the classroom of Sara Stanley, a teacher in Louisville, Kentucky, after the Civil War who taught black children in the basement of the Center Street

Colored Methodist Church. The dialogue is between a government official trying to convince black students that white people are superior to them due to a better education. The government official's statements of white superiority did not bring a submissive response from the black students. He raised the question "What makes them [white students] different from you?" The black students responded, to the official's surprise, "MONEY." The official agreed that money "enabled" the white students to have a better education, but he asked the students how did whites obtained the money. The black students all responded in a "simultaneous" voice: "Got it off us; stole it off we all" (p. 61). Although it is not even mentioned in any textbook or discussed in any classroom in the United States, it is a known fact within the minds and hearts of African Americans that our ancestors, contrary to white beliefs and accepted curricula, built this nation's wealth with their blood, sweat, and tears during enslavement.

Randall Robinson (2000) lays the problem of race in the United States at its roots when he states that "this was the house of Liberty, and it had been built by slaves." The United States has committed a massive crime against humanity in trying to exterminate the Native American population and the enslavement and murder of those of African descent. Neither has the United States chosen to rectify its "complicity" in denying millions of people their basic human rights through three centuries of oppression and genocide. The federal government has denied its involvement in the trade of human beings and has "kept us all—black, brown, white—the chance to begin again as co-owners of a national democratic idea." White supremacy has used education to blind "us all to our past and, with the same stroke, to any common future" (pp. 6–7).

Anglo Protestant nationalism willfully adheres to a colonized education where school curriculum excludes African American epistemological paradigms completely from the dominant curricula. This exclusion is a "willful ignorance and aggression" that basically considers African/African American history and culture not worth studying. America has not only denied our basic civil rights for over three hundred years, but consistently tries to make black people believe its their fault for the oppression they have faced over the centuries. The curricular indoctrination of African American youth strengthens the positivist philosophy of racial enslavement, segregation, peonage, and the erroneous belief in black inferiority. Woodson (1933, pp. xiii, 1) insists this allows the dominant society to control not only the production of knowledge, but also a pedagogy that teaches African Americans to despise their own people. This curricular process legitimizes the notion that people of Anglo/Nordic ancestry have accomplished everything worth knowing and at the same time pulverizes and discourages any spark of genius in African American youth. Woodson concluded that this miseducation of African American students has made it necessary to control their minds, he declared:

> When you control a man's thinking you do not have to worry about his actions. You do not have to tell him not to stand here or go yonder. He will find his "proper place" and stay in it. You do not need to send him to the back door. He will go without being told. In fact, if there is no back door, he will cut one for his special benefit. His education makes it necessary (p. xiii).

This hegemonic ideology is in complete agreement with the words of Elias B. Caldwell when he spoke at the 1836 Annual Colonization Convention in Washington, D.C. He stated:

> If they must remain in their present situation, keep them in the lowest state of degradation and ignorance. The nearer you bring them to the condition of brutes, the better chance do you give them of possessing their apathy. (*African Repository,* February 1836, p. 53).

Caldwell's statement has turned into a pedagogical method manifesting itself throughout American societal and educational history to construct and articulate an idea of differentiation by race, thereby constructing blacks as inferior and alien in the dominant society. The dominant curriculum currently utilizes the white child as its central focus. This approach compels African American youth to feel and see themselves as outsiders and being acted upon despite their acculturation into American society. They are rarely ever seen as active participants in history or the sciences and are taught to honor as heroes those who have vilified and enslaved Africans and those of African decent. African American children are consistently decentralized and must, "if they are to be allowed to become Americans," shed their blackness (Asante, 1987, pp. 4–11).

While African American youth have been historically denied access to their culture and history, white students also have been denied access to African American history as well as their own history in the name of patriotism. When curriculum developers make the necessary changes so African American youth can learn about themselves, their history, and their culture, the curriculum must also include answers why African American history and culture was excluded in the first place. The curriculum also must explain to white students why they were given a curriculum that lied and also colonized their minds ths same as black students. When white supremacist ideologues decided to exclude African American history and culture from the curriculum and lie about the magnitude of the African American contribution to the building of this nation, they also had to lie about everything else in American history. While there have been major changes in some curriculum programs that include multicultural epistemologies, the majority of curriculum programs still only select fragmentary sections of African American history and culture (Wilhelm, 1994).

The famous address of W. E. B. Du Bois, "To the Nations of the World," at the first Pan-African Conference at Westminster Town Hall, London, in July 1900, which denounced the aggressive policies of white supremacy and imperialism throughout the world, appears to be very relevant for the world today—especially for the United States. This is the only nation in the world today that claims itself the world's policeman so it can exploit its resources even if it means death and poverty to the people around the world (Blum, 2000). As Du Bois (1963) analyzed the global consequences of white supremacy and Western capitalism's imperialism, he prophesied:

> The problem of the twentieth century is the problem of the color-line, the question as to how are differences of race, which show themselves chiefly in the color of the skin and the texture of the hair, are going to be made, hereafter, the basis of denying to over half the world the right of sharing to their utmost ability the opportunities and privileges of modern civilization...the darker races are today the least advanced in culture according to European standards (pp. 20–21).

Du Bois accurately understood the global pedagogical consequences of white supremacy and why the white elite, especially in the United States, needed black people as a cheap labor force who were never to be accepted as citizens. He explicitly understood that the quest for racial justice is the respect and the continuation of one's culture and excellence in education. Du Bois also said that the answers to the questions of who will educate children of color, what will be the nature of that education, and whose vision will be imparted was crucial not only for black children, but for all people of color (Du Bois, 1963 & 1973).

Du Bois understand that school curriculum is a form of "cultural capital" and within the current political and epistemological control of elite and middle class whites. This cultural capital can be transformed from economic capital converted into institutionalized forms of educational qualifications and social capital in the form of obligations or connections that can be mobilized to collectively promote a certain idea or belief advocated by the aristocracy (Bourdieu, 1986; Kozol, 1991). African American history and culture is referred to as black history and culture, but never fully accepted as a part of American history and culture. When my children attended school, I suggested to a State College Area School District teacher that I would like my children to read African American literature. The teacher's response was "they need to read American literature, too." One does not have to wonder what the teacher implied. Without saying it outright, the teacher was saying African American literature, history, and culture is not American, but black literature, history and culture; it is the "other," alien and deliberately placed on the margin. Because Anglo Protestant knowledge is full of distortions and silences nonwhite knowledge, it is easy for a teacher to say black literature is the "other" and not American literature. This is very important to understand because to exclude the history and culture of people of color from the curricula implies that not only is Anglo Protestant history and culture all that is worth knowing, but the students who are being devalued, subjugated, and colonized have no history and culture, but also children of color themselves have nothing to offer at all (Asante, 1987; Delpit, 1995; Spring, 1997).

It is imperative to question—at this point—the extent to which the dominant curriculum has discounted and repudiated our cultural heritage, our value system and experience, in favor of its Eurocentric paradigms. Even more crucial is examining how hegemony manipulated us not to protest and demand changes in the school curriculum even though we as black people distrust white dominated school practices. Some of us have been indoctrinated to stand not only silent but to acquiescence to the dominant cultural influences as our children contest the legitimacy of the dominant curriculum and the pedagogy that demeans our own cultural heritage. It is naïve for black people to believe that the curriculum is developed with our best interest in mind or presents a neutral perspective, why is so much of our own cultural history and knowledge excluded? This colonial education in schools is present K–12, where thousands of Hispanic, African, and Native American children (including the author) were and still are taught to live their lives based on a social order that devalues their cultures and people. By distributing specific kinds of knowledge in schools, colonial curricula maintains inequality and presents a picture that convinces society that the status quo is a natural occurrence and is appropriate to the ideological hegemonic control of certain groups (Semali, 1996). This hegemonic saturation is more effective when it is done early (in elementary school) in one's life, designed to maintain and serve the social, political, and economic interests of the ruling white elite and their middle class suburbanites (Apple, 1990; Artz & Murphy, 2000; Keddie, 1971; Kozol, 1991; Mills, 1956).

Hegemonic societies in general allow enough people from the oppressed groups to learn the skills considered necessary to carry out the work desirable to the needs of the dominant group to maintain their racial and socioeconomic dominance. Consequently, in the United States, the "acceptable" chosen leaders from the oppressed groups acculturate their own people into Anglo Protestant cultural values, compelling loyalty to the oppressors (Artz & Murphy, 2000; Zweignhaft & Domhoff, 1991; hooks 2000). Michael Apple argues that schools portray themselves as neutral but start early to imbue children with the appropriate ways of thinking to subtly influence students to accept and protect the cultural norms of the dominant society (Apple, 1990). He says:

> This is particularly important, and will become more so, in urban and working class, among other, students develop positive perspectives towards conflict and change, ones that will enable them to deal with the complex and often repressive political realities and dynamics of power (p. 84).

Those who offer any resistance to this type of education are labeled deviants, criminals, lazy, unworthy to receive or participate in the civil structure of society; they are either imprisoned or left to languish on the margins of society (Kincheloe, 1999; Kozol, 1991; Miller, 1995; Shipman, 1995). White supremacist interests are consistently promoted and protected whereas African, Native, and Hispanic Americans derive very little benefits from education in the United States. Apple asserts social studies textbooks socialize students to accept American imperialism by casting the story in language so students will believe we are the good guys and all others are bad and warlike, trying to dominate or destroying our freedom (Apple, 1990, p. 85).

For two hundred years, some scientists and scholars have been obsessed with a mission to demonstrate that black people, Hispanics, indigenous people of the Americas, poor whites, certain foreigners, and women are innately inferior to upper class Anglo/Nordic white males who descended from the regions of Northern Europe and therefore should receive a basic elementary education and nothing else. White supremacy has camouflaged itself within unambiguous conceptualizations of the character and purpose of schooling. Instead of using overt racist language in the discourse, some scholars have appropriated psychometric and behaviorist theories to promote and maintain their alleged superior racial ideology. They couch their racist philosophy behind methods of positivistic empirical quantification and measurements to analyze purported inferior intelligence in children of color and then seek to influence public policy with their racial agendas (Breggin, 1998; Lewontin, 1991; Selden, 1999). They have promoted their so-called scientific hereditary and racial differences in the various races, or in the various ethnic groups, maintaining that these differences purportedly indicate lesser intellectual abilities. Those with supposedly less intelligence, they argued, should not be allowed to participate in the civic culture of the United States (Jordan, 1968; Spearman, 1927). Today, such white supremacist ideologues influence social and political measures as their predecessors did, and their representation as an oppressive and dogmatic ideology has captured the renewed interest of the American public (Breggin, 1998; Kozol, 1991; Mauer, 1999).

In the early 1900s the theory of scientific management advocated by Franklin Bobbit, W. W. Charters, H. H. Goddard, David Snedden, Edward Thorndike, and the sociologist Edward A. Ross not only argued that black people were a threat to the social order of the United States, but endorsed the superiority of the blond blue-eyed white Anglo Protestant individual. In the minds of these men, schooling for nonwhite children should follow a curriculum that validated their inferiority (Apple, 1979, pp. 47, 71–72; Carlson, 1975; Kamin, 1995; Kliebard, 1995, pp. 77–105). Alongside this theory of scientific efficiency within the school curriculum, they also supported a eugenic agenda to control the birthrate of Southern European immigrants, poor whites, and nonwhite people who were being excluded and disfranchised from society (Callahan, 1962; Selden, 1999; Spring, 1997).

The fear of losing traditional Anglo Protestant values and their way of life compelled Bobbit, Charters, Thorndike, Ross, Finny, Snedden, and others to perceive blacks and other non Anglo-Saxons as a threat to the alleged homogeneous North American culture. They believed in a culture that had been centered on small towns dominated by Anglo Protestant forebears who apparently had carved a civilization out of the wilderness (Carlson, 1975; Doherty; 1962; Hofstadler; 1956). The fear of a drop in the birth rate of Anglo Protestant people led them to influence public policy that reflected social Darwinist and eugenic theories based upon the racial superiority of Anglo-Saxons. The growth of urban centers, the different cultures and religious traditions of blacks and other non Anglo Protestants were seen as threats to the stability of the United States and the democratic experiment.

To ensure the homogeneity and social order in the United States, school curriculum was considered a strategy in achieving the Anglo-Saxon goal of superiority. In other words, the curriculum became the tool to disseminate Anglo Protestant cultural nationalism and restore what was believed lost especially by the influx of Southern Europeans and the presence of African Americans into the cities (Apple, 1990; Carlson, 1975; Ross, 1930; Spring, 1997). Noam Chomsky in *Language and Politics* (1988), says "Students are rewarded for obedience and passivity" and that "schooling is fundamentally subversive" (pp. 393–394). Schools therefore are cultural sites of indoctrination to imbue obedience and forbid any thought that questions power and oppression. Essential to this cultural ideology was and still is an excess commemoration of myths that indoctrinate children first about Americanization and then on the supremacy of Anglo/Nordic history and culture. These myths disguise complex truths while at the same time maintaining cultural hegemony. Those who refuse to accept Eurocentric forms of learning become a threat to the dominant culture as Malcolm X, George Jackson, Pedro Albizu Campos, and numerous others chose to decolonize their minds from the ideological doctrinal systems that manipulate language to falsify reality.

Crucial to understanding the pedagogy of white supremacy in education, is recognizing how old cultural beliefs still influence the way some teachers, administrators, curriculum developers, and those who implement public policy perceive nonwhite students. White people were always characterized as civilized while nonwhite people were labeled "savage"—a term derived from the Latin word *silva*, meaning "wood": *silvaticus*, a man of the wood, not domesticated, a man belonging to a primitive society, a wild man. The mythical image of the wild man/woman created by European superstitions was perceived to lack any social or linguistic abilities, yet possesses extraordinary sexual prowess and physical strength, walks around naked, and resorts to cannibalism. These perceptions were applied to all nonwhites as Europeans set out to colonize America between the sixteenth and eighteenth centuries and Africa in the nineteenth century (Dudley & Novak, 1972; Jordan, 1968; Vaughan, 1995). Thus the purported superior European civil and political capabilities were set in a struggle against the alleged nonwhite savage that was in opposition to the Europeanization of the world. The question we can ask is: How is this myth perpetuated today through the academy? How do these beliefs form opinions about nonwhites in the minds of teachers and students? How does this cause society to see and treat nonwhite people?

Eurocentric epistemological dimensions restrict nonwhite knowledge as unauthentic, therefore, not to be valued. Those regions not under Eurocentric interference supposedly will never achieve any significant cultural or intellectual progress and are permanently subjected to myths and ignorance. Many Eurocentric scholars wrote that Europeans opened up Africa to civilization and saved it from savagery, cannibalism, and heathenism. The scholar C. P. Groves, in his work *The Planting of Christianity in Africa*, Volume I (1948) wrote it was not until the latter part of the nineteenth century that Africa was "opened up" (p. 1). Why are places no Europeans inhabit labeled dark, closed, dangerous, primitive, heathen, savage, and inferior? Eurocentric epistemology, the invasion and theft of nonwhite spaces are easily justified through the school curriculum with words like discoveries, progress, settlers, or civilizing endeavors (Bigelow, 1998). For example, the Spanish conquistadors are absolved for invading and committing mass murder and genocide throughout the Caribbean, Central and South America. They are pardon for burning Aztec manuscripts, which were deemed demonic. Eurocentric archeologists dig up and violate nonwhite grave sites and remove the artifacts to European countries without respect for the indigenous people in the name of science. European scholars concluded that Africans have never produced anything worth learning about: that Benin art, for example, is of Portuguese origin; they claim the architecture of Zimbabwe was Arabic technology; and the elaborate governmental capabilities of the Hausa and the Buganda were borrowed from whites, who, somehow, invaded West Africa in ancient times (Mudimbe, 1988, p. 13). Therefore it is easy to produce Tarzan novels and movies alongside fictitious stories about lost white civilizations in West or Central Africa, which either excludes the presence of indigenous people or presents them as primitive in comparison to Tarzan or the lost white civilization.

White supremacist pedagogy is apparent when nonwhite people are distinguished as contaminators of white spaces. For instance, in colonial situations, racial divisions were labeled clearly through color bars, color lines, apartheid, Jim Crow laws, Niggertowns, and Darktown. Franz Fanon observed the colonized spaces are where all the whites live and the indigenous people live in the village or on the reservations segregated from whites and are labeled "niggers and dirty Arabs" (1963, pp. 38–40). Even today, in the United States, blacks continue to be stereotyped as contaminating, dirty, sexually deviant and are watched even when they have fully assimilated into the Eurocentric culture. What is distressing and proof that hegemony is a powerful tool is black people joining with whites in calling Arabs and other people from the Middle East "Sandniggers or rag heads." When Islamic hatred cools off, the discriminatory racial attention will shift back on those same blacks who sided with whites against people from the Middle East and their Islamic culture. The spaces occupied predominately by blacks are referred to as "urban jungles," while the white spaces are called "suburbs." These white spaces are patrolled by the police for black intruders (even if they live there and have the lifestyle of a middle or upper middle class whites), whose presence somehow threatens the existence of these white spaces. Thus, it becomes clear who benefit from curricula knowledge, whose knowledge is supported, and whose epistemological beliefs are accepted by using certain models and traditions. Why does this fear and hate of the black body, especially black males, prevail in U.S. society?

The hatred and fear of black males has dominated the white mind since colonial times and turned into a sexual paranoia during the Reconstruction period. The abolition of racial enslavement signified to whites that had previously ruled supreme feared black men would seek out revenge upon white women. To supplant the hierarchy of slavery, a social caste system was established and was explicitly enforced above and beyond the law (Day, 1974; Jordan, 1968; Litwack, 1980; Wood, 1970). The lynching of black males was argued to preserve white womanhood regardless of what actually happened. However, the real reasons for lynching black men was to prevent voting registrations, to keep black males from becoming too prosperous, or sheer white rage. Also, when one examines the way in which the lynchings were carried out it suggests an overriding sexual theme (Allen, Als, Lewis & Litwack, 2000; Paterson, 1996; Pinar, 2001; Wells-Barnett, 1969). In addition, the main reasons against school desegregation to keep little white girls away from young black males (Davis & Clark, 1992, p.184; Day, 1974). In a documentary by Deborah Ames of the Minnesota Public Radio on "Thurgood Marshall Before the Court," recalls white resistance to school desegregation was the fear of miscegenation. Ames records someone saying "It was incendiary, the idea of little black boys in school with little white girls." This fear of miscegenation has been preached by whites since the 1600s (McPherson & Katz, 1969, p.2) by both southern slaveowners and northern Puritan leaders and has been the reason for many white families to resort to private or suburban schools (Berwanger, 1972; Fredrickson, 1971; Kerber, 1967)

How does the curriculum address the continual unwritten curfew restrictions that the police still practice upon blacks who "intrude" into the white suburbs? How can teachers formulate a pedagogy that confronts the unwritten laws of white supremacy? Teachers and educators can begin to discern and understand white supremacist discourse, educate and prepare young black males who live in these white spaces—educate them how to negotiate the unwritten laws of apartheid. We can examine the ideological and cultural positions white teachers have when they walk into the classroom or curriculum developers when creating curriculum. These are important curricula concepts and questions to think about given that increasing numbers of black students, along with other students of color, are finding their way into suburban schools

Schools are sites where cultural knowledge is processed but has no relation how black people live and no connection to any antiracist struggle. During the 1960s and 1970s, black children were bussed to predominately white schools where many teachers held racist opinions of black students. African American students were believed to be not as intelligent as white students, have no self-control, are violent, and disrespectful to authority. Some teachers today still believe this and act out their pedagogical methods in systems of privilege and penalty that further validates and exacerbates the subordinate position (Foster, 1997; Howard, 1999; Sleeter, 1993).

Many white teachers believed black children should first to learn to be obedient and quiet in the classroom, used memorization and behaviorist theories espoused by B. F. Skinner in his 1948 novel *Walden Two*. Others such as Arthur Schlesinger, in his work *The Disuniting of America* (1991), argued the core values derived from Anglo Protestant Americanism be reinforced in schools and African culture be excluded, it is not worth learning. He believes that African culture is more oppressive than Anglo-Protestant American culture (pp. 40–55). In *Teaching to Transgress: Education as the Practice of Freedom* (1994) bell hooks says during segregation, black children were taught not just the core subject but were also taught how to survive in a racist society, that education was politicized and "contextualized within the framework of generational family experiences." She emphasizes when schools were integrated she was forced to conform to white images and "education was no longer about practicing freedom. Realizing this, I lost my love of school (p. 3)."

It is no wonder that many of my students (both black and white) come to class at the beginning of a semester with very little knowledge of the vast wealth of African American history and culture. The banking system of education (Freire, 1970) allows teachers to teach students only what they want students to know, memorize certain information, store it, and use it later for the teacher or multiple-choice exams. Any inclination of a student questioning or expressing opinions not in agreement with the curriculum is viewed as a threat to the social order of the classroom and silenced. Students who show enthusiasm about becoming a deposit of memorized information are rewarded and allowed to pursue a false intellectual journey, whereas students who show any independent thought process are forced to conform to the class rules and be quiet. The thought of teaching about racism, poverty, or the various episodes in American history have been silenced and completely excluded from the curriculum. Freire (1985) states: "It would be extremely naïve to expect the dominant classes to develop a type of education that would enable subordinate classes to perceive social injustices critically (p. 102)." The dominant white society will never educate black children to be equal with their children; education for black children will always be a false consciousness, actively stifling the development of a critical consciousness and suppressing the ability of blacks to live in a true egalitarian society.

When I taught an African American Studies course as a graduate instructor, part of the requirement was to study the entire video series of *Eyes on the Prize*. As we studied the videos, there was always a look of shock and disbelief on the faces of both the black and white students, but especially the white students. The black students, while they may not have experienced the kind of extreme outward racism of Jim Crow and may not have seen any vignettes of the Civil Rights Movement, they all had experienced racism and/or exclusion in some form already within American society. What they saw on the videos verified what they already knew existed in America. On the other hand, the white students were astonished as they read the materials and watched the videos throughout the course. They were amazed at the overt and subtle racism, the police brutality, the lynching, the water hoses and dogs unleashed on black men, women, and children, and the violence instigated by whites as they expressed their unwillingness to end racial apartheid in the United States. On many occasions, for example, my students were angry and shocked at the murder a twelve year old black male named Emmitt Till and black elementary school kids in Boston reading books and lyrics approved by the Boston School District that had the word "nigger" used regularly. They were taken aback to see white parents react violently to the idea of having black children bused into their children's neighborhood schools. One white student confessed the videos "made me mad, made me sad, and made me embarrassed because white people acted with no remorse." She continued saying, "How come we were not taught this? I think these videos should be shown in every classroom across the country." Another white student responded he could not understand why he "had not been taught the truth about the Civil Rights Movement." On the other hand, the black students were angered because they had not been exposed to the all the facts about the struggle for equality. Another student asked why was Martin Luther King Jr. valorized and accepted by the dominant society while Malcolm X and Marcus Garvey are disparaged or not even mentioned?

All the students raised good questions and debated among each other about ways of educating Americans about the truth of racism and ways an anti racist collation could be active and viable. They asked: Why is the *Eyes on the Prize* video series not shown and discussed in public schools, on college campuses so students can engage each other in debates with teachers on the issue of race in America? Why is Martin Luther King Jr. valorized and embraced by whites while teachers and society teach us to discard Malcolm X and

Marcus Garvey as our heroes. Why do teachers refuse to discuss the racial conflicts that continually confront us and the enormous poverty that exists in this wealthy nation? Why are students given a history of social amnesia that fail to challenge them or encourage any critical reflective thinking?

Every student in the class, especially the white students, responded to the video series by saying "I didn't know this went on: How could our government participate and sit back and allow blacks to be oppressed like this? How can an alleged God fearing people express so much hatred towards people of color?" Every one of those students (including the author) has been told mythical patriotic stories about the history of the United States. All of us have been indoctrinated as James W. Lowen says in his work, *Lies My Teacher Told Me: Everything Your American History Textbook Got Wrong* (1995) that "[n]ationalism is one of the culprits...[in] indoctrinat[ing] blind patriotism."

As my students were also introduced to the idea of hegemony and the concept of epistemology, we discussed the ways in which all of us have been socialized through school and how Anglo Protestant American knowledge have shaped the way we think. We discussed whose knowledge was instilled in schools and for what purposes were we given certain knowledge. We began to ask ourselves how hegemony presents particular aspects of knowledge in schools as objective, official and legitimatize as unquestioned truths. We debated how this ideology represented the interests of the dominant culture. We discussed ways in which knowledge is produced and used in school settings and whose interest is served by the teaching of certain factoids. The students raised questions why does the curriculum exclude conflicts that reflect badly upon the national character of the United States? Why textbooks include small fragments of African, Hispanic and Native American history? More significant, why have we been told lies about the national character of the U. S.? Why have textbooks excluded how the Founding Fathers proposed and organized to remove or exterminate the Native American population, did not want blacks in this country, went about trying to deport free blacks, while keeping slavery intact and engaging in numerous other events that reflected the criminal acts of this nation? Instead the message we are drilled with is "be a good patriotic citizen; you have a proud heritage and be all you can be" is drilled into the minds of millions of students.

Personal Reflections

As an African American growing up in New York City schools and reflecting back, the question I raise is: What heritage can I be proud of, if it was consciously kept from me? Yes, I am proud of my rich heritage as a person of African descent, learning about the great African civilizations, the rich African culture, what my ancestors went through under extreme inhumane circumstances during and after the Middle Passage. However, the history and cultural heritage public schools hammered into me had nothing to do with who I am as a person of African decent, the heritage they promoted was all white and European. How were other black children and I supposed to create any sense of worth in ourselves if all we learned was how great Europeans are and how they came to save the ignorant blacks from our alleged savage nature? How can we begin to love literature if the only literature we read was about Europeans and white Americans and if black people were mentioned at all, it was only in the light of us living in the shadow and according to Eurocentric culture and history? People gaze upon us in a derogatory manner because we express a sense of pride in our African culture, our sexuality, our music, style of dress, hairstyles, our writings, and our sense of the world. Scholars throughout U.S. history have written about our utter poverty and ghettoization, and our alleged inferior intellectual skills. We have had to live with these accusations and lies and yet we have proven every allegation and fabrication to be fictitious and inaccurate. Also very few textbooks include the the cosmopolitan civilizations of Egypt, Mali, Ghana, or Songhay and the intellectual abundance of these empires. There is very little honest dialogue concerning the issues of white supremacy and race within the public school system; there is mostly talk of tolerance and respect with no mention of the root of the problem: white supremacy, racism, oppression, and segregation. This kind of pedagogy prevents any dialogue of the origin of white supremacy or racism, nor any kind of understanding of oppression and the exploitation of people; instead it places all responsibility on the oppressed group and blames them for their failure to be successful in society.

Black people, for example, who are oppressed and colonized are taught to pledge allegiance to a flag and to support a nationalist ideology set upon preserving white supremacy, since 1619 consistently treated us as if we are inferior, not worth educating, called lazy, and, most of all, seen as a disease to American society. We were all taught to sing patriotic, nationalistic songs like "My Country Tis of Thee," "America the Beautiful," and "The Star-Spangled Banner," written by Francis Scott Key, who himself believed in black inferiority and joined an organization to deport all free blacks from the United States. While some students of color may not be able to articulate why they reject American education, they are not ignorant that there is something inherently wrong with it. Again, many educators and teachers do not make the effort to question why African, Native, and Hispanic American students hate or have no respect for American history nor do they ask students their thoughts or discuss the issue.

I ask myself sometimes why are some teachers and school administrators are so indoctrinated to the point of closing their eyes to the hypocrisy of The Pledge of Allegiance. It is amazing they expect children of color to continue to give allegiance to a government that has violated their identity, endorsed genocidal practices against Native Americans and endorsed the enslavement of black people, denied women their equal rights, and consistently practices discriminatory acts upon people of color.

My first conflict in school was in the second grade, when I refused to pledge allegiance to the United States flag. I was not able to articulate why I refused to pledge allegiance or remember who taught me to resist placing my hand on my left breast and recite the pledge of allegiance, but I knew it was wrong to give allegiance to a nation that repeatedly had devalued me, my people, my culture, and my heritage. I learned years later that the source of this resistance was my father, who instilled in me never to give any allegiance to the United States, which consistently oppresses people of color.

Imagine Native, African, and Mexican Americans and other children of color saying in unison "liberty and justice for all" in the attempt to dull the mind to the hypocrisy of the pledge of allegiance. Even more deceptive is the idea of joining the oppressed with their oppressor in a common cause to maintain the status quo. Teachers have encouraged and forced children of color (whether consciously or unconsciously) to give allegiance to a government and society that historically oppressed them is one of the greatest hypocrisies of patriotism and democracy, and one of the greatest triumphs of hegemony. When students of color resist the hegemonic power of the dominant culture, we become a threat to the social order and must be or neutralized or extracted (Macedo, 1994).

In teaching about white supremacy in the classroom, the teacher needs to understand the historical background of their students; no matter what race or ethnicity they may be, there needs to be respect and care from both students and teacher and the teacher's willingness to learn from his or her students. Teachers are agents of change; therefore, their pedagogy should be to empower students with the confidence to become responsible civic agents for social change. Today, many white students come to class and experience a change in classroom demographics where their "whiteness" ceases to be the norm. Some white students feel personally attacked when they are confronted in class by black students who may express anger at the discriminatory practices they and other people of color have had to endure. Many teachers are not prepared to facilitate when confronted with classroom scenarios about race and class (Howard. 1999; Sleeter, 1993)

Universities and college education departments can offer courses that prepare teachers and teacher candidates to deal with racism and the inequities that permeate our schools and society. Many multicultural education courses do not prepare teachers to facilitate discussions on race, power and class; most multicultural courses are methods on lessons of tolerance or the celebration and respect of other cultures. Many teacher candidates go through their programs without learning the historical struggles of their students. Instead, teachers have been taught or are given a curriculum promoting Anglo Protestantism cultural values. There is no mention of the racial or ethnic discrimination many of their students may face daily (Feagin, Vera & Imani, 1996; McCarthy, 1993; Sleeter, 1993).

Some students feel that multicultural courses lead only to discrediting Western culture and disparage European history. They argue there is no need for multiculturalism or any such discussions of issues of race and class. Those who promote this argument believe that multiculturalism is just a "feel-good" or "self-esteem" topic that has no place in the development of a child's mind, they only need to study the canon that has been empirically validated by scholars as the only source for higher order thinking. These conservative forces fear that multiculturalism and the agendas of people of color are destroying the social fabric of American society, a fear that has plagued this nation since colonial times

CHAPTER THREE

WHITE SUPREMACY'S POLITICS OF CULTURE AND EXCLUSION

I know now that the most damaging thing a people in a colonial situation can do is allow their children to attend any educational facility organized by the dominant enemy culture.

George Jackson, 1970

It would be extremely naïve to expect the dominant classes to develop the type of education that would enable the subordinate classes to perceive social injustices critically.

Paulo Freire, 1985

The purpose of white supremacy has always been to teach black inferiority, miscegenation threatens the purity of white people, threatens the security of the nation, and ensure that all white immigrants are acculturated to accept Anglo Protestant American traditions. They believe they are on a sacred mission and have replaced the ancient Israelites as God's chosen people and their acts to dominate the world's resources are justified by the God of Christianity. This belief that God is only on *our* side is used by conservatives to legitimize a blatant Anglo American superiority over all others, especially today as this government's foreign policy attempts to make the Islamic world accept the American version of democracy and culture as the suitable   lifestyle. Prominent government, religious, intellectual, and other prominent figures made systematic and deliberate efforts to make whiteness and Anglo Protestant culture a necessity for citizenship within this society (Spring, 2004; Adams & Sanders, 2003).

Right wing educators have promoted an ideology that declines to address or attack the social conditions that force nonwhites and the poor into the lowest level of society. Instead they attribute societal problems to black people's alleged depravity and continually claim blacks (especially black youth) pose a danger to the social fabric, and security of the United States (Miller, 1996; Parenti, 1999; Zinn, 1995). White conservative educators and politicians argue blacks display perfect behavior when they shed their blackness, are "Americanized" and conform to the standards of the dominant society. On the other hand, instead of creating integrated housing and opportunities for African Americans and other nonwhites to buy homes in predominately white communities, the dominant white culture continues to embrace residential apartheid that manifests a tendency in the differentiation of race (Lipstiz, 1998). Schools are also sites of racial apartheid, where poverty is the tool to maintain racial segregation, devalues black and other children of color as the "other" and pushes them to the margins of the curriculum (Orfield & Lee, 2005 Yeo, 1997).

Government and other public figures from this nation's inception were determined to create and secure a national culture around Anglo Protestantism (Grant & Davison, 1928). Public schools became the defenders of Anglo Protestant cultural values perceived to be challenged by Catholicism, Native and African American cultures (Apple, 1990; Carlson, 1975; Spring, 1997). Today, conservatives, liberals and various ethnic groups are engaged in a struggle to protect the traditional canon of literature that supports Protestant values while Native, African, and Hispanic Americans believe devalue their own cultural icons and historical heritage. On one side of the debate, the dominant culture with white supremacist support, maintains a curriculum that safeguards Anglo Protestant asocial norms; on the other side of the debate leftists, Native, African, Hispanic Americans are demanding an equal share of representation in the curriculum. (Gomez, 1993; Kincheloe, 1993; Kincheloe & Steinberg, 1997: Macedo, 1994; Spring, 1997).

During the early 1800s, white supremacist ideologues promoted the idea to remove blacks from society. It was believed blacks could never become a part of American society and therefore were a threat to the racial purity of whites (Adams & Sanders, 2003; Bodo, 1954; Jordan, 1968; McIntyre, 1984). Alongside this belief, the intelligentsia began to use science to justify their enslavement and segregation of blacks, but instead of the racist ideology dying out when slavery ended, the alleged scientific truths grew stronger as whites relegated blacks to legal segregation (Friedman, 1970; Hannaford, 1996; Smedley, 1999; Tucker, 1994; Wood, 1970). By the beginning of the twentieth century, academic scholars were publishing outright racist and eugenicist literature and applied it on college campuses. This literature stated that Anglo/Nordic people were superior to all others and deserved the right to dominate and rule the world (Selden, 1999; Tucker, 1994). They referred to their theoretical ideas as social Darwinism or eugenics (Hofstadter, 1944); in the 1990s a theory termed the Bell Curve became the new discourse of old white supremacist ideology intent on excluding Native Americans, Hispanics, African Americans, and even poor whites from educational and economic opportunities (Kincheloe, Stienberg, & Gresson, 1996; Jacoby & Glauberman, 1995).

Throughout the history of public education, black children were segregated and isolated, Hispanics and southern European immigrants were forced to speak English and learn Anglo Protestant cultural values. This idea to Americanize nonwhites and European immigrants into Anglo Protestant cultural values became the main goal of the curriculum (Apple, 1990) While European immigrants were culturalized into Anglo Protestant values, Native, African, and Hispanic American children were deculturalized and in some cases forbidden to express their own cultural or religious values (Carlson, 1975; Perlmutter, 1992; Spring, 1994). Children of color may not know how to articulate that being white means "right" and gives one access to places nonwhites do not have access to; but they understand the concept and seek to become white through assimilation (Spring, 1997; Asante, 1991).

The transformations within curricula have influenced debates over what should be taught in schools, how it should be taught, and why it should be taught (Apple, 1990, Pinar, Reynolds, Slattery & Taubman, 1995). In the 1960s, the Civil Rights Movement confronted white supremacy, seeking to promote more egalitarian principles and public policies; the movement made some headway in a society that believed black people were inferior in every sense of the word. However, since the 1980s, right-wing groups and conservative organizations have put pressure on schools to make textbooks more patriotic, to adhere to the Anglo-Protestant traditions that supposedly made this nation, and to promote capitalism and maintain their dominance (Macedo, 1994; Apple, 1996b; Spring, 1997). E. D. Hirsch (1988) claims education has failed its responsibility to acculturate children in the Western tradition. He argues the future of the English language and traditional western literature is being shoved to the side in place of multiculturalism. He cites China as an example in failing to acculturate its people:

> By the seventeenth century, China had printing presses and a stable written language. But even after the arrival of printing, the oral Chinese language did not become standardized throughout the country. To this very day, China is a ployglot nation of mutually unintelligible dialects.... China is not able to function successfully as a modern industrial and economic unit (p. 76).

Hirsch exposes his white supremacist beliefs by stating that China failed because it has no stable written language. By saying that the Chinese language is unstable, Hirsch fundamentally says that Chinese people are "mutually" not intelligent because they cannot understand each other's dialects! If he believes that about the Chinese, then what are his feelings about Africans and those of African descent and the various dialects among them? Hirsch further argues any nation nationalizing its people under the dominant culture must follow the European pattern. This means in order to acculturate and conform, subordinate groups must be Americanized in the quest for a homogeneous white society (Carlson, 1975). Does Hirsch really expect Chinese or any other student of color to just sit there and accept his demeaning statements?

Former Secretary of Education William Bennett calls for a complete inclusion of Western civilization, arts, and literature in school and college curricula and more of the major achievements of Europeans in the scientific disciplines, as if only Europe has produced anything significant. He also claims this nation's moral Christian values have been thrown to the wayside and we need to get back to the basics of our common knowledge and heritage (Apple, 2001, p.16). In Bennett's book *Our Children and Our Country: Improving America's Schools and Affirming the Common Culture* (1988), he claims the American people want their children to receive the best education. Although it is true that all parents want the best for their children, it should also be questioned what group of American people he is actually referring to. It is not hard to figure out whom he is talking to. Bennett writes:

> In the 1960s and 1970s, we neglected and denied much of the best in American education. We simply stopped doing the right things. We allowed an assault on the intellectual and moral standards. Traditional education practices were discarded, expectations were lowered, and the curriculum was dumb-down (pp. 9–10).

Questions to ask: What was happening in the United States during the 1960s and 1970s? What caused William Bennett to say American education was being neglected? Who allegedly assaulted the intellectual and moral standards and caused this so-called decline in education until we are now dumb? What is the hidden message in Bennett's language and exactly who is he blaming for this decline in education?

During the 1960s black people in the United States were in a struggle against a racist, hegemonic, white supremacist society and a struggle to force the federal government to protect black people and their civil rights, to rid the United States of its system of apartheid in public facilities, housing, and education. Urban centers exploded in riots and African, Hispanic, Asian, and Native Americans mobilized politically in the 1960s and 1970s, radically changing the political and cultural landscape of the nation. While the Civil Rights Movement achieved some degree of success and reformed some of the nation's racial apartheid system, the movement came immediately under attack by right wing and conservative alliances (Edgar, 1981). In preparation for conservative educational reform, people like Chester Finn advocated the Euro-American canon be combined with Judeo-Christian values. Bennett and other conservative scholars believe the Civil Rights Movement corrupted the 1960s and that left wing, multicultural, and Afrocentric educators, along with allowing the undeserving poor into higher education, have somehow lowered educational standards (Gottfried, 1991; Stotsky, 1999).

It becomes easy to blame people of color, especially blacks, for having "dumbed-down" the standards of education. Today, white society still adheres to the beliefs and attitudes created and constructed by colonial and religious leaders about race. Buttressed by elite slaveholders who wanted to sustain their profits and way of living and Puritan religious leaders in the North who wanted to preserve control of their congregations, consciously and deliberately invented the category of "whiteness"—an inherently superior "whiteness"—for the purpose of social control. The Puritans' doctrine of predestination somehow claimed Americans had the divine right to rule over all others who did not adhere to their brand of Christianity, did not physically look like them and rationalized inequality as a natural part of hierarchy, what others have called the "great chain of being" (Lovejoy, 1960; Powell, 1992; Smedley, 1999). This ideology of race has been employed since the eighteenth century as a device to categorize society and allocate privileges, benefits, and rights to some and not to others with the justification of physical differences and superiority, which we still have not transcended in the United States. White supremacy continues to permeate our society through economic inequality, unwritten apartheid laws such as residential and educational segregation, and informal restrictions against socializing, intermarriage, and memberships in private organizations, including the most visible institution in the United States—the church (Bullard & Lee, 1994; Davies, 1988; Kelsey, 1965; Kozol, 1991; Lipstiz, 1998; Massey & Denton, 1993; Orfield & Eaton, 1996).

African Americans historically have lived daily with the internal and external divisions caused by racism within the church. Both clergy and their congregations are complicit in having played a major role in oppressing black people and maintaining white supremacy in the United States. Between the early 1600s up into the Civil War, northern white clergy made efforts to first segregate free blacks from their churches and then sought to send them to Africa (Berwanger, 1967 & 1972; Bodo, 1954; Litwack, 1961; Staudenraus, 1961). Throughout the period of the Social Gospel, and now with the Religious Right and the Moral Majority, despite sporadic humanitarian efforts, Christianity has largely buttressed the racial oppression of black people. Church assumptions of cultural and spiritual superiority, combined with fanatical missionary zeal and a belief in the infallibility of the Bible, assisted in the institution of racial slavery in the Americas. Today, the Religious Right asserts they alone know the "will of God" and everyone else is all beyond redemption; and try to intimidate public schools into conformity with this notion. Christianity now camouflages its racism and stereotypes of blacks behind slogans of morality and clean living as it tries to force black youth to conform to Anglo Protestant traditional values through education (Boesak, 1990; Wood, 1990; Hood, 1994; Edwards, 1998).

The presidential race of George Wallace in 1968 was a campaign to turn back the clock on the limited political, social, and educational achievements of the Civil Rights Movement. As the next decade began, industry went through a period of restructuring and downsizing, and the elimination of jobs displaced thousands of people. However, along with this downsizing, most whites continued to hold a callous opinion of the nation's growing poor, which was predominately African, Hispanic, and Native American and included a large number of poor whites. Middle class whites resented they were supposedly paying for the "underprivileged." They hated the idea that people of color, especially blacks, were receiving alleged preferences in educational and employment opportunities. They also feared traditional values and traditional interpretations of American history were being lost to Afrocentric, Native American, and Hispanic forms of knowledge (Handler & Hasenfeld, 1997; Kincheloe & Steinberg, 1997; Omi & Winant, 1994; Pinkney, 1984).

Public debates about race and white supremacy within curriculum circles and society at large are now expected to vanish without any acknowledgement of the persistence of racism or the renewed entrenchment of racially structured power relations. Because the topic of white supremacy is excluded from debates in education, its supremacist characterizations become increasingly difficult to recognize, especially by those who are unable or do not want to decipher the encoded language. This means the hidden racist arguments can be mobilized readily across racial boundaries and political alignments. Political alliances that were once easily defined as white supremacist, conservative, liberal and sometimes even radical therefore have a tendency to lose their distinctiveness in the face of the seductions of camouflaged white supremacist discourse.

Thus it becomes easy for Bennett to talk about maintaining white Anglo-Protestant hegemonic ideology in education, claiming that affirmative action and multicultural education that can be emancipatory and critical of traditional norms have "dumbed-down" the educational standards of public schools. When he mentions the 1960s and 1970s, white conservatives and neoliberals understand Bennett's language and know he is referring to race and the perceived loss of Anglo Protestant American values and traditions in public schools to the Civil Rights Movement.

Sandra Stotsky in her book *Losing our Language: How Multicultural Classroom Instruction Is Undermining Our Children's Ability to Read, Write, and Reason* (1999), claims learning Swahili or Spanish deprives children of the ability to read, write and reason in English. Questions can be raised: Does the learning of Latin, German, Italian, French, or even English prevent children of color from learning their own cultural identities? What implications does Stotsky provide in writing a book arguing learning European languages that have been forced on people of color through repressive white supremacist societies is any better than learning our own cultural language? And, in any event, what school whether it be predominately white or African, Hispanic, or Native American public school does not promote Standard English as primary? Thus through camouflaged discourse, white supremacist ideology continues to devalue the culture and language of people of color.

Curricula represent the cultural ethos of the dominant group and the debates surround what is allowed in the curricula always involve more than just textbook content. The debate really centers on society and the cultural direction the curriculum should take in educating the masses and the process where the dominated groups are made more obedient, acculturated in the values and beliefs of the dominant culture (Apple, 1990). Students are forced to conform to acceptable behaviors that reflect Anglo Protestant American values and those who refuse to conform are excluded from the classrooms (Figueroa, 1991, p. 122). In Greek mythology, the character Procrustes is a robber and champion who enforce conformity upon the people. He ensnares unsuspecting travelers, drags them to his dwelling, and ties them to his bed. While the travelers have various heights, Procrustes' bed is only one size, and if the traveler is too short, Procrustes stretches them out to conform to the size of the bed. If the traveler is too long, he cuts off the extremities so there is nothing hanging off the bed. Therefore everyone is conformed to Procrustes' standards and desire for uniformity. In the same light, our schools shape students to Procrustes-style curricula and behaviors—to fit into only one kind of sexual union, worship only one certain God, and accept only one worldview.

In other words, white supremacy uses education to implement a "culture of silence" in us, to produce apathy, illiteracy, and passivity to solidify their economic, social, and political domination along with paternalism. Again, the words of white supremacist Elias B. Caldwell come back to mind—he proposed if black people could not be removed from the United States then:

> keep them in their lowest state of degradation and ignorance. The nearer you bring them to the condition of brutes, the better chance do you give them of possessing their apathy. (*African Repository*, February 1836, p. 53).

For two hundred and fifty years, white supremacist attitudes were overt during slavery and denied free blacks any opportunities in education and socioeconomic mobility. Then, from Reconstruction right up to the Civil Rights Movement, overt force lasted in the South while in the North racial discriminatory practices along with a blanket of paternalism settled over the masses of black people to maintain dominance. Northern philanthropy gave assistance to blacks in their quest to gain their rights as citizens only as long as white philanthropists could dictate the progress and was accommodative to Southern racial apartheid polices so they could achieve economic profits (Spivey, 1978; Watkins, 2001). Thus pedagogy is produced by white supremacist ideologues concealed in a false benevolence. This paternalism make objects of their false humanitarianism by treating blacks as hapless and by presenting themselves as models for blacks to emulate (Stanfield, 1985). White Anglo Protestant Americanism has produced an epistemology teaching they have this inalienable right, given by God, to dominate everyone else. White people are supposed to have superior intelligence and technology, acquired their power by their own effort, and pulled themselves up by their bootstraps. Blacks do not have this right because supposedly they are incompetent and lazy.

By projecting blacks as ignorant, they have negated any idea of true education and tried to remove any desire of inquiry from us, justifying not only white paternalism, but also their ideology of oppression. It is imperative white supremacy control education to fill students with predetermined knowledge and memorize the narrated curricula. It is essential to understand since Anglo Protestant Americanism can not have the homogeneous society it desires, it becomes imperative for the elite leadership to politically dominate, determine what is socially acceptable, exercise the most influence upon the masses, and determine what values and skills schools transmit. Therefore, schools become the conduits of transmitting from one generation to the next the knowledge, values, aesthetics, and spiritual beliefs of the dominant group's cultural orientations (Apple, 1990).

The invidious nature of this racism carries so much fear within our society that many right wing proponents fail to remember that most African Americans have been imbued with the same mythology and values of white America. The problem arises because our religious beliefs and values are proud and independent of the dominant white community. Vincent Harding (1981) emphasizes the "spiritual strivings" that characterizes our struggle as African Americans in the United States. What white America has always feared since colonial times is the black tradition to resist subordination and use Afro-Christian religious beliefs to gain some independence from white control. Anglo American ideologues hated the idea that African Americans did not fully embrace "Americanization," blacks resisted and sought to seek the revalorization of our image of Africa, our willingness to accept protest and agitation in the tradition of Denmark Vesey, Gabriel Prosser, Nat Turner, Malcolm X, and numerous others who sought the liberation of black people (Morris, 1993; Wilmore & Cone, 1979 & 1993; Wilmore, 1996).

It is therefore important that the symbolic representations in the curriculum serve the interests of Anglo Protestant Americanism, which in the minds of whites constitute good literature and legitimate political actions. Thus the curriculum will filter out any knowledge that prompts critical reflection upon the dominant society, therefore giving students selective ideas and information to guide students to think and act in a certain passive manner. Paulo Freire (1970) writes why and how the oppressor uses education to maintain dominance:

> The banking notion of consciousness that the educator's role is to regulate the way the world "enters into" the students. The teacher's task is to organize a process which already occurs spontaneously, to "fill" the students by making deposits of information which he or she considers to constitute true knowledge. And since people "receive" the world as passive entities, education should make them more passive still, and adapt them to the world. The educated individual is the adapted person, because she or he is better "fit" for the world. Translated into practice, this concept is well suited to the purposes of the oppressors, whose tranquility rests on how well the people fit the world the oppressors have created, and how little they question it (p. 57).

Thus a Eurocentric epistemology seeks to change the consciousness of African, Native, and Hispanic American students to conform to the dominant standards and to the conditions that oppress them. Within a hegemonic white supremacist society, like the United States, the dominant culture also seeks to maintain control by reaching into the oppressed culture and reshaping the ideology by allowing certain heroes from the oppressed groups into the curriculum to meet the demands of multiculturalism and inclusion. In other words, dominance is maintained through the process of compromising with the oppressed groups by integrating selective parts of the oppressed culture and history into the dominant culture and historical traditions, thereby acculturating the oppressed into accepting the values and beliefs of the dominant group (Artz & Murphy, 2000; Bennett, 1988).

Frederick Douglass, for example, is represented well in textbooks as the most celebrated black man next to Martin Luther King Jr. in American history. Yet both of these influential black men have been silenced concerning their criticism of America's longest lasting institutionalized ideology, white supremacy. One of the most compelling speeches Douglass gave was on July 5, 1852, in Rochester, New York, where he criticized the United States and its hypocritical celebration of the Fourth of July while at the same time supported the perpetual enslavement of over four million blacks and the segregation of free blacks in the North. Douglass's critique of American nationalism, the Constitution, and the Declaration of Independence can allow teachers to pedagogically guide students to critique our form and practice of democracy. Students can begin to question, research and understand how white supremacy and hegemony has millions of people of color celebrating a holiday that historically denied them any voice. Douglass told the crowd of white politicians, religious leaders, and lay people the Fourth of July was not a holiday black people wanted to honor, but it was a contradiction white people took for granted. He said:

> Why am I called upon to speak here to-day? What have I, or those I represent, to do with your national independence? Are the great principles of political freedom and of natural justice, embodied in that Declaration of Independence, extended to us?... I am not included within the pale of this glorious anniversary! Your high independence only reveals the immeasureable distance between us.... The Fourth of July is yours, not mine. You may rejoice, I must mourn. To drag a man in fetters into the grand illuminated temple of liberty, and call upon him to join you in joyous anthems, were inhuman mockery and sacrilegious irony. Do you mean, citizens, to mock me by asking me to speak today? (Asante & Abarry1996, p. 637).

Douglass understood blacks in the North had no rights "white people were bound to respect:" we were denied access to public facilities, could not participate in attaining public lands like immigrant white people, and were pressed into the menial jobs whites refused to accept. Black children were denied access to most public schools and with the rise of Jacksonian politics blacks were totally disfranchised while Jackson tried to exterminate Native Americans. Blacks were even excluded from celebrating the Fourth of July (Harding, 1981). Douglass criticized the United States for celebrating Independence Day while blacks were denied basic human rights. Douglass continued:

> What, to the American slave, is your Fourth of July? I answer: a day that reveals to him, more than all the other days in the year, the gross injustice and cruelty to which he is the constant victim. To him, your celebration is a sham; your boasted liberty, an unholy license; your national greatness swelling vanity; your sounds of rejoicing are empty and heartless; your denunciations of tyrants, brass fronted impudence; your shouts of liberty

and equality, hollow mockery; your prayers and hymns, your sermons and thanksgivings, with all your religious parade, and solemnity, are, to him mere bombast, fraud, deception, impiety, and hypocrisy—a thin veil to cover up crimes which should disgrace a nation of savages. There is not a nation on earth guilty of practices, more shocking and bloody, than are the people of these United States, at this very hour (p. 639).

Douglass struck at the core of what white Americans valued the most and called it all a sham and charged the nation to contemplate its celebration of the Fourth of July. By completely omitting this speech from high school and college history textbooks, the writers withdraw from the responsibility of giving students the opportunity to critically question not only white supremacy and racism, but also the fundamental rationales underpinning racism, and its eradication. Students are not given the chance to critically examine the U.S. Constitution and its support of racial slavery.

Martin Luther King Jr. is perhaps the most celebrated African American leader that white America has chosen to accept and put into the textbooks—his birthday has even been proclaimed a national holiday. School textbooks depict him as the leader of the Civil Rights Movement encouraging black people into nonviolent confrontation with racial segregation. However, the index of *America's History since 1865* (1987, p. xxxv), gives a reference to King's accomplishments on pages 934–935. But when one turns to the pages to read about his accomplishments, there is no list of such deeds. On page 934, students are given a dialogue between King and a young angry black male during the 1965 riots in the Watts section of Los Angeles, California. This is significant because, at the end of the previous page, 1964 is proclaimed the beginning of the "long hot summers" of rioting by urban blacks. The last paragraph talks of "racial turmoil," that sixty percent of Watts' black population is on "relief" (welfare), but the important part of this paragraph is the authors make sure the reader reads "[i]ronically, Watts erupted just five days after President Johnson had hailed passage of the Voting Rights Act of 1965 as the next step toward racial equality" (p. 933). Black people are portrayed as ungrateful to the liberal white community by not restraining themselves and not following King's nonviolent strategy. The narrative ends with King being disappointed with young black urban males allegedly burning down the city—thus undermining King's accomplishments. Why is the Watts unrest inserted into the textbook where the index section says King's accomplishments should be? Could it be the authors wanted the readers to take notice of alleged ungrateful black people rioting right after the signing of the Voting Rights Act? Could it be while the textbook explains black people were tired of discriminatory employment practices, substandard education, being exploited, weary of discriminatory mortgage lenders and being denied access to various public facilities by the white society, the focus was on black people asserting themselves violently who needed to be put back under control and the failure of the liberal policies of President Johnson's Great Society.

The Civil Rights Act of 1964 and the Voting Rights Act of 1965 were passed by Congress and signed by President Lyndon B. Johnson, yet the majority of white people in the United States were already wondering if the demonstrations of the Civil Rights Movement served any purpose anymore. White people's apprehensions were confirmed when Watts broke out in civil unrest five days after the Voting Rights Act of 1965 was signed. As long as Martin Luther King Jr. contained the Civil Rights Movement in the South, only addressing the right of black people as citizens to vote and have access to public facilities, Northern white liberals gave the movement their support.

However, once the movement decided to move into the Northern urban centers bearing a list of grievances greatly enlarged by demands for jobs, open housing, and citizen reviews of police departments and real estate boards, many Northern white allies, labor leaders, various white liberals, prelates, and the federal government began to distance themselves from the Civil Rights Movement. Textbooks tell very little if anything of the stiffening of Northern white resistance to ending segregated schools and allocating equal education to black children and Northern unwillingness to allow blacks to compete in the job market. Fear of their spaces being invaded by blacks has plagued the psyche of whites since colonial days—the right to vote was not as threatening as having blacks living next door, competing in the job market, or sitting next to their daughters in the classroom (Kinkner, 1999; Lipsitz, 1998; Orfield & Eaton, 1996). The eradication of the slums, better educational facilities, and integrated neighborhoods were considered far too much and beyond integrated buses and lunch counters. Northern white allies were not willing to fight against racial segregation in their own backyards and assault the larger issues of discrimination and the struggle against economic exploitation (Kozol, 1991; Massy & Denton, 1993; Lipsitz, 1998). Textbooks like *America's History since 1865* follow the political sentiment of white America and their feelings about the Civil Rights Movement. The textbook *Out of Many: A History of the American People,* Vol. II (1994), gives an extensive account of the Civil Rights Movement in the South, but nothing about it in the North. Similarly, *Nation of Nations: a Narrative of the American Republic* (1991) does not offer much to students on the Civil Rights Movement nor does it give a favorable point of view to the reader.

Neoconservative educators and groups are relentless in their efforts to create and maintain an ideological consensus to uphold traditional Anglo Protestant American cultural norms in public schools. They believe they are saving democracy, which some have never been allowed to participate in or enjoy, and advocate what Allan Bloom, E. D. Hirsch, and William Bennett call the "great books" and ideas of Western tradition are supposed to save this nation and return it to its mythical golden age. They claim by returning to a curriculum that advocates the "common culture," as William Bennett and others claim, student achievement will rise, our international economic competitiveness will grow, and poverty and unemployment will disappear (Bennett, 1988; Bloom, 1987; Hirsch, 1988; Shea, 1989; Martin, 1989). Symbolic representations in books and the media are used to bestow legitimacy on the dominant status of particular social groups. As always, the dominant group uses the media and cultural capital to confirm its own achievements as the only thing to study and research (Bourdieu, 1977).

The fear of black power, alleged propensity towards crime, reverse discrimination, the perception of our presence in their communities will devalue private property, and the economic crunch on white workers, along with the apprehensions that this nation's Anglo Protestant American cultural family traditions were declining rapidly, brought about major debates in educational arenas. While the New Right was careful not to overtly display any explicit racism, it rearticulated a racist ideology under the umbrella of political movements and fundamentalist religion (Apple, 1996 & 2001). Opposition to school desegregation in the South and northern urban centers like Boston nourished fears that their homogenous white communities were threatened. In 1975 the Heritage Foundation, founded by New Right leaders including Colorado's brewer Joseph Coors, the Washington operative Paul Weyrich, and fundraiser Richard A. Viguerie, formed the National Congress for Educational Excellence to coordinate textbook protests across the nation. The organization capitalized on the concerns of white people who fear that their American traditions and values were being diminished for multicultural curricula textbooks (Crawford, 1980; Domhoff, 1998). By arguing for traditional Anglo Protestant American family values and a return to the homogenous society, the New Right conservatives and Christian fundamentalists can continue to exclude blacks and other people of color from the curriculum and society, maintaining the ideology of white supremacy.

Thus the curriculum is very selective in the information it allows students to learn concerning those who were anti-racist and for a true democratic society. The life of Martin Luther King Jr. has been buried under the popular slogan "I have a dream" and his life struggle against white supremacy is erased completely from public classroom discussions. The curriculum does not allow students to investigate the richness of his later speeches against economic greed and poverty. Schools say very little, if anything, about Malcolm X—students cannot examine his life, to see how it always constantly changing, nor are they allowed to study his speeches. There is no mention in the curriculum of June Johnson, the thirteen-year-old black girl who joined Fannie Lou Hamer only to be brutally beaten by white men, or Viola Liuzzo, a white activist who left her four kids to join hundreds of other African Americans who were determined to cross the Edmund Pettus Bridge in Selma, Alabama, in 1965 and was later killed by Klansmen on a highway (Carson, Garrow, Gill, Harding & Hine, 1991; Mills, 1993). It is evident that the exclusion of these people who counted the cost of freedom and refused to back down raises questions for us as educators. Why is so much history excluded from our textbooks? Why are so many ordinary people who criticized, fought for, and died for this nation's apparently great ideals excluded from our curricula? As Vincent Harding asks in his book *Hope and History* (1990) what is the purpose of our teaching? Where do our assumptions, actions, and content direct students? How do we confront conservatives and New Right groups in their argument against a multicultural society?

Conservatives and other New Right groups promote textbooks that reproduce, revere, and honor Anglo Protestant American forms of knowledge and continue to depreciate African American forms of knowledge (Asante, 1991; Banks, 1992; Lee, Lomotey & Shujaa, 1990). While textbooks praise the Anglo Protestant American way of life and the men who led this nation in its early years, they do not tell us that that almost every president up till Abraham Lincoln were slaveowners. Nor do textbooks mention that the Protestant leaders of New England praised and gave honor to their God for giving them the strength to exterminate the Native American population (Jennings, 1975). I wonder what Bennett has to say about Native American resistance to emulating Anglo Protestant culture in reference to the Puritans praise to God in their quest to exterminate the Native American population. Alan Bloom argues in his book *The Closing of the American Mind* (1987) for a curriculum whose focus is the "great books" of Western tradition and Western philosophy, especially the Greeks. Both Bennett and Bloom want African, Hispanic, and Native Americans to cherish and study the works of Western philosophy, yet Bloom and Bennett are asking us to ignore Voltaire's racist viewpoint:

> The Negro race is a species of men different from ours....If their understanding is not of a different nature than ours it is at least greatly inferior. They are not capable of any great application or association of ideas, and seem formed neither for the advantages nor the abuses of philosophy (Gossett, 1963, p. 45).

How can I or any other black student study the great works of the Western canon, encounter bold racist statements such as Voltaire's, and be expected to respect Eurocentric literature? We have seen what happens to the psyche of black youth who comply with a curriculum claiming Africa has no history or civilization or those who have descended from African ancestry are inferior and have no ability to think in abstract terms.

Bennett and Bloom want African American children to be instructed on the preeminence of European culture and history, while their own heritage and values are disparaged. I believe to comply with Bennett and Bloom or any others who believe only the works of the Western canon are worth learning and studying is insidious to the minds and hearts of African, Native, Hispanic, and even white Americans. This epistemological process not only validates the notion Anglo/Nordic ancestry has achieved everything worth knowing, but at the same time it pulverizes and discourages any brilliance in African American youth by making them feel all Africans, and those of African descent, have never amounted to much nor will they ever be on equal footing with the white race. Carter G. Woodson (1933) insists this allows the dominant society to control not only the production of knowledge, but also a pedagogy committed to teaching African Americans to despise their own people and once this is completed there is no need to worry about their actions. Paulo Freire spoke of this hegemonic ideology when he argued students are turned into "containers" and "receptacles" filled by the teacher and denied the ability to create their own forms of knowledge through the process of investigation. African American youth are alienated from their own history and cultural heritage; they accept their ignorance, never create their own knowledge, and become tools of the hegemonic power structure.

Bennett (1988) wants black children to esteem James Madison as one of our greatest leaders. Yet, how can black children honor a man who became the third president of the American Colonization Society and left over one hundred enslaved blacks to his heirs? How can Bennett expect black children to even listen to the words of James Madison, who served as president of an organization that argued blacks were inferior and this nation would be better off without any black people (O'Reilly, 1995)? By excluding the history of the American Colonization Society and the white supremacist attitudes of the leaders of this nation, both blacks and whites are taught to believe in racial superiority and inferiority. To teach black children to venerate men who believed in white superiority and black inferiority in the name of patriotism and loyalty is not only wrong, but very deceptive!

Throughout my public school life, I always wondered why my teachers never once discussed anything about black history. For example, they never told me, nor do teachers still acknowledge, Alexandre Dumas was black and from Haiti, a general under Napoleon, and wrote the *Three Musketeers*, the *Nutcracker*, the *Count of Monte Cristo,* and numerous other works, nor will they ever acknowledge Alexander Sergeyevich Pushkin, the father of Russian literature, was also black (Rogers, 1967). Even when we studied the Civil War, there was never any mention of the 180,000 black soldiers who fought bravely under racist conditions (Cornish, 1956). The only reference to black people was that Abraham Lincoln freed us from slavery; hence we should be forever grateful to him. Yet we were never told that Lincoln, in a speech in 1858 in Charleston, Illinois, stated he was never in favor of allowing black people to serve on a jury or allowing social or political equality between white and black people. He further announced "there must be the position of superior and I as much as any other man am in favor of having the superior position assigned to the white man" (Nicolay & Hay, 1894, pp. 369–370). We were never told Lincoln strongly favored colonizing blacks from the United States; in every annual speech to Congress during his administration, he spoke of funding colonization. With all this knowledge, should black children continue to look upon Lincoln as the "great emancipator" or begin to see that he, too, held the belief that blacks were inferior?

In my courses, students and I discussed why Africa and its civilizations are never studied during social studies in high school. Why were black people never in the textbooks we used? When classes study Africa, or the Discovery Channel shows Africa in a program, there always seems to be more discussion, interest, and care for the animals in Africa than there is for the people unless the men and women are half-naked, thus showing how great the need is for the United States and Europe to bring civilization to a purportedly savage Dark Continent. There is no mention of the great African civilizations, ancient or modern African leaders, or the numerous rich cultures that make up the whole African continent.

Today, as classrooms begin to discuss Africa, there is still no dialogue about Africa ever having any great civilizations or leaders or about European and American imperialism, neocolonialism, and the proxy wars between the United States and Russia from the 1960s to 1980s, which have all contributed to the enormous degradation Africa faces today (Harding, 1993; Mazrui, 1986; Pakenham, 1991; Rodney, 1982; Stockwell, 1978). Also, on most college campuses, Africa, its history, and its culture are examined within a Eurocentric paradigm. There is no mention of Africans sailing and trading with the indigenous people in the Americas hundreds of years before Columbus landed in the Caribbean. The possibility of Africans reaching the Americas before Europeans is just not believable to the European or American mind (Wuthenau, 1992). In denying or excluding this history from textbooks, the words of David Hume come to mind:

> I am apt to suspect the negroes, and in general all the other species of men (for there are four or five different kinds) to be naturally inferior to the whites. There never was a civilized nation of any other complexion than white, nor even any individual eminent either in action or speculation. No ingenious manufactures amongst them, no arts, no sciences (Jordan, 1968, p. 253).

Teachers only taught and discussed how the supposedly godly Pilgrims came to the North American shores and established themselves and were friendly towards the Native Americans. We are not told that the Pilgrims consciously set out to enslave and exterminate the Native American population because they felt God had ordained them to inherit the land (Jennings, 1975). We were taught about George Washington's leadership during an alleged Revolution (or was it a rebellion of the colonial elite against the British crown?), but nothing is ever said that Washington held over two hundred blacks in slavery and even went after those who ran away to get free from his oppression. We were taught the Founding Fathers (I ask who's Founding Fathers?) came up with the ideas of the United States Constitution. There is no mention the Iroquois Confederation was the premise upon which the present United States Constitution was formulated. I was taught the United States is the "land of the free and the brave," and there is justice and liberty for all, and we all have a patriotic duty to uphold the tenets of the United States. I was given no knowledge nor did my teachers tell me these men who they claimed were my Founding Fathers held my ancestors in slavery and proposed to remove all free and emancipated blacks from the United States in order to maintain slavery and a homogeneous white society. Also not one teacher revealed to me that the same men, whom I was taught to revere and honor, believed blacks were inferior to whites all because of our skin color and our cultural heritage. So how do teachers expect us or any child of color to learn, respect, and honor these white men as national heroes or even respect and honor their words when they did not even consider my ancestors as part of the human family, but rather as some other species closer to animals?

White supremacist expressions of these men that go from blatant to subtle are not the words and acts of unlearned men, but come from the minds and mouths of leaders, supposedly "great" men, in science, politics, and law. For example, curriculum textbooks portray Thomas Jefferson as the ideal American statesman and seek to promote his assertions that "everyone has an equal right to Life and Liberty, and the pursuit of Happiness," but they diminish the focus of his belief in the racial enslavement of Africans whose presence in the United States affected his actions on foreign policy. In the textbook *A People and a Nation: a History of the United States* (1991) published by Houghton Mifflin, the author state that Jefferson "was deeply concerned about the issue...What troubled Jefferson most was the impact of the system of slavery on whites" (p. 60). Jefferson's concern had nothing to do with how enslaved blacks felt about being held in bondage; he was concerned only with how it affected whites, especially white children. While *A People and a Nation* does give a brief description of the brutality of the enslavement of blacks, the authors shift the brutality from the United States on to the Caribbean, South and Central America by saying that "the physical cruelty of slavery may have been less in the United States than elsewhere in the New World" (p. 186). The brutality and violence against free and enslaved blacks witnessed by Jefferson provides a glimpse of the unmitigated power whites had over blacks throughout American history. Jefferson knew that the power and racism exhibited by adult whites was being transmitted to white children. Even though he knew that white children were getting an education in tyranny, yet he refused to stop punishing, selling, and buying enslaved blacks himself.

Jefferson's only concern for black people was his fear of blacks rising up and exacting revenge upon white people for treating them so horribly. He comments:

> And can the liberties of a nation be thought secure when we have removed their only firm basis, a conviction in the minds of the people that these liberties are of the gift of God? That they are not to be violated but with his wrath? Indeed I tremble for my country when I reflect that God is just: that his justice cannot sleep for ever: that considering numbers, nature and natural means only, a revolution of the wheel of fortune, an exchange of situation is among possible events: that it may become probable by supernatural interference! The almighty has no attribute which can take side with us in such a contest (Jefferson, 1787, p. 163).

While Jefferson supposedly hated slavery, he never condemned it publicly or joined any antislavery organization. He associated the abolitionist movement growing in the nation with the enslaved black population's nefarious desire to liberate itself. Jefferson even proposed buying land in the West (west of the Mississippi River, beyond the U.S. border at that time) for blacks out of fear of their revenge but Southern slaveholders wanted free blacks as far away from those still in chains so they could not instigate and support any attempts to free any enslaved blacks (Berry, 1971).

Again the fact that Jefferson could not find anything positive to say about black people and instead proclaimed that we were a "problem to the security of this nation" (p. 163) raises one question and one answer. How can any teacher expect to teach me or any other child of African descent to hold Thomas Jefferson in respectful awe when he claimed blacks were ashamed of their color and want to be white and black women preferred orangutans as sexual partners because we "secrete a very disagreeable odor?" First of all, Orangutans are not found in Africa. Secondly, in 1829, a black abolitionist from Boston, David Walker, eloquently refuted Jefferson's assertions when he stated "that it has pleased God to make us black" (Walker, 1829, p. 32).

Personal Reflections

As I contemplate upon American society, I see there can be no solution to racism until there is some open dialogue about its origin and the power relations supporing it. I wonder if teachers really expect black and white students to revere and honor Thomas Jefferson and others when they find out these men proceeded to create an ideology that required whites not only to retain their racial purity, but also to degrade and treat blacks as animals. College curricula can begin to explain white power as it served to exploit black labor, sexually abuse black women, and then make their own children invisible, as the children became property to be sold and exploited. These courses can begin to discuss how white men practiced interracial sex while at the same time passed laws prohibiting sex between black men and white women (Higginbotham, 1978; Nash, 1992). By excluding this dynamic scenario from the curriculum, students are left without ever knowing how white supremacy solidified its power and why it still persists. Without curriculum change, students will never be able to understand that white supremacy maintained its absolute power in American society through schools, the economy and interracial activity as long as it involved white men and black women.

We can also discuss with students how the colonial elite in Virginia consciously and deliberately devised an ideology of "whiteness" or the idea that white becomes superior right after Bacon's Rebellion in 1676 and aligned the poor white immigrant worker/slaves with them against the enslaved black population to maintain social control and their lofty positions in society (Webb, 1984). If educators continue to deny students the opportunity to examine colonial Virginia's hegemonic society, it is not only a flagrant disservice to our students, but we are allowing our society to remain ignorant of the formulating building blocks of racism in the United States. Students can research how the ruling class of Virginia gradually and covertly separated the precarious poor whites from the alleged dangerous black population by building a wall of racial contempt—and how the elite benefited thereby. Edmund Morgan wrote after Bacon's Rebellion the Virginia elite realized: "there was an obvious lesson in the rebellion. Resentment of an alien race might be more powerful than the resentment of an upper class" (1975, pp. 269–270).

Morgan alluded to the enslaved black population, but what is more insightful is the Virginia elite knew blacks were not happy and content being enslaved—the white elite therefore had to formalize their exploitation of free labor by passing laws enforced not only racial enslavement, but also a clear separation of black and white (Berry, 1971; Higginbotham, 1978). White colonial elite perceived both the enslaved black people and the poor white servants as lazy, shiftless, irresponsible, unfaithful, ungrateful and dishonest (Morgan, 1975; Allen, 1994). Students can discover the fear of enslaved blacks attempting to liberate themselves from perpetual domination was great, but not as extensive as the fear of discontented poor whites aligning themselves with the blacks in overthrowing the existing social order established by the wealthy white elite. Teachers and educators need to find ways tol allow students to investigate and examine the complex issues that brought into play the racial and class structures of the early English colonies and still guide race relations today. They can research why the colonial elite established laws that made black inferior and white superior; they can examine how white supremacist ideology was evolving. They will begin to see and understand the colonial elite had to justify their capitalist gains at the expense of black and white labor and also justify their economic status to the masses of poor whites who were immigrating to the colonies and being forced to labor to further enrich the planter class. Through examining documents and various other materials, students can begin to become agents of social change in out society and work to bring about a more egalitarian society.

As I searched for answers to this social cancer called "racism" and "white supremacy" that has destroyed the lives of millions of people, I have come to the same conclusions others before me have—that the colonial leaders needed a way to justify the physical and psychological brutality of black people by creating stereotypes, pseudoscientific beliefs, and an economic slave system on which the United States depended for its survival and way of life. The theory of race, therefore, is a socio cultural invention—constructed as a set of beliefs and attitudes about the differences in humanity and created for a specific purpose (Bennett, 1969; Higginbotham, 1978; Zinn, 1995; Fredrickson, 1981; Allen, 1994; Hannaford, 1996).

Students are taught democracy is a form of government where its citizens can be trusted to govern themselves through elected representatives, who are liable to their constituents. We are taught all who live in the political community have the right to take part in the political process no matter what differences we may have in our private lives.

These principles were the basis for a kind of voluntary pluralism in which all European immigrants and their progeny were free to maintain affection for their ancestral religions and cultures while at the same time claiming citizenship in the United States. The people embraced the founding myths and participated in the political life of this republic. This civic culture was not tested as long as those immigrants were predominantly Anglo/Nordic stock. George Washington, in his farewell address, said that the United States must be built upon a people who are united by the same religion, manners, habits, and political principles (Grant & Davison, 1928; Nagle, 1971; Marty, 1970). Thus for the next two hundred or more years white supremacy would outwardly structure itself as an expansionist, dominating ideology in the quest for wealth and power. This attitude and the feeling white supremacy engendered have nothing to do with genetics; they are extra somatic, learned, and transmitted through an enculturation process

THE AMERICAN COLONIZATION SOCIETY

If they must remain in their present situation, keep them in the lowest state of degradation and ignorance. The nearer you bring them to the condition of brutes, the better chance do you give them of possessing their apathy.

Elias B. Caldwell, 1836

What right, I demand, have the children of Africa to an homestead in the white man's country?... The ready answer is, because the African race is despised...that the descendants of Ham are inherently and naturally inferior to ourselves and others, the children of Shem and Japhet.

Washington Parke Curtis, 1831

No matter how great their industry, or how abundant their wealth—no matter what their attainments in literature, science or the arts—they can never, no never be raised to a footing of equality.

Cyrus Edwards, 1831

On August 14, 1862, President Abraham Lincoln invited five black leaders, headed by Edward M. Thomas, president of the Anglo-African Institute for the Encouragement of Industry and Art in Washington, D. C. to meet with him concerning the "Negro problem." According to the accounts of the meeting by James McPherson (1965), it turned into a condescending speech by Lincoln on the racial differences between blacks and whites and the impossibility of the two races living together as equals. According to Lincoln, blacks "suffer very greatly" from living under the racist beliefs and practices of whites, "while ours suffer from your presence" (Basler, 1953, pp. 371–375; O'Reilly, 1995). He further stated it would be better for the two races to separate due to the unwillingness of whites to live with blacks. Thus he suggested African Americans be colonized to present-day Panama to work the coal mines (Aptheker, 1951; Adams & Sanders, 2003). In essence, Lincoln agreed with the Swiss naturalist Louis Agassiz, who came to the United States in 1846, who expressed shock at the physical features of blacks and wanted to run away in fear and disgust: "[W]hat unhappiness for the white race....God preserve us from such contact" (Gould, 1981, p. 40). The account of Lincoln's meeting spread quickly throughout Northern newspapers and the response was quick and sharp by the African American community. John S. Rock, a black abolitionist and lawyer in the United States, asked the question: Why is it that the white people of this country desire to get rid of us...that much of the wealth and prosperity found here is the result of the labor of our hands (McPherson, 1965, p. 92)?

The suggestion that the "Negro problem" in the United States could be solved, or lessened, by removing all people of African descent (or a portion of them) to distant lands beyond the boundaries of the United States has persisted since the colonial period. The northern black community responded quickly to the idea of colonization. While some African Americans did choose to emigrate to Africa, the majority refused to leave the land of their birth. During the antebellum period, African American communities throughout the North mounted an effective opposition to the colonization plan. Vincent Harding makes it clear that Lincoln was no friend of black people and states that Lincoln the Emancipator is a "mythology," that history fails to give credit to the "thousands of black people" that broke away from slavery. Harding also shows that Lincoln had no interest in giving black people equality; he "could not see beyond the limits of his own race" and tried to remove all blacks from the country (Harding, 1981, p. 236). The idea that radical militant blacks, free and enslaved, could independently move and coerce whites to end slavery is hardly ever mentioned.

The idea of a homogeneous all white nation and of removing "free" blacks from living next to white people began in 1691 when the governing body in the colony of Virginia prohibited any further emancipation of enslaved blacks unless the owner provided transportation beyond the limits of the colony (the wilderness) within six months after emancipation (Hurd, 1858, p. 237; Higginbotham, 1980, pp. 47–50). As recently as 1939, Senator Theodore G. Bilbo of

Mississippi introduced into Congress a bill calling for the federal government to support a large scale voluntary migration of all blacks to Liberia (Congressional Record 76, Vol. 84, pp. 1647, 4650–4676). Senator Bilbo believed this was the only solution to racial discrimination, the abuses, and hardships endured by African Americans. Throughout the history of the United States numerous schemes and plans to colonize African Americans somewhere outside the national borders have been promulgated and given support by prominent public figures of this country (Osofsky, 1967).

Following the successful revolt by the English colonists in North America against British rule, the new republic of the United States was a politically and militarily weak nation. The new nation was composed of diverse racial and ethnic groups with no official communal religion and able to claim neither a common ancestral geographic territory nor a distinctive national culture. Hans Kohn (1957) and other scholars of American nationalistic development have characterized nationalism as "a conscious effort by a people to maintain a common language, historical traditions, geographic terrain, governmental and social institutions, and a common art and literature." They have called patriotism the most effective vehicle to cultivate loyalty to the state and society, as it fostered enthusiasm for the federal government, a common Anglo Protestant American language and geography, and a distinctive national history (Curti, 1943; Marty, 1970; Nagel, 1971). Russel B. Nye (1966) stated:

> A nation is, in many ways, a product of its ideology. Ideas provide necessary forces in the making of civilizations and express that complex of motives within which a people live, think, and move (p. ix).

Thus, since the 1600s, Anglo Protestant Americanism has preached that America is the land in which God will create a new heaven and a new earth, and it has maintained a sense of divine mission.

From the moment the Puritan leader John Winthrop delivered his famous sermon "A Modelle of Christian Charity" in the middle of the Atlantic on the deck of the *Arbella* in 1630, Protestant clergy have referred to the land mass now called the United States as the "Promised Land" and its Puritan inhabitants as the "chosen people." The early Puritans believed England was the new Israel and the Anglo-Saxon race a holy people favored by God. In their view the

Church of England had fallen into error under King James, and the Puritan invasion of North America, from 1630 to 1642, was nothing more than an extension of the divine mandate. Puritan leaders like William Bradford, Edward Johnson, and Cotton Mather believed that God had picked them out for a special destiny as heirs of the ancient Israelites, God's chosen people. They saw America as a flawless utopian paradise (the New Jerusalem) emerging in a world of sin and discontent. These Anglo Protestants living in what became the United States believed they had become or would become superior to all other nations and peoples and fulfill God's mission as his chosen people (Bremer, 1976; Carlson, 1975; Johnson & Miller, 1938). They believed God had chosen the Anglo-Saxon race and the nation's color had to be defined and affirmed. The Puritans believed only a white America could provide security for God's chosen race. Thus the flawless utopia and the racial ideology that emerged were often viewed as the only remedy to reconcile the irreconcilable—perfection in America (Horseman, 1981; Marty, 1970; Washington, 1967, 1984, & 1988). In Cotton Mather's treatise *The Negro Christianized: An Essay to Excite and Assist that Good Work, the Instruction of Negro-Servants in Christianity*, he counseled Boston slaveholders in 1706 black people caused not only physical concern, but also God had no intention of blacks being a part of New Israel. He stated, while Christianized blacks made better slaves, "my Negroes will not prove a part of the Israel of God and will not be gathered unto the Lord." In other words, black people could never become participants in the "Promised Land" nor gain entrance into heaven (Osofsky, 1967, pp. 34–39).

Before the English colonies in North America revolted against the British crown, racial ideas were being voiced in the colonies. Anglo Protestant American beliefs claimed God had arranged humans into perpetual categories called "races." This belief in such groupings became more widespread and more invidious as time passed. A belief in the existence of races was usually accompanied by the conviction that the difference was qualitative, one's own race was innately superior in physical, mental, and moral attributes. Although this misconception has now been widely discredited in scientific literature as intellectually unsound and socially pernicious, the misconception profoundly shaped European and Euro-American relations with Africa from the beginning (Smedley, 1999). When epidemics killed thousands of Native Americans in New England during the 1620s, many Protestant theologians concluded that God was preparing the land for them. Puritan leaders preached the extermination of Native Americans was nothing more than God's way of getting the land ready for occupation by the Anglo-Saxon race. They were convinced the epidemics that depleted the Native American population in New England, the annihilation and enslavement of the Pequots in 1637, and the defeat of King Philip in 1676 were all a part of God's divine plan to give the land to them (Jenning, 1975; Segal & Stineback, 1977). They also believed God had chosen the Anglo-Saxon race to conquer the world for Christ by dispossessing the feeble races and God had chosen the United States as guardian and trustee of the world's progress. While God's selection brought destruction and inferiority upon the Native Americans, Africans and those of the African Diaspora, and other people of color, it meant power and conquest for Anglo Protestant Americans (Carlson, 1975; Marty, 1970; Smedley, 1999).

English contact with Africa in the sixteenth century spawned a vast range of literature revealing a profound antipathy towards African appearance and culture. Winthrop D. Jordan convincingly demonstrated in his book *White Over Black: American Attitudes Toward the Negro, 1550–1812* (1968) that the English described the people of Africa as unattractive, unchristian, and grossly uncivil. From the dawn of Anglo-Saxon intellectualism, articulated superior attitudes towards Africans and an abhorrence of the African's skin color, stature, facial features, and hair texture. Color, cultural, and religious prejudice placed Africans in a tragically inferior status with respect to the English and other Europeans, who believed Africans were inherently and immutably inferior, fundamentally unable to assimilate even if they adopted English culture (Hannaford, 1996; Hood, 1994; Smedley, 1999).

In 1700 the abolitionist Samuel Sewall of Boston in his essay *The Selling of Joseph*, defended the equality and liberty of enslaved black people, but Sewall's antislavery views included fears of miscegenation, more specifically a fear of black men cohabiting with or marrying white women. "As many Negro men as there are among us, so many empty places there are in our Train Bands, and the places taken up of Men that might make husbands of our Daughters." Sewall confessed he preferred white servants and believed blacks could never mix with whites. He wrote:

> All things considered, it would conduce more to the Welfare of the province, to have White Servants for the term of Years, than to have Slaves for Life. Few can endure to hear of a Negro being made free…. And there is much disparity in their Conditions, Colour & hair, that they can never embody with us, and grow up into orderly Families, to the Peopling of the land: but still remain in our Body Politick as a kind of extravasat Blood (Mcpherson & Katz, 1969, p. 2).

It was one thing to oppose slavery in theory, but quite another to accept blacks into the social and political process. Sewall's views show how contemporary Puritan racism regarded Africans and those of African descent as inferior alien beings that could never be integrated into New England's Christian society (Greene, 1942; McPherson & Katz, 1969). This raises the question: Was this the opinion of a person who opposed slavery or one who could not accept the presence of Africans? If Sewall could not accept the presence of a black person, then he had more in common with contemporary white supremacists, future colonizationists, and the later Free Soil Party of the antebellum period than he would have had in common with the abolitionists. The fear of sexual relations between black men and white women drove the colonies to pass anti-miscegenation laws. Virginia passed legislation in 1662 mandating that "any Christian committing fornication with a Negro man or woman" be punished severely, but there were no laws against white men sexually abusing black women. Other colonies followed suit. In 1662, Maryland banned marriages between white women and black men, as did Massachusetts in 1705, South Carolina in 1717, North Carolina in 1718, Delaware in 1721, and Pennsylvania in 1725. Over and over, lawmakers referred to sexual relations between white women and black men as a "disgrace to the nation" and a "dishonor to God" (Johnston, 1973, p. 184).

In 1751, Benjamin Franklin voiced his preferences of color for North America in his *Observations Concerning the Increases of Mankind.* He believed the Saxons and the English "make up the principal Body of White People on the Face of the Earth." He was convinced North America belonged to the white race and hoped the numbers of white people would increase. He added:

> Why increase the sons of Africa, by planting them in America.... I am partial to the complexion of my country. (Feldstein, 1972, pp. 67–70; Labaree, 1961, pp. 225–234).

Patrick Henry echoed Franklin: "our country will it be peopled. The question is shall it be with Europeans or with Africans" (Henry, 1891, pp. 115–116). Earlier, in 1663, Maryland prohibited white women from marrying black men in reaction to "freeborn *English* women, forgetful of their free condition, and to the disgrace of our nation, do intermarry with negro slaves." In 1691, Virginia passed laws "for the prevention of that abominable mixture and spurious issue of Negroes, mulattoes, and Indians intermarrying with English or other white women" (Davis, 1966, pp. 139-140; Donnan, 1969, pp. 131–132; Hurd, 1858, pp. 236–249). In 1736, William Byrd of Virginia voiced his apprehensions of the growing black population:

> They import so many Negroes hither, that I fear this Colony will soon some time or other be confirmed by the Name of New Guinea. I am sensible of many bad consequences of multiplying these Ethiopians amongst us.... We have already 10,000 men of these descendants of Ham fit to bear Arms, and their numbers Increase every day as well by birth as importation (Tingling, 1977, pp. 487–489).

Byrd feared the black population would become the majority and the white population the minority in South Carolina. He also feared what white people called insurrections, where enslaved blacks would forcefully try and liberate themselves. In a race war—such as those beginning to take place in the West Indies—whites would be at a disadvantage in numbers as enslaved blacks attempted to free themselves. The fact these men expressed fears of the growing black population is strange, especially coming from large slaveholders such as William Byrd and Patrick Henry who kept buying and breeding blacks.

On October 18, 1798, Thomas Law, a landowner in England, sent a letter to James Madison telling him he sought neither to immigrate nor to seek citizenship in America but wanted to maintain lands in Virginia. Law continued on the subject of immigration, stating "Virginia should particularly adopt every method to introduce whites and if possible to diminish the black" (Mattern, 1991, pp. 51–52). The preference for a white United States was institutionalized soon after the Constitutional Convention. Naturalization was limited to whites; the federal militia was restricted to white male citizens (even though some five thousand enslaved and free black males had fought with the English colonists during the Revolution). Only white males could deliver the United States mail, city officials for the District of Columbia had to be white, and the District's Capital Square was restricted to white people (Adams & Sanders, 2003; Jordan, 1968, p. 412; Litwack, 1958; Litwack, 1961, pp. 31–32; Robinson, 1969).

While the idea of Anglo Protestant American nationalism was pervasive in the early days of the United States, the idea of colonizing black people—removing free and enslaved black people from white society—was widespread and even more pervasive. As stated earlier, in 1691, Virginia's colonial officials required emancipated blacks removed beyond the limits of the colony. Throughout the 1700s even the antislavery Quakers advocated the expulsion of blacks from North America. Two days after the signing of the Declaration of Independence, Virginia slaveholder Landon Carter declared, "if you free the slaves, you must send them out of the country" (Drake, 1950, pp. 121–123, 138–139; Greene, 1965, p. 1055; Jordan, 1968, pp. 550–551). Benjamin Rush, the father of psychiatry and one of the signers of the United States Constitution, presented a paper to the American Philosophical Society in 1792, "Observations Intended to Favor a Supposition that the Black Color (as it is called) of the Negroes is Derived From the Leprosy," in which he argued the African's skin color was a form of leprosy and the physical symptoms of the disease were the physical features of black people (McIntyre, 1984; Ruchames, 1969, pp. 215–225). Rush also believed that if black men were allowed to cohabitate with white women, the latter would be infected with leprosy and give birth to leprous babies. Yet he never mentioned whether white men were being infected when they sexually abused black women. Rush advocated blacks be colonized in Bedford County, Pennsylvania, and isolated from whites until they were cured from their disease and their skin color turned white (Feldstein, 1972, pp. 58–66; Takaki, 1979, p. 34).

In line with the idea that Anglo Americans were virtuous and on a sacred mission to redeem the world from European tyranny and heathenism, they saw themselves as victims of the Atlantic Slave Trade and blameless in importing Africans into the North American colonies. Thomas Jefferson included a clause in his draft of the Declaration of Independence blaming the king of England for the enslavement and importation of Africans into the colonies. This was done despite the fact Puritan entrepreneurs were heavily involved in the Atlantic slave trade, which was well known to everyone in Congress. Anglo American Christians had very little to say about human bondage when commercial opportunities beckoned them to brush aside the brutality of slavery in order to realize enormous profits. This made what most Americans have always considered a virtue—the Puritan work ethic—complicit in the subjugation of an entire race of people. Thus Jefferson and his contemporaries avoided offending not only fellow slaveholders, but also the Christian ship builders (which transported the slaves) and dealers of Newport, Boston, Providence, New York, and Charleston (Alderman, 1974; Hennessy, 1968; Spears, 1900; Plimmer & Plimmer, 1973).

At the close of the Revolutionary War, Thomas Jefferson declared any continuation of the two races living side-by-side would probably end in the extermination of one or the other and proposed the emancipation and deportation of all persons of African ancestry (1787, pp. 137–140). Although the attempt by Gabriel Prosser to liberate enslaved blacks in Henrico County, Virginia, in the summer of 1800 failed, it caused a heightened uneasiness among whites. Governor James Monroe and other public officials of Virginia passed laws strengthening the local militia and restricting the internal slave trade, fearing slaveholders might sell blacks they deemed as dangerous to unsuspecting whites in other states. Virginia authorized Governor Monroe to begin discussions with President Jefferson about the possibility of purchasing lands where free blacks could be sent (Ammon, 1971, pp. 185–189, 198–200). Although Jefferson was sympathetic to the proposal, he refused to use federal funding. The problem was finding a region where colonized free blacks could not organize to support their enslaved brethren attempting to free themselves by force. While the colonization effort failed, Virginia's legislature passed laws requiring free and emancipated blacks to leave the state. Other Southern—and even Northern—states fearing freedom conscious blacks would encourage other enslaved blacks to rise up and terrorize the white population, enacted laws to prevent the entry of blacks through their borders (Bancroft, 1931, p. 17; Egerton, 1993; Kates, 1968; Johnston, 1970; Litwack, 1961, p. 16).

The American Colonization Society

In the early 1800s, Francis Scott Key, Bushrod Washington, Henry Clay, Elias Caldwell, James Madison, Daniel Webster, and other prominent Anglo-American nationalists formed the American Society for the Colonizing the Free People of Color in the United States, known as the American Colonization Society (ACS), to promote white nationhood. The large increase in the number of free Africans and those of African descent within the new nation caused many whites from both the North and South to look upon the idea of colonizing black people as the only solution to maintaining a homogeneous and "virtuous" white nation. Many proponents of colonization contended it was a philanthropic enterprise—colonized African Americans would Christianize Africa and implement civilization in a degraded continent. In 1773 the Reverend Samuel Hopkins of Newport, Rhode Island, began his crusade for voluntary African colonization (Feldstein, 1972, pp. 84–101; Staudenraus, 1961, pp. 15–24).

The ACS recruited support from four sections of American society in order to promote the organization's reasons for colonizing black people. First, they recruited the slaveholders in the Chesapeake Bay region who fretted over the fact that a race war like the one in Haiti, where blacks had won their freedom from white slaveholders, could take place in Virginia, especially after Gabriel Prosser's brief attempt. Slaveholders in Virginia and Maryland feared the growing free black population in the Chesapeake region, whom they believed to be troublemakers and a menace to the security of slavery. By 1804 blacks were prohibited from gathering together for religious services at night, a common practice among both free and enslaved black people (Hurd, 1858, Vol. II, p. 7).

As stated earlier, Governor James Monroe corresponded with Thomas Jefferson concerning the idea of colonizing free blacks out of Virginia. While Jefferson did not agree with Monroe on colonizing blacks west of the Mississippi River, he did approve of the West Indies as a suitable place for colonization. Affirming his vision of an all white American republic, Jefferson replied to Monroe that a more homogeneous white society would one day cover the North American continent. As Virginia looked for a suitable place for colonization, the state concurrently took steps to curb the growth of the free black population. While Virginia did not restrict slaveholders from emancipating their slaves, its emigration requirements, along with many other states' denial of permanent residence, restrained slaveholders from emancipating any of their slaves. At the same time many slaveholders in Delaware, Maryland, Virginia, Kentucky, and Missouri were selling thousands of their slaves to the Deep South for profit and to prevent emancipation (Bancroft, 1959). Although Virginia supported colonization, not all approved of the idea. Slaveholders along the James River viewed colonization as an abolitionist movement. Like many of the slaveholders in North and South Carolina, some Virginians considered colonization a mischievous scheme whose principles disturbed the relationship between the master and slave, thereby jeopardizing the peace and tranquility of the South. They supported the removal of the free black population only, thus strengthening the chains of slavery (Clark, 1941; Fox, 1919; Freehling, 1982).

The second group, consisting of men such as Henry Clay who were also slaveholders, wanted to limit the free black population stable while increasing the white population. The scheme to increase and stabilizing the white population would be popularized by the Wilmot Proviso of 1846. David Wilmot, a Pennsylvania congressman, declared:

> I plead the cause and rights of white freemen. I would preserve free white labor in a fair country, a rich inheritance, where the sons of toil, of my own color, can live without the disgrace which association with negro slavery brings upon free labor (Litwack, 1961, p. 47).

In other words, not only was slavery to be barred from the West, but free blacks were to be barred altogether from the Western states so white labor would not have to compete with black labor and homestead rights could be maintained as an exclusively white privilege (Allen, 1994, p. 138). In the West, slavery was abhorred not because of any love for blacks, but because settlers were opposed to amalgamation or any kind of integration. Their concern for racial purity contributed to the movement against slavery in Ohio, Illinois, Indiana, Kansas, Nebraska, Wisconsin, and Oregon. Many colonizationists in the West sought to preserve the territories for free "white" labor. The governor of Indiana called for the removal of all free blacks and urged heavy fines to prevent free blacks from settling in Indiana. He candidly stated in a speech in Springfield, Illinois, separation of the races was the only way to prevent amalgamation (Rosen, 1972; Berwanger, 1976; Foner, 1965; Fredrickson, 1975). On September 18, 1858, at his fourth joint debate with Stephen Douglas in Charleston, Illinois, Abraham Lincoln declared:

> I will say then that I am not, nor ever have been in favor of bringing about in any way the social and political equality of the white and black races—that I am not, nor ever have been, in favor of making voters or jurors of negroes, nor of qualifying them to hold office, nor to intermarry with white people; and I will say in addition to this that there is a physical difference between the white and black races which I believe will forever forbid the two races living together on terms of social and political equality. And inasmuch as they cannot so live, while they do remain together there must be the position of superior and inferior, and I as much as any other man am in favor of having the superior position assigned to the white race (Nicolay & Hay, 1894, pp. 369–370).

The third group ACS recruited were old school Federalists such as Gerrit Smith and James Gillespie Birney who characterized free blacks as disorderly, lazy, and dangerous to the social order of the United States. The Federalists formulated rigid political and social philosophies in the 1790s and never parted with their theory of a perfect republic. They favored colonization out of an irrational belief that it would provide some relief to the dangerous and disorderly egalitarianism of Jeffersonian America. Federalists declared blacks as the main source of disorder and the abolitionist movement as the cause of the "mob spirit" between the 1820s and 1850s. In seeking a way to regain social control which had been lost with the decline of the hierarchical society and the deferential politics of the colonial period, they relied upon colonization to restore order in American society. Once the cause of egalitarian disorder (free African Americans) was removed, old school Federalists believed the colonization movement could be turned into private philanthropy projects and could devot their attention in the North and to the Border States. However, the rise of the radical abolitionist movement in the 1830s provided the final blow to the conservatism of the old school Federalists (Dumond, 1939; Fischer, 1965; Harlow, 1939).

Finally, many Protestant clergy favored colonization because they were anxious over the anarchy and licentiousness apparently on the rise in American culture. They worried about political and social upheavals, deplored the new moral standards, and lamented the decline of religion in an increasingly secular age. Some blamed the social problems on the lack of cooperation between state governments and the churches, and most clergy turned to reform groups like the American Bible Society and other temperance groups. There was a feeling of agreement among prominent Northern theologians there never would be any room for blacks in America. This group reasoned removing the troublesome and anarchistic blacks was divinely mandated and would help restore social order in the nation (Bodo, 1954; Cole, 1954; Murray, 1966).

The Presbyterian Church was the first to embrace colonization in 1818 and the Reformed Dutch Church soon followed in 1825. Although the Congregationalist churches had no policy on colonization, they endorsed it by supplying missionaries to the ACS. By 1830, Episcopal, Methodist, and Baptist churches had joined the movement and collected funds for the ACS. Most of the agents of the ACS who traveled throughout the United States collecting funds were prominent clergy. They preached the necessity of maintaining social control and racial purity as the mediating and binding factor in prohibiting free African American men from entering into interracial relationships with white women and forbidding slaves attempting to gain their freedom. The decision was either uphold perpetual enslavement or expel him from America completely (Bodo, 1954, 112-128; Cole, 1954; Murray, 1966, 75-87; Fredrickson, 1971, 6-30).

Samuel Miller, a faculty member of Princeton's theological seminary, declared free blacks were a danger to whites nor could they be trusted as loyal citizens. Other clergy proclaimed that blacks were a danger to the national security of the United States. Archibald Alexander, also from Princeton's seminary, castigated the Reverend Samuel Cornish, a black abolitionist, preacher, and editor of *Freedom's Journal*, for encouraging blacks to abhor colonization. Alexander told Cornish the ACS knew what was best for blacks, that he was "inflicting" great harm on the "posterity" of black people. He further stated:

> If I were a coloured man, I would not hesitate a moment to leave the country where black people faced prejudice and where black skin was held in the lowest degree of degradation and no amount of good conduct can...overcome (Alexander, 1854, pp. 395–397).

The *African Repository*, a journal of the ACS, published an article in October 1836 originally published in the *Christian Observer* by Alexander on how to give religious instruction to enslaved blacks. He stated the usual rhetoric that Christianized blacks made good servants. Cornish refuted Alexander and the ACS in the black newspaper *Freedom's Journal* September 7 & 21, 1837 and in the *Colored American* October 14, 1837.

White clergy who promoted the ACS preached sermons emphasizing Northern urban blacks were "idle, ignorant, and depraved;" to prove this they told their congregations to "visit our jails and penitentiaries and you will find them crowded with coloured convicts." White clergy exaggerated "beyond a doubt their moral character is far [more] debased than any part of the white population." One white preacher, whose sermon was published in *Freedom's Journal*, March 30, 1827 was quoted saying:

> until human nature is radically changed, they will never attain or participate in the privileges of American freemen....Remaining here they must continue ignorant, degraded and depraved.

Samuel Cornish reminded the white preacher "there is a just God who reigns" and the white preacher's sentiments "are the very strongholds of slavery and oppression." Cornish wrote the majority of the black urban population did not fit that description. He continued with his response calling attention to the fact that the majority of the people in New York City's almshouses and prisons were whites (Curry, 1981, pp. 112–135).

It also needs to be understood why white clergy who supported colonization were angry with the black opposition to colonization. From the beginning, the ACS suffered from lack of support in the free black community. Northern free blacks saw themselves as Americans by birth and were not interested in leaving by force or voluntarily the land of their birth; this did not sit well with whites who wanted a homogeneous society. Other factors that discouraged African Americans from emigration was the high mortality rate in West Africa, armed conflicts with various African ethnic groups, and the difficult living conditions in Liberia.

White clergy denied blacks full acceptance, socially and ecclesiastically, they encouraged separate black churches to avoid having to openly deny blacks from attending their churches. White clergy, who financially assisted free African Americans, resented many blacks had deliberately rejected their solution to the race problem. Ironically, when separate black churches decided to make decisions without white input, white clergy put black clergy who needed to solicit funds from white churches in an awkward position. White philanthropic churches saw free African Americans as immature children who willfully disobeyed the paternal benevolence of their parents (Murray, 1966, pp. 30–39).

During the antebellum period, the Federalists with the assistance of Protestant clergy believed they were the keepers of American society for God's glory and the "Promise Land." Political and religious leaders attempted to promote stability within society when traditional ideas and practices of the chosen people appeared outmoded, constricted, and ineffective. Throughout the Northeast, they set out to increase the number of ministers and Sunday schools, handing out Bibles and tracts to control and put a stop to perceived sinfulness within society. Theses groups formed various temperance societies against drunkenness, immorality, and slavery to encourage godly behavior. Both Federalists and clergy consolidated their efforts to mold and bring the nation back in line with its mythical sacred mission (Bodo, 1954; Cole, 1954; Marty, 1970). They also set out to restore stability to the nation by establishing institutions to incarcerate unwanted people, whom they called "deviants." The erection of penitentiaries, insane asylums, almshouses, orphanages, and reformatories by philanthropists, state legislatures, and clergy coincided with the growing popularity of the removal of free African Americans (Rothman, 1971; McIntyre, 1984).

The scheme to eliminate disorderly elements (i.e., free African Americans and other alleged deviants) from the mainstream of American society would insure the nation's cohesion. The various factions within the ACS believed they could restore social balance to the new republic and at the same time eliminate longstanding social problems. In their perverted rationality, white clergy and other public officials publicly acknowledged the racist and discriminatory attitudes of whites, which demeaned free African Americans in the North and South and forced them into a degraded position, yet they refused to improve the social and economic proscriptions free African Americans were forced to live under. They also refused to pass laws, which would of protected blacks from racial discriminatory practices, and did not encourage the general white population to change its racial opinions or discriminatory actions against African Americans. Instead they chose to blame the victim: they placed the entire responsibility of racism and disfranchisement upon free African Americans by advising them to exhibit exemplary behavior. This belief that flawless behavior by African Americans would change the hearts and minds of whites was, and still is today, erroneous. Further, they continued to label blacks as drunkards, infidels, and other deviant elements of society to be colonized or incarcerated along with other delinquent whites and the insane.

Throughout the antebellum period, the ACS relied on staged celebrations on the Fourth of July and private donations to cover its costs. Organization officials urged churches to demonstrate their patriotism via Independence Day sermons designed to influence their congregations to give financially for a white United States (*African Repository*, July 1833, June 1835, & June 1837; Staudenraus, 1961; Fredrickson, 1971, p. 7). These patriotic and religious events became the financial lifeblood of the organization. While the ACS never collected enough money to remove significant number of African Americans, the organization did obtain some impressive endorsements. Between 1816 and 1820 state auxiliaries were formed throughout the North and in the Border states. The ACS also received verbal support from men like Presidents James Madison and Andrew Jackson, John Taylor, prominent men such as Noah Webster, John Randolph, Stephen Douglass, and Roger Taney, to name a few (Bodo, 1954; Cooke, 1957; Litwack, 1961, p. 24).

By pledging itself to cleansing and restoring purity to America by removing blacks, the ACS attracted and received support from Protestant clergy, slaveholders throughout the South and numerous northern abolitionists in words and with whatever small finances they could gather in meetings. While the slaveholders praised colonization for eliminating free blacks in the South, believing they were eradicating any hope of freedom among the enslaved population, many northerners supported the ACS simply because they did not want blacks around them, free or enslaved. This conglomeration of slaveholders, antislavery philanthropists, extreme negrophobes, and religious leaders were all united in the desire to purify the United States. The ACS avoided alienating any single group that supported them; instead they evaded any controversial arguments on slavery or emancipation. They promoted patriotism and issued appeals for sectional reconciliation so that the North and South could unite behind the concept of establishing a white man's country. This satisfied the proslavers who perceived the program as removing free blacks, while the abolitionists and the negrophobe elements were satisfied as well since white nationhood would require the eventual removal of all black people (*African Repository*, May 1834 & December 1837; Adams, 1973, pp. 205-206; Berwanger, 1972; Campbell, 1971, pp. 9-10).

In 1825, Ralph R. Gurley became the secretary of the ACS and proceeded to make colonization a national movement. He turned colonization into a moral crusade, united the reformist groups, sought the support of the New England abolitionists and various church leaders who were concerned with reform in the United States, hoping to soften the problems between the North and South. He invited white "Christians [both North and South] to offer up [their] minor differences" and controversies of interest "on the altar of an undivided patriotism and philanthropy" (*African Repository*, August 1825, October 1825, & January 1828; Staudenraus, 1961). The *African Repository* supported Gurley's position on the race question and his plea for white nationalism and sectional reconciliation. Others within the ACS agreed with Gurley and noticed white nationalism preserved the "fraternal feeling throughout the Union." The rhetoric of reconciliation, white nationalism, and patriotism gave leading proponents of colonization a language, which they used to build argumentative smoke screens in hopes of obscuring their real intentions and motivations (*African Repository*, August 1825, p. 1; October 1825, p. 225; May 1829, pp. 88-89; September 1830, p. 207; Staudenraus, 1961). The notion of eliminating blacks was popular among the general public throughout the nation. Northern white males feared sexual relations between black men and white women, competition with black males in the work force, and believed blacks in general "upset the order and tranquility" of their communities (*African Repository* May 1833, p. 85; March 1836, pp. 80-81; Adams & Sanders, 2003; Tice, 1987).

Leading colonizationists stressed free blacks and whites could never live together in peace as equals. "Nature has made the distinction of color...and of the repugnance which turns us from those who do not resemble ourselves." Colonizationists declared that "endless jealousies and strife would be the natural fruits of any egalitarian society....The black and white populations are in a state of war" (*African Repository* June, 1831, p. 100; October, 1831, pp. 230-231). They argued, because whites detested blacks, racial discrimination was inevitable against the egalitarian principles of the Declaration of Independence. Plans to unite the two races was never considered as a solution; the only proper way to honor any egalitarian principles and end racial discord was to remove all free African Americans from the shores of the United States. George Washington Parke Curtis (1781–1857), a colonizationist, grandson of George Washington and descendant of Lord Baltimore through his mother Eleanor Calvert; his daughter married the Confederate general Robert E. Lee. In 1831, at the fourteenth annual meeting of the society in Washington D.C., Curtis told delegates:

> What right, I demand, have the children of Africa to an homestead in the white man's country?... The ready answer is, because the African race is despised...that the descendants of Ham are inherently and naturally inferior to ourselves and others, the children of Shem and Japhet (*African Repository*, February 1831).

Cyrus Edwards, in an address delivered at the statehouse in Vandala, Illinois, declared the complexion of black people "will forever exclude them from the rank, privilege, the honors, of freemen. No matter how great their industry, or how abundant their wealth—no matter what their attainments in literature, science or the arts—they can never, no never be raised to a footing of equality." Similarly, it was argued, "This is not the black man's country.... [H]e has no home, no position, and no future" in white America (*African Repository* November 1834, pp. 262-263).

Many ACS members belonged to groups like the American Bible Society, the Home Missionary Society, the American Temperance Society for the Prevention of Licentiousness and Vice, and the American Education Society. These societies urged the spread of Christianity and social control both within the nation and throughout the world in their subjugation of nonwhite cultures. Seeking to extend the boundaries of Christianity, they argued partially civilized blacks could civilize the so-called Dark Continent (*African Repository* March 1831, p. 14; July 1831, pp. 131-132; September 1831, p. 218).

This claim for Christian uplift was shabby and deceitful, for if African Americans were lascivious, sexually permissive, and subverting the United States, how could a deviant and vicious black population improve Africa? How could a degraded and repressed people somehow transmit to Africa the higher qualities of learning? The colonizationists, however, never considered their contradictions. Instead, Protestant clergy declared the ACS made up for the cruel Atlantic Slave Trade that had wrongly carried Africa's sons and daughters to America. It was compensating for all the degrading treatment black people received through their demand for colonization. According to many Protestant clergy, the ACS's program atoned for whatever sins white Americans had inflicted upon black people; it expunged the misdeeds of centuries. Yet the racial arrogance of Protestant clergy was exposed when they emphasized that missions to Africa were supposed to make civilized people of barbarians. Barbarians? If there was one thing that exemplified the raw racism of American Christianity, it was this sort of name calling (Mathews, 1965; *African Repository* February 1828, p. 374; April 1833, p. 59).

Colonizationists agreed with Thomas Jefferson's conclusion that blacks had unusually ardent sexual appetites. These white men felt they had a responsibility to prevent any racial mixing; if it did occur, it meant whites had lost control of their lustful passions and the American experiment of self-government had failed. Jefferson's solution was not to allow blacks to stain the white population through miscegenation. Since blacks were considered sexually promiscuous, especially free blacks, they posed a distinct threat to the racial purity of white America and had to be removed to Africa. The ACS decided, therefore, the removal of African Americans would ease the threat of sexual assaults upon white women. On the other hand, the colonizationists did not address the sexual abuse black women suffered at the hands of white men. This clearly exposed a deep element within white America's libidinal recesses—a fear of, along with an attraction for, white and black relationships—that sexual contact could result in amalgamation and the undermining of white civilization. When the English first arrived in the Americas, they disliked red–white sexual liaisons, but few regarded it with horror. However, they persistently feared and fretted over relationships between black men and white women (Jordan, 1968, pp. 162–163, 458–459, 469–475; Takaki, 1979, pp. 42–55).

To completely understand the colonizationist's mind, one cannot focus entirely upon the African's color. For most ACS activists, the African's complexion was the outer sign of their inner impurity. In addition to being condemned for sexual excess, the African was called a sick "black element," the "deadliest blight," "vile excrescence," a "blotch," "polluting," and a "foul stain" upon the United States. African Americans were considered dangerously "contaminated." They were accused of spreading all kinds of vices and diseases throughout the nation, particularly cholera, and it was claimed that they would, inevitably, "infect" whites and "undermine the nation." The American people were forced "to keep in their midst an uncultivated, degraded and inferior race." According to the colonizationists, there was only one way to cleanse the country of its contamination: the impure blotch had to be expelled. Colonizationists, slaveholders, evangelical clergy, and other prominent figures spoke of "cutting off a morbid excrescence" and "throwing off the suffocating" and "infectious load" by deporting free African Americans to the shores of West Africa. Thus the United States would be "relieved from its heaviest curse." They declared that white people would experience the "relief" and "satisfaction" that comes from "cleansing" the nation. The United States would regain its purity and renew its mission to establish a true "Promised Land" (Berwanger, 1967, pp. 34–40, 51–55; Foster, 1953; Logan, 1943; *African Repository* September 1831, p. 211; October 1831, p. 230; March 1833, p. 3; May 1838, p. 143).

For all the talk of removing African Americans to Africa, the ACS never came close to accomplishing its goal. Between 1822 and 1832, the ACS succeeded in transporting some 1,857 emancipated blacks back to Africa. Between 1816 and 1876, the ACS colonized about 6,000 emancipated blacks to Africa, while at the same time the enslaved population increased by more than 50,000 annually before the Civil War. If the aim of the ACS was to remove blacks from the United States, the colonizationists were noticeable failures.

They proclaimed the abolition of the Atlantic Slave Trade was one of their goals, but many ACS members engaged in the internal slave trade (Rosen, 1972; Elben, 1972). For example, Henry Clay, one of the leading spokesmen of the ACS, was busy multiplying his stock of enslaved blacks. The number of enslaved blacks owned by Clay increased to fifty at various times; by the time of his death in 1852, he possessed thirty-three African Americans in bondage. He bought and sold African Americans and collected the earnings of those he hired out to other whites (Van Duesen, 1937, p. 137). Bushrod Washington, the organization's first president, consistently participated in the domestic slave trade. Charles Carroll, the second president, owned over 2,000 African Americans and never once offered to transport a single enslaved black person back to Africa. James Madison, the third president of the ACS and the fourth president of the United States, left over one hundred blacks in bondage to his heirs.

Many slaveholding colonizationists throughout the North, Virginia, Maryland, Tennessee, and Kentucky surreptitiously sold blacks into the Deep South (Bancroft, 1959). Clay even favored extending slavery into the Western territories and encouraged breeding (Sutch, 1972). If all African Americans were removed, influential slaveholders who were presidents of the United States, congressmen, governors, and mayors, men such as Henry Clay, Bushrod Washington, Andrew Jackson, James Madison, Charles C. Pinkney, and James K. Polk, for example would have lost their wealth and social status. Although Gurley favored deporting African Americans, he knew "we must have the blacks for our servants" (Cohen, 1963; Dillon, 1959; Elben, 1972; Ruchames, 1969, p. 393; Pease & Pease, 1972, p. 101; Van Deusen, 1937, p. 137).

Colonizationists struggled to retain enthusiasm for a crusade of purity that would keep whites free from black contamination. However, the slaveholders contradicted themselves by maintaining sexual contacts with their enslaved property and constantly augmenting their slaveholding, while recommending in regard to free blacks, an organized procedure to "drain them off." The ACS members also proclaimed that they abhorred slavery and pleaded for its demise, while at the same time defending slave breeding, the domestic slave trade, the recovery of fugitive slaves, and the stability of a slave society (*African Repository* October 1836, p. 297). Through expulsion, the "noxious" problems of the United States might be remedied. Clergymen and their congregations imagined the United States as the New Jerusalem, a shining "city upon a hill," and themselves as building a godly community on earth. By expelling the "noxious" free black people, white Christian Americans hoped to gain a fresh start (*African Repository* January 1838, p. 38; Bercovitch, 1978)).

However, the ACS quickly discovered free African American opposition caused them serious problems. Most free African Americans simply balked at the idea of colonization, contending the United States was their country and they should not be asked to depart for the shores of Africa. Alarmed by the rising tide of repression, leading African Americans struck back and utilized, for perhaps the first time, mass pressure technique. In 1817, at Philadelphia's Bethel AME Church, in resistance to colonization, blacks gathered for the largest and most significant meetings prior to the Civil War. Although, a few African Americans thought favorably about emigrating from the United States, the majority of those in attendance denounced the ACS and published the following statement:

Whereas our ancestors (not of choice) were the first successful cultivators of the wilds of America, we their descendants feel ourselves entitled to participate in the blessings of her luxuriant soil, which our blood and sweat manured...having a tendency to banish us from her bosom, would not only be cruel, but in direct violation of those principles, which have been the boast of this republic. Resolved, that we view with deep abhorrence the unmerited stigma attempted to be cast upon the...people of color, by the promoters of this measure.... Resolved, That we never will separate ourselves voluntarily from the slave population in this country (Aptheker, 1951, pp. 70–72).

Post revolutionary and antebellum periods saw the rise of free African Americans in protest against racial discrimination and slavery in the North and South. Early in 1827 black activists including Nathaniel Paul, the founding pastor of Albany's First Baptist Church; William Hamilton, one of the original trustees of AME Zion Church; Peter Williams Jr., pastor of Saint Philip's African Episcopal Church; Lewis B. Woodson, pastor of Bethel AME Church in Pittsburgh; and John Russwurm, the first black to graduate from college, joined the Reverend Samuel Cornish in the house of Boston Crummell, Alexander Crummell's father, and started *Freedom's Journal*, the first African American newspaper in the United States. They, along with numerous other blacks, were angry over the abusive language used to characterize black people and the support for colonization in white newspapers. *Freedom's Journal* attacked colonization, supported temperance, education, racial unity, and the editors hired agents from Maine to Maryland to promote the paper in their communities (*Freedom's Journal*, March 16, 1827; Aptheker, 1951, pp. 82–85; Mullane, 1993, pp. 63–66).

Freedom's Journal embraced a wide variety of issues—abolition, education, fugitive slaves, civil and political rights—that greatly affected the lives of black people in the United States. Instead of colonizing the free black population, the editors proposed that the solution to the degradation of free blacks was to uplift the race. Other black activists founded, edited and published newspapers, unmasking white supremacy implicit in the colonization movement. They attacked white clergy for maintaining segregated "nigger pews," seats labeled the "African Corner" and for practicing a segregated Lord's Supper in their churches. They organized vigilance committees to help fugitive slaves and held all-black conventions that aimed to win civil rights for blacks through legislation (Curry, 1981, pp 143–173).

At the same time, thousands of African American children were excluded from educational facilities or were segregated into all black schools. While some blacks were able to pursue intellectual learning, the majority of blacks were refused access to education. Others saw it as irrelevant to their survival. In many Northern cities such as Boston, Providence, and Philadelphia, no Jim Crow laws existed, but intense harassment of black children effectively prevented them from attending public schools. Private schools discontinued accepting the few black children able to enroll in their schools (Mabee, 1979; Ripley, 1991, Vol. III, p. 437). For many black children, the only available learning facilities were in black churches. A few schools were financed by white philanthropists, for example New York City's African Free School, which produced some of the brightest African American minds of the 1800s was well attended until it came under the umbrella of the public school system (Mabee, 1979; Andrews, 1830; Moses, 1989, p. 17).

African Americans organized vigorous protests to break down the peculiar and racist alliance between white abolitionists and slaveowners who advocated colonization. During the early 1800s, white abolitionists and other reformers such as William Lloyd Garrison, Lewis and Arthur Tappan, Gerrit Smith, and Benjamin Lundy believed slavery was evil; nevertheless, they argued the nation needed to be relieved of its black population. They asserted black people were inferior and feared that slave rebellions would lead to race wars. For instance, before Gerrit Smith became a radical abolitionist, as a member of the ACS he wrote Gruley that educating blacks did not sit well with whites. He added the "editors of *Freedom's Journal*, a paper I was at first disposed to patronize" was not a beneficial newspaper for the country and "my heart is fully set on discharging the patriotic duty of contributing to relieve our country of its black population." Until Garrison published his *Thoughts on African Colonization* in 1832, white abolitionists believed there was no time to wait until prejudices abated and a peaceful biracial society was facilitated. The Haitian Revolution in 1791 caused fear and anxiety throughout the United States—whites dreaded the thought of "black savages" sweeping throughout the South causing death and destruction. Many colonizationists agreed with Thomas Jefferson that God would side with black people if they decided to liberate themselves by force (Abzug, 1970; Litwack, 1961, p. 27; Pease & Pease, 1974, pp. 100–104, 220–223; Staudenraus, 1961, pp. 128–129; Fox, 1919, p. 32).

While the majority of African Americans refused to leave the United States, they struggled against Northern Black Codes. Although northern states made steps to end slavery, emancipation merely redefined the subordinate status of African Americans into Black Codes. Henry Clay was correct when he acknowledged the "prejudices" of white people were "more powerful than any law," for it was white men who introduced the bills to pass as laws, and it was white men that interpreted the laws as they sought ways to keep the distance between black and white. As Northern states abolished slavery, they enacted laws to bar interracial marriages, to expel all blacks who were not citizens of the states they sought to live in, and denied blacks the right to vote or hold any political office (*African Repository*, March 1830; Litwack, 1961, pp. 3, 16; McManus, 1966, pp. 164–165). Elias B. Caldwell stated very clearly:

> If they must remain in their present situation, keep them in the lowest state of degradation and ignorance. The nearer you bring them to the condition of brutes, the better chance do you give them of possessing their apathy.(*African Repository*, February 1836, p. 53).

By focusing on African Americans as inferior and degraded, whites reassured themselves of white supremacy and justified continued discrimination against black people. Discriminatory laws were very important to the legal process because they treated blacks as a distinct class whose loyalty in war times and capabilities generally were automatically suspect. This reinforced white perceptions of blacks as a danger to American society. The exclusionary laws in the Northeast and the denial of citizenship in Illinois, Iowa, Indiana, Oregon, and Ohio reflected the belief whites and blacks could never form a harmonious community.

Colonizationists believed sending free blacks to Africa would compensate for all the wrongs slavery had imposed upon Africans and those of African descent. They insisted the removal of blacks would solve the race problem and revitalize the nation's mission as God's new Israel. The hypocrisy of the American Colonization Society revealed itself through its white supremacist speeches and its members' profiting from the domestic slave trade by breeding and selling of enslaved blacks. Consequently, there were nearly four million black people living in bondage at the beginning of the Civil War. By 1860, the ACS had transported only about fourteen thousand African Americans in contrast to the one million free black people and the four million still in bondage.

The ACS failed from lack of support because the various groups who wanted separation of the races but had economic ties to slavery while others saw the contradictions of the ACS pronouncements. Slaveholders in the lower South did not want to part with their valued "black gold" that enriched their pockets and gave them status in society and power in the government. These slaveholders were suspicious of anyone advocating the abolition of slavery or emancipation for removal. On the other hand, many philanthropists, for example Gerrit Smith, who had fully endorsed the ACS at first, began to see through the smoke screens and rejected the deprecatory pronouncements and suggestions about the innate negative characteristics of black people. In 1832, William Lloyd Garrison published his *Thoughts on African Colonization*, which provoked serious and sometimes heated debates among the white abolitionists who supported colonization.

Conclusion

From its inception, most blacks distrusted and regarded the ACS as a racist organization. They stripped away the façade of philanthropy, revealed the ACS had no antislavery goals, no sincere concern for the condition of free blacks, and no serious commitment to Christian missions to Africa. As opposition to colonization mounted in the 1820s, blacks chose to respond against the incessant references to black inferiority and the increasing oppression suffered by both free and enslaved blacks. Black people knew that the Black Codes in the North worked with the ACS to encourage blacks to seek sanctuary in Africa. African Americans understood the importance of remaining in the United States and refuting the claims of inferiority by demonstrating their capacity for moral and economic uplift. Free blacks believed their citizenship, opposing colonization, and creating a place for themselves in American society threatened the ACS and slavery.

The colonizationists' concern with cleansing the nation of free blacks due to their physical differences and maintaining white supremacy attracted learned people and scientists, even as race-based ideology was evolving as the foundation of social, political, and economic oppression. Racial enslavement in the United States gave white people unrestrained power to create and impose their beliefs on society, to view blacks as subhuman and treat them as beasts. It also allowed American society to create a discrete social category for free blacks and impose laws that forbid interracial relationships and created cultural differences, discriminatory actions to refuse education to black children, left free blacks largely illiterate, without any rights as American citizens, property rights, and excluded from political and economic processes.

With the rise of Western science in the beginning of the nineteenth century, white supremacy was able to address American society with the same old pedagogy of alleged black inferiority, now buttressed by supposedly scientific evidence that suited white interests. Classifications emerged led to hierarchical structures that enforced inequality between whites and peoples of color. Thus white supremacist scholarly and academic epistemologies legitimized "natural" and God-given superior qualities to whites and inferior qualities to all nonwhites. As the twentieth century began, this pedagogy of racial classification showered the American people with images not just of black inferiority, but also of black "bestiality," which fed fears about the safety of white womanhood. Thus a program of scientific scholarship, or eugenics, emerged that rationalized the maintenance of social and economic segregation in the United States.

CHAPTER FIVE

THE PEDAGOGY OF EUGENICS

Mistaken regard for what are believed to be divine laws and a sentimental belief in the sanctity of human life tend to prevent both the elimination of defective infants and sterlization of such adults as are themselves of no value to the community. The laws of nature require the obliteration of the unfit, and human life is valuable only when it is of use to the community or race.

Madison Grant, 1916

Human racial crossing in general is a risky experiment, for it interferes with social inheritance which after is the chief asset of civilization.

William F. Castle, 1927

If you look, for example at male monkeys, especially in the wild, roughly half of them survive to adulthood. The other half die by violence. That is the natural way of its males, to knock each other off and, in fact there are some interesting evolutionary implications of that because the same hyperaggressive monkeys who kill each other are also hypersexual, so they copulate more and therefore they reproduce more to offset the fact that half of them are dying. Now, one could say if some of the loss of structure in this society, and particularly in the high impact inner city areas, has removed some of the civilizing evolutionary things that we have built up and that maybe it isn't just careless use of the word when people call certain areas of certain cities jungles.

Frederick Goodwin, 1992

Introduction

Today scientists know that there is no scientific purpose or value to the study of innate differences in abilities between various races, ethnic groups, and the two sexes. Yet, for over two hundred years, white supremacists have used professed scientific investigations, often under the rubric of eugenics, to prove the existence of innate differences in ability between the races, ethnic groups, and sexes. This spurious research has been used to rationalize white supremacy, define the social and political inequality in the United States as the unavoidable consequence of natural difference. The chapter will briefly trace the evolution of the eugenics movement and describe how its research on genetic difference was used in particular eras to support specific political and racist agendas. Also how it is still used today under a different umbrella to mask those some agendas.

Scientific researchers have consistently argued their research is not based on objective and putative disinterest but rather on their professional expertise. This positivist paradigm has gained so much support in the social sciences that it has been used to justify claims of innate differences in races and ethnic groups and has not been sufficiently challenged enough publicly for supporting an imperialist capitalism and its subordinate ideals. It is on this paradigm the eugenics movement and the racist theories it propagates were founded. In the eighteenth century, the English physician Charles White declared he and other colleagues desired only to investigate truth and to discover the established laws of nature, even as they concluded black people were biologically closer to apes than to humans (White, 1799). The biometricist Karl Pearson, in his essay "The Problem of Alien Immigration into Great Britain," printed in the *Annals of Eugenics* (1925, p. 8), claimed he had no "axe to grind" when he stated the Jews were a "parasitic race" and should be excluded from England. This conclusion, according to Pearson, was founded on the premise seeking the truth was his only motivation (Tucker, 1994). In the United States, nativist, racist, and hegemonic ideologues feared the alleged superior Anglo/Nordic blood in the United States was in danger of being spoiled by inferior races. Scientists like Raymond Pearl, a liberal biologist, publicly denounced Anglo/Nordic racism, but furtively advocated race superiority and called for universities to discriminate against potential Jewish applicants (Barkan, 1992). Doctor Carl C. Brigham argued he presented not theories or mere opinions but facts when he itemized the threats posed by what he called Mediterranean and Alpine immigrants to the national progress and welfare of the United States.

In the 1960s and 1970s, Nobel Prize–winning physicist William Bradford Shockley, an engineer at Stanford University, and Arthur Jensen, an educational psychologist at University of California, Berkeley , claimed their only interest was to conduct research as competently and carefully and then report their methods and findings as carefully and accurately as possible. Both Shockley and Jensen concluded Lyndon B. Johnson's War on Poverty would lead to the "genetic" enslavement of blacks within the United States (Tucker, 1994). These arguments would lay the foundation for right-wing conservatives in the 1980s during the Reagan and Bush administrations. They rearticulated whiteness and recoded racist ideologies by presenting African Americans and other people of color as irresponsible, undeserving, delinquent, immoral, and a menace to society, who sucked up the tax money of white middle-class suburbanites (Quadagino, 1994; Gans, 1995). Within this culture of racism and white superiority, the eugenics movement has consistently mobilized white resentment and fear to maintain and reconsolidate the white hegemonic order.

The scientific debate over genetic differences between groups now continues into the twenty-first century. Unlike other scientific controversies, where the argument diminishes as new discoveries are made or as scientists with opposing views retire or die away, the bitter dispute over race, intelligence, and whose culture will prevail remains a continuous debate. Denigration of the poor has gained renewed strength all over again today in almost exactly the same terms at the beginning of the century, but with a fervor that seems more theological than empirical. The issue of race inferiority became heated in 1994, when Richard J. Herrnstein and Charles Murray published the most incendiary piece of social science to appear within the last twenty years, *The Bell Curve: Intelligence and Class Structure in American Life.* Herrnstein and Murray have rearticulated the racist ideology through academic protocol, without any overt racist language, even acknowledging contrary viewpoints and hiding behind so-called scientific data. While the authors hide behind alleged academic scholarship and scientific data full of warnings and falsifications, the Bell Curve became a explosive device. Herrnstein and Murray's book received top billings throughout the media and was sold on most bookshelves in the country, including those of Kmart nationwide. The argument has not confined itself to academic journals and scientific conferences; the subject of racial differences was debated from university classrooms, bars and living rooms. Their book received unprecedented coverage in the nation's popular culture and media.

The idea that academicians allied themselves with politics gave scientific authority a powerful strategy for influencing public policy. The results of this kind of scientific investigation that groups people as genetically inferior have facilitated organizational or informal alliances between scientific racial research and right-wing political groups, often fascists or racists who have been more than pleased to use this scientific authority as a source of prestige for their own agendas. The use of science to promote race superiority and whiteness has been accomplished with the cooperation of or at the very least without protest from even those who do not support the eugenic ideology.

Since 1945, Americans has increasingly been associated with a strong civic culture that is supposed to sanction and safeguard the assertions of every ethnic and religious group based on individual rights, in the attempt to reduce antagonism among the various religious, ethnic, and racial groups of the country. This civic culture is supposed to bring together the people of the United States and protect their freedoms—including their right to have racial and ethnic differences. Civic culture is based essentially on three points made by those men who framed the basic principles of the American republic: First, ordinary men and women can be trusted to govern themselves through elected representatives. Second, those who live in the community are supposed to be able to participate in the political process. Here lies one of the foundational problems: The rule of naturalization in the U.S. Constitution, signed into law on March 26, 1790, provided "any alien, being a free *white* person...may be admitted to become a citizen" of the United States. Essentially, the signers of the U.S. Constitution were making only adult white males eligible to participate in public life as equals (Smith, 1997).

As stated earlier this was the basis for voluntary pluralism in where European immigrants and their progeny were free to maintain affection and loyalty to their ancestral ethos, while at the same time claiming United States citizenship. They embraced the founding myths and participated in the political life of this republic. There were no problems as long as the immigrants were predominately English or Scottish. George Washington, in his farewell address in 1796, understood this when put forward the idea for a homogeneous society (Grant and Davison, 1928). Thus, for over the next one hundred or more years civic responsibility was reserved only for white Protestant males, while white women were not even considered citizens and over 40 percent of the population was enslaved for the first 250 years of this new experiment.

Since the founding of this republic, the civic culture of the United States has been constantly challenged by some individuals and extremist groups whose ideology centered on scientific racism. They promoted their belief that there existed scientifically identifiable, hereditary racial differences in the various races or ethnic groups, and those with supposedly less intelligence should not be allowed to participate in the civic culture of the United States (Spearman, 1927; Jordan, 1968). Today, such thinkers are influenced by social and political events, as their predecessors were, and their representation of an oppressive and dogmatic ideology has captured the renewed interest of many. For over two hundred years, some scientists have been obsessed with demonstrating that Native Americans, Africans, those of African descent, Hispanics, poor whites, foreigners, and women are innately inferior to upper-class white males descended from the Anglo/Nordic stock of Northern Europe.

Aristotle was one of the first to promote distinctions between those who are intended to rule and those who are intended to be ruled, but it was not until the nineteenth century positivist ideologues made the linkage between science and politics explicit. Positivist academic doctors and anthropologists began to assess intelligence through various anatomical and physiognomic characteristics in scientific attempts at linear evaluation of racial and ethnic groups.

Beginning with the enslavement of black people to the present publication of Herrnstein and Murray's incendiary *The Bell Curve*, white scientific pedagogues have advocated and campaigned through the media their racial superiority, but also political policies of exclusion based on race and ethnicity. A critical multicultural civic pedagogy, therefore, must be practiced not only in the classroom, but also in communities to educate the masses in general and educators, labor leaders, politicians, and cultural and social workers in particular about the invidious agenda of eugenics. A critical multicultural pedagogy can be designed to teach students to become responsible civic-minded citizens ready to participate in the political system. In other words, a critical multicultural pedagogy is imperative to repudiate scientific racism which oppresses not just Americans but a scientific racism exploiting people around the globe (Bigelow & Peterson, 2002; Kincheloe, Gresson, & Steinberg, 1996; Kincheloe & Steinberg, 1997;).

While this nation's civic culture was allegedly formed on sound principles, it was in open violation of those very principles from the beginning with the enslavement of Africans and their descendants. Americans today have a tendency to project their cherished political values back to the 1700s and impute a modern moral vision upon the framers of the United States Constitution. The enslavement and belief in the cognitive inferiority of Africans and those of African descent is so sickening to many teachers they cannot conceive that decent people—much less those who framed the Constitution—would embrace them. So today, we naturally want to believe that the ideology that justified the enslavement of blacks was incompatible with the constitutional order that was established and which we, as citizens, revere. We try to persuade ourselves the Declaration of Independence manifests the real values of the United States governmental order and the enslavement of black people somehow sneaked in to the Constitution eleven years later (Franklin, 1989).

Most Americans have been kept from really understanding and engaging in an epistemology of civic action that would refute the concept of genetic perfectibility of the Anglo/Nordic race. Whites have been taught to believe in their superiority, to achieve socioeconomic success and global dominance (Grant, 1933; Hofstadter, 1944; Dyer, 1980). This belief in the importance of whiteness was rearticulated in the latter part of the nineteenth century as social Darwinism and later eugenics. Eugenic supporters described it as a science of human improvement through controlled breeding. Eugenicists sought policies that restricted immigration of non–Anglo/Nordic Europeans, segregated and excluded blacks, and controlled children of interracial unions, and used eugenics as a venue to legitimatize their racial ideology (Hofstadter, 1944). Critical multicultural teachers need to understand and raise questions within the eugenics debate concerning technocratic education and capitalism, along with champions of racial birth control. Right-wing conservatives have lined up, knowingly or unknowingly, to advocate the idea of controlling the birth rates of allegedly inferior races and ethnic groups (Quadagno, 1994; Roberts, 1997) and encourage the breeding of more Anglo/Nordic people (Ingle, 1973). As informed critical multicultural teachers we can question how eugenics has come to exert such powerful influence in education, the political, and economic arena, and how it has gained such appeal in this land (Roberts, 1997). Whose interests does eugenics serve? How has the ideology of population control, especially in nonwhite communities, employing arguments to justify Malthusian-inspired solutions of restrictive immigration and eugenic sterilization, become palatable to broad segments of the American people (Reed, 1978; Crook, 1994; Larson, 1995)?

Curtailing the fertility of selected racial groups, or classes, is the goal of Malthusian-based programs. Birth control has appealed to policy makers because fertility appears to be the most easily manipulated variable with which to alleviate problems such as poverty and inequality. Furthermore, this approach provides a technocratic solution to educational and other social problems by altering the behavior of the poor rather than redistributing power or resources. Therefore, a critical civic pedagogy to educate the masses to prevent the government from maintaining the power to decide for the ordinary citizen is crucial to begin to address the issue at hand. Instead of the popular will, the government has always responded more often to the webs of power—the interests of economic organizations and concentrated wealth and influential elites surrounding them. It is imperative to understand how this invidious agenda came about and how it has camouflaged itself under the umbrella of objective science (Ingle, 1973; Reed, 1978; Greider, 1992; Crook, 1994).

Historical Origins of Scientific Racism

As early as 1684, in the *Journal des Scavans,* Francois Bernier, a French physician, became one of the first to publish an article on racial classification and human differences (Bernasconi & Lott, 2000). In 1735, Charles Linnaeus, a biological taxonomist, published his *General System of Nature,* a preliminary attempt at racial classification. Linnaeus attributed several character traits to each race: Europeans were sanguine, brawny, gentle, and inventive, while Americans were choleric, obstinate, content, and free. Asians were melancholic, rigid, haughty, and covetous, and Africans were phlegmatic, crafty, indolent, and negligent. Johann Friedrich Blumenbach, a professor at the University of Göttingen, added his aesthetic judgments to personal traits as possible elements of racial classification and coined the term "Caucasian." In his publication *On the Natural Varieties of Mankind* (1775), he wrote the most beautiful race originated in the Caucasus Mountains, a mountain range in present-day Republic of Georgia (Bernasconi & Lott, 2000; Jordan, 1968; Gossett, 1963).

The concept of the "great chain of being," rooted in the Aristotelian belief that inequality was the foundation of the natural order of things, flourished throughout the eighteenth and nineteenth centuries. Its basic premise was the existence of hierarchical structures as a "new ordering" based on the logic that establishes a relationship of superiority and subordination. This theory allocated every form of life to its appropriate rank in the great chain, from the lowest to the highest position; thus biological diversity was synonymous with inequality. This hierarchical order of human beings was natural to Europeans as they came into contact with each other and peoples of other cultures around the world. They began to attach personal traits and aesthetic judgments to skin color, which soon merged with the assumptions of the great chain of being and the creation of a vertical ordering of the races became an accepted task of science (Lovejoy, 1966; Vaughan, 1995).

In 1799, Dr. Charles White, a member of the Royal Society of London, argued black people were biologically nearer to apes than to Europeans and blacks were of a completely different species. He maintained his only purpose was the investigation of truth. Yet while he argued he had no desire to see blacks oppressed, his opinions consistently fed the capitalist slave traders, proslavery supporters, and those who could not see black people having any civilizable traits, making them fit only for enslavement. White's claim of unbiased objectivity would be echoed by many scientists over the next two hundred years. Even those who supposedly opposed enslaving blacks agreed with White's claims. Thomas Jefferson, in his *Notes on the State of Virginia* (1787), wrote in query 14 on the alleged inferiority of black people and even went on to say black women preferred to mate with apes. Based on the theory of the great chain of being, Jefferson and others of his day implicitly assumed blacks were by nature subordinate to whites and slavery was in harmony with nature and the social order (Jordan, 1968).

As antislavery advocates gained momentum, both black and white abolitionists engaged in civic action, produced an epistemological pedagogy exposed the contradictions between, on the one hand, the Declaration of Independence and the nation's claim of being Christian and, on the other, its engagement in the racial enslavement of Africans and those of African descent (Ripley, 1991 & 1993; Jacobs, 1993). Proslavers responded to the abolitionists by moving from implicit arguments to a more explicit premise of black inferiority. While American proslavery thought is believed to be a Southern ideology, it is far from an invention of the slaveholding Southern planters. Proslavery epistemology and its pedagogy concerning black inferiority had its origins in the crucible of conservative New England's academic and religious circles (Tice, 1987).

Proslavery doctors, including New York's John H. Van Evire, wrote on the anatomy and physiology of black people. In his book *Negroes and Negro Slavery: the First an Inferior Race: the Latter its Normal Condition* (1863), Van Evire argued blacks were inferior to whites from skin color to intelligence. In 1868 he published a second edition, changing the title to *White Supremacy and Negro Subordination: or Negroes a Subordinate Race and Slavery its*

Normal Condition with an Appendix, Showing the Past and Present Condition of the Countries South of Us. He arguing any effort to educate blacks would only render them utterly incapable of locomotion or an upright position at all. In other words, it would be impossible for blacks to stand upright (Van Evire, 1863 & 1868; Smith, 1993a).

However, even before 1868, black people had already proven Van Evire's theory wrong. In the 1830s, the segregated African Free Schools in New York City already had trained and laid the educational foundations for future black activists who became doctors, businessmen, scholars, clergymen, and actors—inarguably intelligent black people in the United States during the nineteenth century. There were also many black innovators: Onesimus, a slave owned by the Puritan leader Cotton Mather, developed a cure for smallpox; Ned, an enslaved black, invented the cotton harvester in 1857; Benjamin Bradley constructed the first steam engine in 1840. There were several others such as Benjamin Banneker, James Forten, and Norbert Rillieux—who developed a sugar refining process that revolutionized the sugar industry in 1843 (Andrews, 1830; Moses, 1989; Ripley, 1991; Brodie, 1993; Asante & Abarry, 1996). In spite of black intellectual achievements of the 1800s, the American public, influenced by white supremacist ideology and supposedly scholarly sources, continued to believe the so-called scientific opinions being used to defend the racial theories of black inferiority and the perpetual enslavement of African Americans.

The general arguments printed in journals and newspapers declared blacks were destined to be slaves to whites. Dr. Samuel Cartwright received wide attention in the 1850s declaring freedom was the cause of mental and physical diseases among black people. He contended a disease called "drapetomania" attacked blacks who liberated themselves from the chains of enslavement. He argued the cure for this was to treat blacks as children, but only so long as they were submissive; if they dared to raise their stature to the same level as whites, then violence would whip the devil out of them and return them to the submissive state nature intended for them. White supremacists even used the Census Bureau to promote black inferiority by claiming freedom drove black people insane (Fredrickson, 1971; Horsman, 1981).

In 1844, Senator John C. Calhoun's letters to Richard Parkenham, a government official from England, utilized the writings of Edward Jarvis and used data from the 1840 census, asserting freedom caused vice, pauperism, deafness, blindness, insanity, and idiocy in free blacks. Conversely, enslaved blacks had proved Calhoun wrong (Cralle, 1855; Jarvis, 1844). James McCune Smith, a graduate of the African Free Schools in New York City, the first African American doctor in the United States and considered one of the most scholarly black men of the nineteenth century, responded to Calhoun's racist rhetoric by publishing an article in 1843 titled "What Shall We Do with the Insane." In his rebuttal, Smith proved carelessness had virtually invalidated the statistics on black insanity. Then, in 1846, *Hunt's Merchants Magazine* published an article by Smith, "The Influence of Climate upon Longevity," in which he refuted the erroneous claims made by Calhoun and Cartwright. Smith revealed in another essay, "The Memorial to the United States Senate: Dr. James McCune Smith Refutes Secretary of State John C. Calhoun's Remarks Concerning Negro Inferiority," the 1840 census reported 133 African Americans in the mental institution in Worcester, Massachusetts, when in fact the 133 were all white patients (Aptheker, 1951; Morias, 1967; Fredrickson, 1971; Litwack, 1961).

During this period certain individuals began to study the dichotomization of nature and nurture, which eventually led to the psychometric tradition. Scientists such as Harvard professor Louis Agassiz in the late 1840s wrote when he first came into contact with black domestic workers in Philadelphia he thought they were hideous, and that he would rather be served by white domestics. Agassiz expressed grief that white people had such close contact with blacks and prayed to God to "preserve us from such a contact" (Gould, 1978). The scientist Samuel George Morton, in his *Crania Americana* (1839), declared the racial characteristics of white people were the fairest and possessed the highest intelligence of all races. He reserved the worst classifications for black people, claiming they were the nearest to animals, filthy, gluttonous, licentious, and repulsive. Josiah Clark Nott argued for far more than just black inferiority; the focus of his scientific race theory became a new ideology of Caucasian or Anglo-Saxon racial pride and articulated racial homogeneity. It must be remembered racialist epistemology was emerging in Europe and the United States was being articulated to justify more than the South's institution of slavery. This racist epistemology emerged to serve and defend a pedagogy of subordination and, in some cases, the extermination of people of color throughout the world. It was also used pedagogically to explain the ever-increasing gulf in power and progress separating the Anglo/Nordic whites from the people they were forcing into subjugation. It should be noted all the racist statements considered here issued from schools of higher learning and respected men of intellect. The damage from this is thousands of men and women have been imbued with these invidious theories and have encouraged public policies which still cause harm to blacks today (Fredrickson, 1971; Horsman, 1981).

As these two lines of investigation merged at the turn of the century, a movement arose that attempted to derive moral and behavioral guidelines from what were claimed to be scientific-physical laws. Questions of human rights and freedoms—who should vote, who should be educated, who should have children, and who should be allowed into the country—were transferred from their appropriate place in the domain of political discourse to the domain of science (Adams & Sanders, 2003; Smith, 1995). In particular, an understanding of racial differences was claimed to be the key to social progress. Public education, social harmony, national welfare, and, indeed, the future of the Anglo/Nordic people were all said to depend on the eugenic/nativist movement (Grant, 1916; Ingle, 1973; Horsman, 1981; Smith, 1993a). What began as the study of hereditary characteristics thus quickly burgeoned into a presumptuous field marked by immodest pronouncements on the limits of democracy, the necessity of racial segregation, the futility of education, the biological inevitability of vast socioeconomic disparities, and the necessity of controlling the birthrate of certain groups.

Charles Darwin influenced the development of natural selection a spurious social science arguing biological evolution as proof that white Anglo Protestants evolved much further than other races. It was seized upon by the Western intelligentsia in the later part of the nineteenth century by men like Herbert Spenser who argued this concept of biological evolution will weed out the unfit and make room for the survival of the fittest (Hoffstadter, 1944). Darwin's theory assisted the intelligentsia to categorize the belief of self-determination and the self-justification of the rise of a social science that helped people perceive and interpret issues from the differences between the races and classes to the implications of state intervention in the economy.

Social Darwinism was welcomed and perhaps the most powerful store of ideas conservatives appealed to when they resigned poverty stricken people to languish in dilapidated conditions and blamed the horrible living conditions on the victims. Social Darwinism also defended the political and economic status quo, the laissez-faire conservatives, who were the first to pick up the idea that any attempts to reform society were efforts to remedy the irremediable, that to interfere with nature would lead only to social degeneration (Hoffstadter, 1944). This ideology became one of the leading strains in conservative thought whose primary conclusion was that state assistance to the poor and disfranchised should be kept to the barest minimum. Also, more important, was conservatism tried to dispense with sentimental or emotional ties with the disadvantaged. Social Darwinism brings to mind the ideas of Christian fundamentalism in which man's connection to nature is as hard and demanding as man's relation to God under the Calvinist viewpoint (Hofstadter, 1944).

Social Darwinism was a mixture of oversimplified biology, racism, opportunistic politics, and capitalism. While Darwin was very careful to explain his theory of the struggle for existence and limit its relevance to the biological realm, Herbert Spencer, the leading exponent of social Darwinism, combined Malthusian socioeconomic theory and pseudo-Darwinian evolutionary theory and applied them to social and political institutions. He repudiated any state aid to the poor, state sponsored education, sanitary supervision, and regulation of housing conditions, claiming poor people were unfit and should be eliminated. He insisted humanity was divided into superior and inferior races, which the dominant civilized races must overrun the inferior savage races, and technology had been reserved for the biologically advanced Anglo/Nordic peoples. Black people, according to Spencer, were of another, inferior species. His ideas became vogue and provided frameworks for the moral decisions of governmental and other powerful figures. Spencer vehemently believed the suffering of inferior beings was the inescapable price of the evolutionary process and any attempts to ameliorate it would only impede nature's method for preventing the pollution of the master race. In other words, the benign neglect of the weak—the losers in the social Darwinist struggle—and their ultimate extermination were viewed as nature's way of ridding society of its dross. Philanthropy and traditional notions of humanitarian assistance to the poor and needy were seen as pointless; preventing starvation, diseases, and suffering in general was seen as scientifically unsound (Hofstadter, 1944; Gossett, 1963; Hawkins, 1997).

In accord with Spencer's pronouncements, social Darwinists were adverse to all governmental programs of benevolence, welfare, or any other humanitarian assistance for the so-called undeserving inferior. Social Darwinist rationale was used to beat back demands for minimum wages, maximum working hour regulations, child labor laws, restrictions on convict labor, free public education, and any other measures that would improve the circumstances of the poor or shield them from the allegedly just consequences of their own inferiority. Even modern advances in healthcare were viewed as interfering with the biological process, since they preserved the weaklings and elderly of society. Spencer's message of misguided philanthropy allowed business leaders in the United States to lobby for relief of government taxes. In fact the business leaders who were the major proponents of imperialism strongly believed in Spencer's laws of science, which sanctified avariciousness. Science, social progress, and prosperity could now be solidified by suppressing and eliminating the weaklings and people of color, by the machine gun triumphing over the bow and arrow, by unrestrained trade and competition, by getting rid of the other guy with impunity (Hofstadter, 1944; Gossett, 1963; Fredrickson, 1981; Hawkins, 1997).

Spencer's influence can be seen in the lives of corporate giants like railroad tycoon James J. Hill, who believed the prosperity of the railroads rested upon the survival of the fittest. Andrew Carnegie, for instance, was a strong disciple and intimate friend of Spencer, while

John D. Rockefeller taught Sunday school classes and claimed the growth of big business was merely the survival of the fittest and evidence of the law of nature and the law of God in action. Social Darwinists applied the notion of the struggle for survival to larger spheres of debate—nations versus nations and race against race. It was believed the contest between the strong and weak races could be settled by waging war against the inferior, war for control of trade routes, resources, and food supplies. Social scientists claimed their empirical studies had proven blacks were inferior to whites, which had significant theoretical consequences. With the idea that only the strongest races would survive, to admit to any black achievement in the minds of many scientists would cause serious damage to the proclamations of white superiority (Hofstadter, 1944; Gossett, 1963; Perlmutter, 1992).

During the antebellum period, bogus scientific investigations proclaimed black people flourished under the system of enslavement. George Fitzhugh and others asserted black inferiority justified their enslavement and they were being shielded from nature's struggle. Some believed blacks as a whole were on their way to becoming a degraded and criminal race. However, at the turn of the century social Darwinism claimed freedom would eliminate blacks because the two races could not coexist together. Social Darwinist scholars believed science had proven blacks could not compete evenly with whites and a racial struggle would eliminate blacks in an unequal contest. While this kind of ideological determinism may or may not have been premeditated the way Nazi Germany's Final Solution would be, yet there are many similarities between the two worldviews, which makes one wonder if many of the social Darwinists shared the later Nazi goal of scientifically justified genocide.

With its scientific rationale, the potential extermination of blacks was seen as a remedy rather than a tragedy. Physicians such as Charles S. Bacon suggested assisting nature in the extermination of black people, although Bacon realized that to exterminate three million black workers would have dire consequences for the U.S. economy (Bacon, 1903; Bennett, 1969; Lacy, 1972; Spivey, 1978; Oshinsky, 1996). Social Darwinists concluded any attempts to educate black people were not only useless but also a waste of government funds. In 1913, Professor James Bardin of the University of Virginia stated in his *Popular Science* article "The Psychological Factor in Southern Race Problems," that 'no matter how much we educate black people, no matter now much we better his position in society...he will remain a Negro physically." In other words, education only made blacks imitators of whites without leading to any real, biological progress (Smith, 1993b).

Blacks were not the only targets of the social Darwinists; many European immigrants at the turn of the century were viewed by scientists as not far removed from blacks in the evolutionary process. For instance, Anglo/Nordic solidarity articulated Irish immigrants as being inferior and doomed to extermination. Edward A. Freeman, a professor at Oxford, declared the best remedy for the racial problems in the United States was for "every Irishman to kill a Negro and be hanged for it." While some white supremacists called for African Americans to be returned to Africa (Smith, 1993d), the social Darwinists wanted restrictive immigration laws to exclude the hordes of allegedly uncivilized Europeans coming to the United States. Even as the African American population failed to decline despite predictions, the number of white non–Anglo/Nordic immigrants to America soared. Jim Crow laws and geopolitical isolation in the South kept African Americans separate and unequal, whereas the white Southern and Eastern European immigrants were beginning to pose not only a numerical threat, but also a political threat in major cites throughout the nation (Reed, 1913; Ward, 1920; Smith, 1993c).

The concept of genetic perfectibility was widely accepted by middle class people who lived in the United States, Canada, and England and in certain other parts of Europe. Francis Galton, best known for his pioneering work in statistics and its application to the problems of human heredity, invented the term *eugenics* for his program of selective breeding in 1883. Eugenics comes from the Greek word *eugenes,* which means "well born" or "good in birth." Galton defined eugenics as a science, which improve the inborn qualities of a race; also with those that develop to the utmost advantage. Eugenics looks to improve the stock and takes cognizance of every influence that tends—to whatever small degree—to give the more appropriate races or strains of blood a better chance of prevailing speedily over the less suitable (Blacker, 1952; Roberts, 1997). Galton later advocated the study of agencies under social control, which may improve or impair the racial qualities of future generations. He wanted science to deal with the influences that would improve the inborn qualities of a particular race and develop them so they would have the utmost advantage. He suggested the government promote men and women of hereditary fitness to marry each other and produce as many children as possible (Hofstadter, 1944; Larson, 1995).

Galton's positivist eugenics sought to replace traditional religion with a new faith based on the natural laws of the universe, which included heredity influences. Galton and other social Darwinists were worried about the growing numbers of black people and the more "prolific Celts" over the Teutonic race; from a scientific point of view they warned of the folly of allowing these supposedly inferior racial groups to grow. The next few years brought a flurry of activity both in the United States and England as journals were started, fellowships were endowed, and laboratories and public information societies (now called think tanks) were established. Galton was also interested in eugenics as scientific support for his social programs. More significant was the impact that Galton's theory had over society even after his death. Galton's ideas not only endorsed Spencer's by justifying the intrusion of public policy into a competitive survival of the fittest, but also rearticulated its opinions to the public under the umbrella of impartial objectivity. Galton believed that without proper government intervention the supposedly inferior black people and inferior European ethnic groups would take over. Social Darwinists and eugenicists moved to ensure that laws were passed and social plans and polices were enacted so that the Anglo/Nordic race would be victorious in the evolutionary struggle. Thus Galton set the tone for the eugenics movement, which moved with religious fervor, encouraged the most oppressive policies, and justified them with moral arrogance, claiming they were the unavoidable social consequences of scientific truth.

According to eugenic theory, biology along with psychology and sociology would solve the world's problems, thereby removing many of the social ills from the nonscientific realm of politics. As far as its proponents were concerned, eugenics would replace religion, emotions, and other irrational ideas for implementing social policy. The intelligentsia at major universities taught courses on eugenics including universities like Harvard, Columbia, and Cornell. Eugenics attracted progressive thinkers and liberal social reformers like Emma Goldman, Bernard Shaw, Margaret Sanger, and Scott Nearing (Freeden, 1979; Paul, 1984; Larson, 1995). Eugenics appealed to many New Deal advocates who supported sterilization bills while at the same time pushed for old age pensions, free textbooks in schools, and clinics for babies. However, white supremacist politicians like Georgia's Governor Eugene Talmadge vetoed proposed sterilization bills along with everything else the New Deal supporters tried to pass. Eugenic sterilization was finally passed in Georgia in 1937 by a progressive Democratic governor, E. D. Rivers (Larson, 1991).

The debate to legalize birth control was strongly connected to eugenics. Many felt it was disgraceful middle class taxpayers were rearing only one or two children per family while society allowed the racially negligent, the careless, the feebleminded, and the lowest dregs of society to produce innumerable thousands of inferior children. Others believed that a simpler way to deal with this chronic problem was to sterilize the poor. These supposedly civilized and civic-minded individuals and groups supported involuntary sterilization upon the allegedly racially inferior, immoral, and undesirable; whose behavior reflected a benighted biological heritage. Between 1910 and 1939, Harry H. Laughlin, a school teacher in the Midwest and a zealous propagandist of eugenics, led a small group of prominent physicians who promoted the passage of laws designed to protect the racial purity of the United States (Reilly, 1991).

Eugenicists were especially concerned with the role of women in society. While some conservatives supported legislative acts for birth control, those who were opposed to birth control based their opposition on the premise college educated women had dangerously lowered the birth rate and birth control would further harm the posterity of the race. Margaret Sanger, the founder of Planned Parenthood, and Nora Nixon of the prestigious Augusta Junior League, who operated a baby clinic for poor black and white women during the Depression, were worshipped like gods. Nixon's facility became the first birth control clinic to make an attempt to reduce the number of unwanted children among the poor and uneducated (Roberts, 1997). Eugenicist Clarence James Gamble, a philanthropist and physician, supported Sanger and Nixon by promoting and disseminating model sterilization laws. Political involvement in the eugenics movement was extensive: Nora Nixon's husband, a prominent civic reformer, whose father was a superior court judge and a progressive candidate for the Democratic gubernational nomination in 1936, was also committed to eugenics. Eugenicists believed the future of the United States was at stake; hence it was their patriotic duty to control the behavior of inferior groups. The eugenics movement sought technocratic solutions to the social problems that the nation faced (Larson, 1991; Crooks, 1994).

Eugenics attracted to its ranks biologists, animal breeders, psychologists and other social scientists, public and private executives, criminologists, social workers, and overt racists and nativist political organizations. They feared that the traditionally dominant Anglo/Nordic race was being overwhelmed and in serious danger of succumbing to the sheer numbers of degraded people of color and other European ethnic groups. In the minds of the eugenicists the poor, degenerates, and the supposedly inferior races were prolifically increasing their numbers, outpacing the so-called superior Anglo/Nordic people. In response the eugenicists articulated technocratic, repressive policies on the grounds of scientific necessity. Eugenic influences upon social issues were supported by Anglo/Nordic elite and upper class people who held eugenicists as experts who reflected the social Darwinist opposition to assistance to the poor. They opposed even looking for cures of diseases on the basis that any attempt to eliminate poverty would only increase the numerical population of the poor, degenerates, and black people. The eugenicist Edward M. East declared in his publication *Heredity and Human Affairs* (1927) "a complete triumph of civilization, with gases and bombs annihilating whole populations, will restore the biological value of warfare."

Paul Popenoe and Roswell H. Johnson, in their publication *Applied Eugenics* (1935) claimed people with natural superior abilities for prosperity and foresight provide for their own retirement, thereby relieving the government and individuals of caring for the elderly. Social programs for the elderly, now known as social security, were viewed as dysgenic since it would reduce the economic obligations of able bodied workers. Many eugenicists believed that eight-hour workdays, minimum wages, and free medical assistance would only encourage so-called degenerates and the weaker races to increase rather than decrease (Larson, 1995). When Nazi Germany put into action the eugenic ideas of American and British scholars, Popenoe in 1934 supported the Nazis arguing that is was not racially motivated but was a solution to eliminate all inferior and undesirable people (Degler, 1991)

Southern and Eastern Europeans, black people, alleged degenerates, and the masses of working class people were judged as too listless to provide any meaningful contributions to the political process and society in general. The new immigrants were not considered Anglo/Nordics, who over the centuries had unparalleled success in the world. Eugenicists viewed the passage through Ellis Island by purportedly weaker or inferior Europeans a threat and a contamination to Anglo/Nordic purity. Established immigrant families were considered a threat as they moved from the inner cities into the suburbs to escape African Americans migrating from the South and Hispanics migrating from Puerto Rico. In response to this perceived menace eugenicists campaigned vigorously for legislation; they were rewarded when the Immigration Restriction Act of 1924 and closed Ellis Island (Daniels, 1991; Permutter, 1992). Black people, regarded even more undesirable than white immigrants, were basically kept from participating in the civic culture. Eugenicists encouraged and defended the already established antimiscegenation laws and Jim Crow policies that kept blacks segregated and unequal. Since the American public considered black people inferior in every regard, eugenicists did not feel any need to persuade the public to further implement policies against blacks. The white supremacist scholar Madison Grant (1916) proclaimed blacks were not a volatile political force and had no interest in socialism or labor movements.

Eugenicists proposed and eventually sterilized over forty thousand individuals in thirty states under state laws. The statutory language used terms like *socially inadequate persons* and eschewed the emotional term *degenerate*. Included under the description of the socially inadequate were the feebleminded, the insane, alcoholics, criminals, epileptics, the diseased, those with impaired vision, and the cripple; in some cases dependent orphans, the homeless, vagrant, and paupers were also included. While sterilization was directed at individuals, eugenicists made sure the civic culture knew these laws would referred only to European immigrants and black people. They ensured the public that good old Anglo/Nordic stock would not be included in the sterilization process (Larson, 1995; Reilly 1991). Eugenicist pedagogy suggested full entitlement to United States citizenship had been too generous and the right to be educated be disallowed to immigrants and black people. Some eugenicists even argued science had raised serious doubts about the feasibility of democracy.

Many eugenicists believed science was the answer to major social problems—if they had their way, blacks would be excluded from ever participating as full citizens of the United States. Harvard professor Edward M. East, in his publication *Heredity and Human Affairs* (1927), concluded that the genetics of whites were the ones that counted. He believed the United States would experience no internal problems and should have nothing to fear as long as the Anglo/Nordic race remained pure and an acceptable percentage of the total population. He argued if sterilization laws were enacted, millions of socially inadequate persons would be prevented from reproducing and wasting taxpayers' money on free education. East concluded that the existing government was not compatible with scientific research and a scientific approach would lead to the termination of the premise that all men are created equal. He claimed the idea of molding children in schools to participate in a Jeffersonian democracy was a failure; to correct this; he suggested the voting process be reserved for those with higher grades of intelligence. These repressive ideas were not referred to as political suggestions, but viewed as the rational utilization of scientific research.

During the early years of the twentieth century, sociology and psychology held low academic status, enduring ridicule and criticism from the more recognized fields of study. In their quest to gain respect, many in both fields abandoned any impartial attempts to understand behavior and the ideological support for a Darwinist social order. In return for selling their souls to pseudoscience, sociologists and psychologists received recognition, authority, and status within academic and political circles. Edward L. Thorndike, a psychology professor at Columbia University, became the most influential educational psychologist for over forty years, publishing some fifty books and numerous articles arguing that the most intelligent people are the most clean, decent, and gentle. Intelligence, to Thorndike, was the quantifiable measure to be used to rank genetically transmitted abilities. Thorndike was very important in endorsing eugenic ideas in education such as the theory of inherited mental capacity. He believed and supported the theory that absolute achievements of men can be affected by their environment and training, but relative achievements, the comparative performances in competition with each other, were due to genetic superiority. In other words, individuals endowed with greater worth, with better test scores, should be entitled to greater socioeconomic rewards, thus—in circular fashion—proving their genetic superiority. Existing racial and ethnic beliefs were now reaffirmed with the ultimate scientific support—measured "data"—in the form of I.Q. scores (Thorndike, 1927 & 1940; Hofstadter, 1944; Tucker, 1994).

While Thorndike promoted I.Q. scores to determine superiority, other scientists formed a coalition to enact restrictive immigration legislation. With the combination of social Darwinism and genetics, white supremacist scholars offered their accounts of political and racial history. Madison Grant published *The Passing of the Great Race*, (1916), which received great praise from many scientists such as geneticist Frederick Adams Woods, while Lothrop Stoddard's *The Rising Tide of Color against White World Supremacy* (1920) became popular. Both Madison and Stoddard exerted enormous influence as legislators quoted passages from their books during congressional hearings on immigration. Even President Theodore Roosevelt praised Madison Grant's work and, during the 1920 presidential campaign, on September 14, the *New York Times* carried an article in which Senator Warren G. Harding made references to the danger of racial differences within the United States. After Harding won the election the *New York Times* carried another article describing a speech of Harding's to a white audience in Birmingham, Alabama, which he referred to Lothrop Stoddard's work. He stated in his speech that he was not in favor of black people gaining any kind of social equality with the white man. Calvin Coolidge added that scientific research reveals that certain people should not be allowed to mix with those of superior genetic endowment (Dyer, 1980; O'Reilly, 1995).

In support of the eugenicists, Congressman Albert Johnson, who chaired the House Committee on Immigration and Naturalization and who held strong racial prejudices, was in favor of immediate immigration restrictions and the denial of citizenship to certain European immigrants. Eugenicists presented Congress with an analysis of the alleged melting pot lowering the I.Q. of Anglo/Nordic Americans. They wanted each immigrant investigated biologically and statistically for their mental and moral quality. With such so-called scientific facts, the Immigration Restriction Act of 1924 was passed, which contained the ideas of Madison Grant on selective racial and ethnic quotas, restricting immigration from each country in proportion to the United States population. Congressman Johnson was rewarded for passing the 1924 Immigration Restriction Act by being appointed president of the Eugenics Research Association (Daniels, 1990).

In order to avert any social disaster, eugenicists agreed on an efficient surgical method of accomplishing their goal of race purity. They called for the sterilization of millions of people over the next two generations, thereby ridding the nation of a social menace. In 1923, Oregon, Montana, Delaware, and Michigan enacted sterilization laws. In 1924, Virginia passed its own sterilization laws and in 1925, Idaho, Utah, Maine, Kansas, and a few other states followed suit. During the early part of the 20th century, total of thirty states passed bills authorizing involuntary sterilization of the insane, criminals, imbeciles, epileptics, and other undesirables. Although eugenicists claimed their research was apolitical, in fact they acted as if science should be used to define certain social goals and values (Reilly, 1991; Larson, 1995).

In the 1960s sterilization debates were refueled when University of Chicago professor Dwight J. Ingle decided to breathe new life into the idea of how to control the productivity of alleged genetically inferior people to justify racial differences and intelligence (Tucker, 1994). Ingle claimed he was concerned about the very high birth rate among lazy and unfit blacks and the consequent threat to the success of the race. He proposed sterilization or some other method of controlling the birth rate of blacks because of their alleged lack of cultural heritage, ability to provide their children any reasonable opportunity to achieve happiness, self-sufficiency, and knowledge of the civic culture. In order to protect society from corruption by their harmful genes, Ingle proposed a group of professional physicians and scientists arrive at some conclusion regarding the social, economic, behavioral, and parenthood abilities of these people. He proposed a mandatory implementation of an antifertility agent under the skin of every woman able to bear children (Ingle, 1973). Although Ingle's conclusions were widely regarded as preposterous in the 1970s, in 1990 the Food and Drug Administration approved the use of Norplant, an anti-fertility agent placed in a woman's arm for long-term birth control.

In December 1990, editorials in the *Philadelphia Inquirer* and the *New York Times* discussed the debate around the issue of offering this new technique to welfare mothers. Eventually the American Civil Liberties Union published an essay, "Norplant: A New Contraceptive With the Potential for Abuse" (December 31, 1994), explaining the coercive use of Norplant. Others began to see how doctors were hesitant to remove the implants from the body thereby forcing black and other poor women to keep them regardless of the possibility of physical harm due to Norplant's side effects. Thus, Norplant became an early weapon in the Right's struggle for welfare reform (Roberts, 1997).

While the United States was engulfed in nativist pedagogy and race purity politics in the 1930s, Germany, in an attempt to prevent any further national decline, took notice of America's advanced eugenic implementation. German scientists considered sterilization their first priority and emphasized the importance of racial purity to Germany's health. Like the American scientists, German scientists justified their conclusions as having nothing to do with the superiority or inferiority of a race, but merely with the scientific consequences of impartial research: the putative facts of hereditary traits of every race had evolved through thousands of years of natural selection and nature's harmony would be destroyed by racial mixture. Germany followed the lead of U.S. segregation laws. According to German scientists, the Nordic race was the superior one, even over other European people, who in turn were considered superior to the colored races. The Nordic race was supposed to have provided all the great discoveries and be the model of truth, honor, and self-control; to protect their alleged genetic capabilities, German scientists and doctors felt they had to purge their land of all non-Nordic people. Again, following the lead of the United States, German scientists and doctors believed that legalized compulsory sterilization was the step first to racial purity. While Hitler was writing his *Mein Kampf*, German eugenicists had already supplied the intelligentsia with the scientific foundation for the Final Solution (Weindling, 1985; Lifton, 1986; Paul 1995).

Back in the United States after World War II, with the Civil Rights Movement on the horizon, the scientific community was going through a paradigm shift. Franz Boas's notion of cultural differences replaced Darwinian evolutionary development as the dominant explanation for the diversity of human behavior (Tucker, 1994). Scientists gathered at UNESCO conferences and concluded—as seen in their publications *The Race Question in Modern Science: Race and Science* (1950) and *The Race Question in Modern Science: the Race Concept* (1951)—given an equal opportunity to reach their potential, the average achievements of individuals would be about the same. At the same time UNESCO convened another group of scientists and anthropologists who held different opinions. They acknowledged it was possible that innate intelligence and responses are more evident in one race than in another. Even though these were scientists who were experts on human differences and therefore qualified to speak impartially on the issue, their conclusions were clearly political. While they stated equality was an ethical principle, they also stated implicitly that innate differences legitimated differences in rights. Their conclusions were published in the 1961 edition of *The Race Question in Modern Science: Race and Science*. As UNESCO was debating these issues in Europe in response to the racist policies of the former Third Reich, the United States was trying hard to hold on to its white supremacist ideology, exemplified by its Jim Crow statutes and customs that kept blacks separate and unequal, disfranchised politically and relegated to inferior facilities in public transportation, education, and healthcare. In the South and in some Northern cities, black people were excluded completely from many public libraries and from public recreational facilities (Cell, 1982; McMillen, 1990; Tucker, 1994; Higginbotham, 1996).

As the 1954 Supreme Court decision in *Brown v. Board of Education of Topeka, Kansas*, threatened the wall of racial segregation, right-wing social scientists and Southern segregationists were terrified by the possibility of racial amalgamation. Social scientists held tenaciously to old theories that racial prejudice protected blacks from the injuries of integration. There was also the age-old fear of black men and white women cohabiting, which scared many whites into believing young black male classmates would reap revenge on their daughters (Hurd, 1858; Higginbotham, 1978; Day, 1974). Harry H. Laughlin, in his article "Race Assimilation by the Pure-Sire Method," in *The Journal of Heredity*, Vol. 11 (1920), concluded "the salvation of a great nation is the virtue of its women....[This] is true racially as well as socially and morally." Professor Henry E. Garrett, president of the American Psychological Association and the Psychometric Society, was the nation's most eminent scientific spokesman in the defense of racial segregation between the 1940s and the 1960s. Another segregationist and wealthy Northern businessman, Carleton Putnam, published *Race and Reason, a Yankee's View* (1961), in which he stressed blacks were not victims of political oppression but of biology. Putnam was completely against integration and any enfranchisement of blacks participating in the political process. When President Kennedy sent U.S. marshals to escort James Meredith when he enrolled at the University of Mississippi in 1962, Putnam wrote letters that were published in the *New York Times* on October 3 to Kennedy deploring his use of federal troops to protect Meredith or any other black (Tucker, 1994). *Science*, Vol. 134 (1961), reported the Louisiana State Board of Education made Putnam's book a requirement for all college faculty and students enrolled in anthropology, sociology, and psychology; Governor Ross Barnett of Mississippi declared October 26, 1961, Race and Reason Day, a state holiday for people to study Putnam's book. The *Journal of Heredity*, Vol. 52 (1961), listed other Southern white supremacist politicians who endorsed Putnam's work such as Georgia's Richard B. Russell, Harry S. Byrd of Virginia, and South Carolina's Strom Thurmond (p. 190).

Right-wing college and university scholars and scientists were given the freedom to promote neo-Nazi ideology in their crusade to preserve apartheid in the United States. They focused their attention on alleged black inferiority while at the same time maintaining a shrewd space in their theoretical constructs for the Jewish population. Putnam's purported conspiracies to promote racial equality and integration by Jewish scientists and scholars were used by right-wing academicians to influence and validate the social polices of apartheid. The writings of Putnam, Madison Grant, and others would later influence white supremacists such as David Duke and Tom Metzger (Tucker, 1994; Dees, 1996; Rowan, 1996).

In 1937 textile millionaire and Nazi sympathizer Wycliffe Preston Draper established the Pioneer Fund, a tax-exempt private trust fund to promote research for the betterment of the white race (it financially supports the journal *Mankind Quarterly*) and aid for the education of whites descended from the original English North American colonies; the fund also supported sending blacks back to Africa (Lane, 1995). Douglas A. Blackmon wrote an article in the *Wall Street Journal*, "Silent Partner: How the South's Fight to Uphold Segregation was Funded Up North" June 11, 1999 that revealed Draper's Pioneer Fund financially supported those who fought to maintain segregation during the Civil Rights Movement. On December 11, 1977, the *New York Times* published Grace Lichtenstein's article "Fund Backs Controversial Study of Race Betterment," listing college and university scholars who have received grants from the Pioneer Fund and also schools who were embarrassed by the grants. She also cites Richard Arens, a staff director of the House Committee on Un-American Activities, who was forced out of his congressional employment in 1960 for being a consultant to the Pioneer Fund. Henry R. Garrett, professor of psychology, former president of the American Psychological Association (APA), and supporter of the White Citizen's Council (the political arm of the Klu Klux Klan),

Pennsylvania Congressman Francis E. Walter, chairman of the House Committee on Un-American Activities, and Mississippi Senator James O. Eastland were instrumental in obtaining grants for the Pioneer Fund for scholars to conduct research on black inferiority. Adam Miller states in his article "The Pioneer Fund: Bankrolling the Professors of Hate," in *Journal of Blacks in Higher Education*, No. 6 (Winter 1994/1995, p. 58), eugenicists have now gathered themselves under the umbrella of the Pioneer Fund and have focused their attention not only on the inferiority of blacks and Latinos, but also on the notion that people of color have been used by Jews to undermine the white race so they can take over the world. The certificate of incorporation of the Pioneer Fund can now be read on the Internet. With the Civil Rights Movement becoming more of a threat to the maintenance of white supremacy and race purity than immigration, the *Nation* published an essay by R. W. May, "Genetics and Subversion," Vol. 190 (May 14, 1960), which states Draper provided grants to leading geneticists to conduct supposedly objective research in major university departments to prove the inferiority of blacks and promote their repatriation back to Africa. White supremacist scientists and other supporters formed the International Association for the Advancement of Ethnology and Eugenics (IAAEE), applying the scientific findings of eugenics, entomology, history, archaeology, and any other research to support their ideology of racial purification. The goal of the IAAEE was to publish pertinent scholarship for individuals with an interest in an epistemological pedagogy that different races were not scientifically entitled to the same rights and those of certain genetic stock should be excluded from the civic culture under the law. The IAAEE's journal, *Mankind Quarterly*, first published in England in 1961, transferred to Washington D.C. in 1979 and currently under the umbrella of the Council of Social and Economic Studies. *Mankind Quarterly* provides a respectable academic platform for opinions in line with those of extreme white supremacist groups.

By the end of the 1960s the United States was forced to confront the contradictions between its professed ideals and the apartheid system that refused millions of its citizens access to schools, neighborhoods, restaurants, and public facilities. Lyndon Johnson's

War on Poverty produced the Great Society programs and social welfare legislation, which provided impoverished citizens (black and white) access to health care, nutrition, and education. However, many eugenicists opposed the War on Poverty, relying on the old social Darwinist ideology that predicted the imminent demise of the black race in America (Gams, 1995). This allegedly scientific conjecture impeded many social programs intended for blacks on the grounds they interfered with the natural extinction of an inferior group. Eugenicists claimed social programs such as state medical care, better nutrition, and educational opportunities for blacks and other people of color were only justified if such people were genetically equal to white people—which, of course, the eugenicists claimed was not the case (Pinkney, 1984; Steinberg, 1995; Hasian, 1996).

Eugenicists claimed attempts to improve the quality of life through baby clinics and child development programs for supposedly inferior blacks were misguided and ineffective, they wanted the government to sponsor a sterilization and birth control program. During the 1970s, Arthur Jensen championed the eugenic cause by claiming the I.Q. of blacks was much lower than whites. On March 10, 1969, *U.S. News and World Report* summarized Jensen's views in an article titled "Can Negroes Learn the Way Whites Do?" On March 31, 1969, "Born Dumb" was published in *Newsweek,* and "Intelligence: Is There a Racial Difference?" was published in *Time* on April 11, 1969. The timing of the media's focus on race differences could not have been more significant because, as the Civil Rights Movement shifted its efforts to improving the conditions of the masses of poor people, the white middle class assumed further improvement would come at too high a price. Compensatory education meant higher taxes and affirmative action was costing middle class white people jobs (Pinkney, 1984; Steinberg, 1995).

Richard Nixon won the presidential election in 1968, riding to victory on the growing impatience of whites with the Civil Rights Movement and the general increase of racial intolerance within the nation. John Ehrlichman, an advisor to Nixon, would later write in his book *Witness to Power: The Nixon Years* (1982),that Nixon not only used racial epithets on a regular basis (O'Reilly, 1995, pp. 292, 311), but that his policies, especially those in education and housing, were designed specifically to appeal to rising antiblack sentiment. Nixon along with thousands of other whites blamed the civil unrest of the 1960s upon blacks and set out to "devise a system that recognizes this while not appearing to" target them (Parenti, 1999, p. 12). After taking office, Nixon quickly attempted to slow down school integration by cutting funds for the Department of Health, Education, and Welfare. He threatened to seek legislation or a constitutional amendment to prevent the courts from promoting racial integration. Nixon's attorney general, John Mitchell, even recommended that the Voting Rights Act of 1965 not be renewed, proposing a weaker bill in its place that passed the House of Representatives but failed in the Senate. Thus in the early 1970s conservatives and white supremacists stonewalled the quest for equality with measures that ensured continuing inequality and deprivation for blacks, other people of color, and poor whites (Ehrlichman, 1982; Franklin, 1988; Pinkney, 1984).

The Civil Rights Movement had begun to decline, even as the winds of eugenics and social Darwinism began to sweep, however surreptitiously, through the nation's bureaucracy. On January 27 and March 4, 1970, the *New York Times* recorded President Nixon's veto of an educational appropriations bill; in private sessions Nixon stated federally funded programs could not benefit blacks because they were genetically inferior to whites (Ehrlichman, 1982; O'Reilly, 1995, p. 327). The *Boston Globe* on January 4, 1992, reported White House aide Pat Buchanan's questioning of the worth of federally funded programs for blacks arguing supposed genetic differences in intelligence were not the fault of whites. The eugenicist Arthur R. Jensen concluded in his article "The Price of Inequality," published in *Oxford Review of Education* (1975), white job applicants were five to six times more qualified than black applicants and confirmed affirmative action programs provided jobs for black applicants who could not read, write or do mathematical calculations, thus "proving" affirmative action scientifically worthless (Steinberg, 1995).

As the New Right was being influenced by eugenicists, its adherents became the new designers of political strategy in the 1970s. White supremacist intelligentsia within the academy, looking for allies in their crusade for segregation, provided leading eugenicists with financial support for their research and assisted them with distributing their findings beyond the boundaries of the scientific community. The Pioneer Fund provided funds for eugenics research and was quoted in the *New York Times*, April 26, 1976, for supporting Southern private schools that excluded black students by claiming discrimination was not a bad thing. Many white citizens were beginning to believe blacks were not underprivileged, but *over* privileged. Just as many whites claimed in the eighteenth and the nineteenth centuries, blacks were aliens, a threat to the republic, and could never become a part of the political process, the eugenicists, reconstructing and rearticulating this old ideology, argued segregation and black inferiority was the natural order of nature and science.

Eugenicists and segregationists in their quest for respect in academic circles refrained from the white supremacist discourse. They adopted a more agreeable conservative approach when they founded the Council on American Affairs and the *Journal of Social and Political Studies*, later changed to the *Journal of Social Political and Economic Studies*. People such as Jack Kemp, Roger Pearson and Jesse Helms wrote essays for the journal including South Africa's admiral H. H. Bierman who wrote an essay on the global strategic importance of South Africa and the need to support a white supremacist government there in order to fight the perceived communist threat in Africa. Other prominent academicians contributed articles to the journal.

Many segregationists funded by the Pioneer Fund also received support from the Foundation for Human Understanding and the Testing Research Fund. Scholars who were funded by these organizations wrote books and essays on heredity, intelligence, and black inferiority and distributed Arthur Jensen's book *Straight Talk about Mental Tests* throughout the nation to college presidents and admission officers. Jensen's book was distributed with the hope of influencing administrators' decisions concerning who gets admitted into college and who does not. The Foundation for Human Understanding paid for a full page in the *New York Times Book Review* on September 1, 1974, in support of Jensen's book.

Conclusion

The obsession and phobia with racial differences has continually been of service in the political realm. Ever since Europeans decided to use Africans in the Americas as free laborers, they and their American descendants employed science to justify the enslavement of millions upon millions of black people. Following emancipation, they had to scientifically justify segregation and nativism; today they depend on science to justify sociopolitical inequality. Despite occasional humanitarian efforts, the preponderance of Christian thought and conduct has buttressed racial oppression and notions of cultural and spiritual superiority and given life to the belief in white supremacy and black inferiority as being sanctioned by the divine order (Wood, 1990; Washington, 1984 & 1988). During the latter part of the nineteenth century, science became the dominant factor in rationalizing inequality, a position that had been previously been held by religion.

Today the movement within this supposedly God-fearing republic to pass laws restricting immigration under the claims of protecting Americanism has grossly exaggerated the ability of   Caribbean newcomers to succeed, arguing these new immigrants lack self-reliance and initiative. It is claimed these new immigrants do not possess the Anglo/Nordic conceptions of law and order and government and their arrival tends to corrupt "our" civic culture. The mythical superiority of white America was sanctioned by the United States Congress, which authorized returning shiploads of Caribbean and Latin immigrants back to their countries. America ignores the inscription "Give me your tired, your poor, your huddled masses yearning to breathe free. Send these, the homeless, tempest-tossed to me. I lift my lamp beside the golden door" on the Statue of Liberty standing tall in New York City's harbor. To understand the ideology of ethnic and racial superiority that lies behind much American policy making, one must understand the philosophical paradigm of positivism and the claims of objectivity in scientific study on the natural selection and eugenics.

Because the civic culture is the common culture of the people of the United States, a new critical multicultural pedagogy must be implemented to teach the people to act on the basic principle of equal rights and overthrow caste and race superiority. Just as African Americans and with their allies led a movement to overthrow Jim Crow in the South. It forced the United States government to reshape its relationship to Native Americans, eliminated racial and ethnic considerations from the nation's immigration policy (although they reemerged in the 1990s), and expanded rights to aliens. As W. E. B. Du Bois put the United States and Europe on notice the problem of the twentieth century was the problem of the color line, this new century's biggest challenge for those who believe in equal rights lies not only in enhancing educational and economic opportunities for people of color and all children born into poverty, but in formulating and instituting a critical multicultural pedagogy will expose and openly critique the white supremacist ideology that is deeply lodged in academic scholarship. Hopefully, if we can begin to honestly discuss this ideological cancer, we will be able to eliminate the various forms of spurious science that support the notion any human being is biologically inferior. However, the question remains for the people of the United States must decide: Are we going to use our gift of citizenship for or against those who are poor and less fortunate, for or against those deemed inferior because of the color of their skin.

CONFRONTING DISPARITY IN AMERICAN SOCIETY

A privileged class never surrenders its tyranny, neither can it be expected that the capitalists of this age will give up their rulership without being forced to do it.

Albert Parsons, 1883

If there is a poor man among your brothers in any of the towns of the land your God is giving you, fo not be hard hearted or tightfisted toward your poor brother. Rather be openhanded and freely lend him whatever he needs.

Deuteronomy 15:7–8

As stated in the previous chapter, *The Bell Curve* is the latest statement of a white supremacist philosophy that regained extensive credence in the 1990s. It is ideologically driven to reconstructed the old Mathusian/social Darwinist philosophy, which claims the widening inequalities among the people of the United States has developed in the last twenty-five years are inevitable. *The Bell Curve* argues science proposes natural selection and its relationship with the economy is more and more by social class than race. The essence of the book insists success in life is mainly determined by inherited intelligence and there are inherited significant differences that exist among the races. The book maligns affirmative action policies in the workforce and discredits public schooling, but the most pernicious damage has come from the argument that steady investment of public funds in the education and training of Hispanic, African, and Native American children along with other immigrants of color is futile. This philosophy is a doctrine without any scientific foundation, for research has shown "nature" decides neither the level of inequality in the United States nor who will be privileged or disfranchised—social conditions and national policies do (Adams & Sanders, 2003; Gans, 1995; Lipsitz, 1998; Vidal, 1996). In this context inequality is planned and carried out for the sake of maintaining white supremacy over people of color. Similarly, economic competition does not require people to accept inequality for the sake of growth.

As in the early part of this century, today many public figures and lay people are calling for the government to withdraw its support to the poor and minimize welfare rolls, to balance the budget, lower taxes, lessen regulation in the economic sector, and stabilize the economy for the middle class (Gans, 1995; Hofstadter, 1944; Omi & Winant, 1994). Conservatives claim the government took away from the poor their initiative, drive, pride, and morality and welfare reform, as we know it, will restore all the qualities ensuring economic success. They argue social programs, particularly welfare, need to be abolished, because the War on Poverty was costly and did not yield any promising results, given the relatively unchangeable purported genetic nature of welfare recipients (Quadagno, 1994; Gans, 1995; Handler & Hansenfeld, 1997). Alongside welfare reform, many are claiming nothing can change the mindset of the poor—nature has set limits on the cognitive abilities of certain groups and therefore inequality drives the competitive nature of our economy.

As the debate rages over the widening and destructive gap between the elite and the rest of the citizens of the United States, this chapter will argue is disparity is planned and carried out in the United States to maintain a racial hegemonic social order (Lipsitz, 1998; Adams & Sanders, 2003). Also this chapter will briefly investigate the malignant myth of innate racial inequality; I argue racial differences in achievements are consequences, not causes, of social disparity. By refusing to blame skin color and the poor for the inexorable market, and excuses that lead to resignation and passivity towards the underprivileged, this chapter will show the people of this nation can make opportunities available for all.

White supremacist ideology argues disparity is natural and necessary in a free market economy. However, discrimination is planned, hides behind public polices and the market forces to be carried out in the United States to maintain a racist hegemonic social order (Hofstadter, 1944; Muwakkil, 1995; Lipsitz, 1998; Apple, 2000). White supremacist academic scholars claim intelligence explains disparity and have used their positions to produce literature suggesting public funds for education is useless and tracking students into academic or vocational slots necessary. In turn, scholars like Herrnstein and Murray can influence public policy that undermines any desire to achieve and regulates thousands of our youth into dead-end jobs across the country. However, there is an alternative explanation that stresses economic fortune depends more on social circumstances than on I.Q., which is a product of man. More critical to this debate is that patterns of disparity must be explained by looking beyond the attributes of individuals and to the structure of our society (Lipsitz, 1998; Feagin, 2001; Noguera, 2003). Social policies set the rules of society, which affect opportunity, individual abilities and efforts to achieve. And recent white supremacist policies have, on the whole, widened the gap between the rich and the rest of the people of the United States.

Not only does the wealth of individuals' shape their chances for a good life, but also national government policies ranging from labor to investments in education and to tax deductions. The United States, the most economically unequal society in the industrialized world, unevenly distributes rewards through regulation of the market, taxes, and corporate welfare. The belief that disparity fosters economic growth, reducing economic inequality requires enormous welfare expenditures, and there is little we can do to alter the extent of inequality must be exposed and put to rest. We need to be reminded the efforts to expand public education and universities, the drive for a truly multicultural society, social security, and fair minimum-wage laws, and support for strong unions have assisted in reducing inequality in the United States since the 1950s. However, since the 1970s and with even more fervor in the 1980s, the theoretical endorsement of neoconservatives, along with the state, began to lead a national retreat from and abandonment of racial equality and institutionalized even more regressive social policies in the United States (Phillips, 1990; Edsall & Edsall, 1991).

Background

The United States has three different societies living isolated from each other: First, there is the more prosperous, the elite who control and influence public policy to favor their lifestyles (Mills, 1956; Domhoff, 1998). The elite, alongside corporate leaders and their political allies, wages an unrelenting class war against working-class people. Corporate America and its neoconservative political allies want to roll back all the social programs and ensure the government works only for the rich and destroy the regulatory apparatus and thus improving their options and profits. The powerful elite uses its ability to control ideology to deprive the masses of any awareness of their own rights, ensuring the political, educational, and economic sectors are run by the rich and powerful, reproducing their cultural values. Chomsky, in *Understanding Power* (2002), states:

> the media will present a picture of the world which defends and inculcates the economic, social, and political agendas of the privileged groups that dominate the domestic economy,...elite perspectives will be reflected in the media (p. 15).

This group does not want decision makers and participants; they want a passive and obedient population of consumers and political spectators—a decapitated community of people isolated to the point where they are unable to harness their limited resources to chip away at the concentrated power of the elite (Greider, 1993; Chomsky, 1996).

The second group, the middle class, is being squeezed by stagnant incomes and rising economic pressures. In the 1970s the coalitions between blacks and whites disintegrated during the nation's steady economic decline and arguments over policy emerged from thirty years of economic turmoil and disappointment. Many of the issues black people protested for during the Civil Rights Movement—such as political representation, the quest for economic development, and the battle for community control of traditional institutions such as schools—came into conflict with traditional white support. The white middle class believed the opportunities for them and their children were coming to a halt by the end of 1973.

The Middle East oil crisis, stagnating wages, rising prices, husbands working longer hours, and their wives being pressed to seek employment to help maintain their lifestyles caused many to critically assess the situation. Discussions around less government intervention in public policy began to dominate the nation as the call went up for less economic regulations, less taxes, the need to cut social programs for the poor, the end of so-called preferences for blacks and women, and eliminate funding for urban schools. The federal government was blamed for wrecking the economy and for wasting hard earned tax dollars and stunting initiative, by rewarding inferior and lazy people and penalizing the superior and talented middle class. Many felt the federal government should unleash the market and stop restricting those who could generate economic growth. Public support for less economic regulation, less spending on social programs, and more tax cuts for the wealthy became the cry of the middle class (Chomsky, 1996; Handler &b Hasenfeld, 1997; Levy, 1987; Schor, 1991).

By the 1990s, the economic dilemma had not eased up for the middle class it had become more perplexing. From 1959 into the 1990s the trend of family income showed income for the rich increased tremendously and the poor sunk very low after 1970, while the middle class gained very little. The middle class managed to maintain their stability by its women taking employment and its men working longer hours. However, this stability was increasingly being shaken by the growing economic insecurity, which led to anxieties concerning the purported American Dream (i.e., college education, stable jobs, and an affordable home), which was slipping away from them and their children's grasp. While the 1980s was called a decade of economic boom, the average U.S. citizen worked harder and longer hours to just break even. Many began to question why the gaps between the rich, middle class, and poor were widening (Danziger & Gottschalk, 1993; Karoly & Burtless, 1995). Some social scientists rearticulated old theories of natural selection as the cause for the disparities. They argued inequality was the inevitable result of superior genes intelligence and talent controlled the marketplace, while the inferior unskilled and lazy people sank into oblivion (Hasian, 1996; Apple, 1996; Lugg, 1996).

The blame for this economic decline was placed in the hands of education as industry emphasized schools were not producing qualified workers. With the call for traditional Anglo Protestant values, free market values and, on the other hand, the panic over alleged moribund standards, dropouts, illiteracy, and the fear of youth violence, many neoconservatives felt the need to regain control of American society. They called for the deregulation of the market, only certain knowledge and values to be taught, standardized tests to be administered, and the Protestant example of hard work had to be articulated in schools. The racist discourse that came forth was Americans are hard working, thrifty, and Christian as opposed to those who are lazy, immoral, permissive people of color getting something for nothing through social programs and preferences. Also, the blame of declining standards was placed upon students of color who supposedly had no cognitive skills to understand or do the work required by teachers.

As stated previously, President Lyndon B. Johnson's signing of the Civil Rights Act of 1964 and the Voting Rights Act of 1965 caused many whites to wonder whether demonstrations served any purpose anymore. As long as Martin Luther King Jr. kept the Civil Rights Movement in the South, addressing the right to vote and access to public facilities, Northern whites gave the movement their support. However, once the movement moved North, bearing a list of racial grievances greatly enlarged by demands for jobs, open housing, citizen review of police and real estate boards, equal education, and economic boycotts of racially unresponsive businesses, many white allies, labor leaders, various white liberals, prelates, and the federal government began to distance themselves from the Civil Rights Movement. Whites now felt the government was taking away their rights. Northern white resistance to so-called discount education given to blacks stiffened and jobs were harder and costlier to create than the right to vote. The eradication of the slums and poverty was considered far too much and beyond integrating buses and lunch counters. White allies were not ready in the battle against racial segregation to assault the larger issues of racism, which would lead to their own doorsteps and the final struggle against economic exploitation (Pinkney, 1984; Massy & Denton, 1993).

During the 1980 presidential campaign, Ronald Reagan gave a speech in Philadelphia, Mississippi, the same town where Klansmen murdered civil rights workers James Chaney, Andrew Goodman, and

Michael Schwerner in 1964. Articulating old Southern rhetoric and speaking to an all-white crowd, Reagan said he favored state rights and clearly demonstrated his racist hostility towards the aspirations of black people. He set out to resurrect nativist language, reverse discrimination, traditional values, and anti-immigration; he used camouflaged white supremacist appeals in his discourse to appeal to middle-class whites. He mobilized the white middle class by referring to the putative unfairness of social policies such as quotas, affirmative action, and special treatment extended to women, blacks, and other people of color and by claiming Anglo Protestant American traditions and values were being disregarded. In essence, Reagan turned on the intricate post–civil rights discourse in general and blacks in particular. He referred to black women as welfare queens and black men as a menace to society, law, and order and employed the historic racialized discourses about welfare and social programs for the disadvantaged against working white people. Essentially, Reagan and the New Right, regardless of the historical and contemporary complexities of ethnicity, class, and racial composition, effectively appealed to the notions of whiteness in opposition to blackness, which was conflated with and came to stand as the other or as "alien" (Edsall, 1984; Wilkins, 1984; Quadagno, 1994; Omi & Winant, 1994).

Intelligence and the Maintenance of Hegemony

Herrnstein and Murray's *The Bell Curve: Intelligence and Class Structure in America* concluded intelligence is innate and largely determines how successful people will be in life. According to them, the rich are smart, the poor are dumb, the middle class possesses average intelligence, and, therefore, inequality cannot be stopped. Government spending on social programs only slowed down the inevitable and did injustice to the talented and damaged the nation's economy. They argued the rising tide of global trade, technological development, and the emphasis on the sciences in education makes intelligence more important today than ever before. Again, they draw another conclusion from their research on the rising tide of disparity in the United States, claiming there is a strong correlation to race and ethnicity. Black and Latinos, by nature, are not as intelligent as whites nor will they ever do as well economically; therefore, little can or should be done to alleviate inequality. Because the majority of the American public relies on academic empirical evidence as truth, most do not question Herrnstein and Murray's claim of black inferiority. However, when one begins to study white supremacist scholarship, eugenics and other racist literature promoting scientific black inferiority, *The Bell Curve* is revealed as nothing more than a reconstructed and rearticulated ideology of Herbert Spencer's old Malthusian/social Darwinist philosophy of biology and evolutionary theory brought to bear on social and political institutions. Spencer's opposition to any state aid to the poor caused him to repudiate state interference with the natural growth of society.

Marouf A. Hasian, in his work *The Rhetoric of Eugenics in Anglo-American Thought* (1996), shows how philosophers, scientists, and politicians preached theories of natural superiority, attempted to state the rights of individuals against the duties of the state, and used science to justify their social and political projects. He notes, concerning the philosophy and beliefs of the Rev. Thomas R. Malthus, in "An Essay on the Principle of Population" (1830):

> a person did not have any inherent "right" to food or "liberty" to procreate if the natural "necessities" imposed limits on the ability of a nation to take care of its citizens....For Malthus, allowing the poor to believe in the false necessities spelled moral, political, economic, and social disaster (pp. 15–16).

According to Malthus, the poor and inferior races were unfit and should be eliminated. In other words, *The Bell Curve* is an old form of scientific racism reconstructed in a different language that proposes racial differences in I.Q. are substantially genetic in origin and cannot be altered by any known environmental interventions. When this kind of ideology is selectively filtered down to the masses of middle class white people, one can now understand how neoconservative politicians market "white anger" toward the inner city and argue, through coded language arguing blacks refuse to live by white standards. It becomes clear why Northern white allies of the Civil Rights Movement began to question their continued support for the redress of social grievances when they perceived inner-city blacks were ungrateful by bringing the Civil Rights Movement to the North and black youth were lawless (Hasian, 1996; Edsall & Edsall, 1991; Pagano, 1996).

However, individual intelligence has not satisfactorily explained who succeeds, nor does it explain where people end up in life. The discrimination and inequality people experience is the result of social policies affecting a myriad of circumstances such as family, locality, school, and community, which contribute to or withhold the means of securing access to a higher class position in the United States. Social policy determines the quality of healthcare for families, affects educational opportunities, and influences rewards individuals receive for achieving their place in society—for example, the salary scales for professionals versus manual laborers, how much tax they pay, and their standards of living, which, in turn, are determined entirely or partially by the government (Chomsky, 1994 & 1996; Young, 1990). Therefore, disparity and intelligence are not natural nor the result of Malthusian/social Darwinist philosophy, but always is socially constructed as a product of the conscious effort of public policy. The people of the United States must understand disparity is a social construction and a result of this nation's past. In other words, some people in the United States have created inequality and have maintained it to their benefit (Zinn, 1995). The advantages and disadvantages people have inherited from their parents, their resources or lack of resources, the quantity and quality of their education, along with the historical baggage that accompanies them will either allow individuals to climb the ladder of success or hold them at the bottom (Lipstiz, 1998; Adams & Sanders, 2003). For example, the children of accountants, professors, and academicians have more opportunities than the children of manual laborers (Kincheloe, 1995).

Policy makers within the United States have chosen, at various periods, to either regulate or deregulate the economy, to either loosen or tighten the marketplace for the benefit of certain groups. Thus public policy provides citizens with opportunities to climb the economic ladder by subsidizing some groups more than others while, on the other hand, dissimilar policies are implemented to repress and deny other groups the full freedom to participate within the marketplace (Lipsitz, 1998; Moore & Stansel, 1995). Therefore, public policy reflects the attitude and ideology associated with the rise of blatant forms of dominance. These policies make malicious distinctions that are primarily, if not exclusively, based on physical characteristics and ancestry (Franklin, 1988, p. 453; Lipsitz, 1998, p. 27). This means a self-conscious effort to implement public policy in the form of color bars, racial segregation, and a restriction of meaningful citizenship (Lipsitz, 1998; Feagin, 2001). If public policy, today, were truly equal and economic equality existed between the various racial groups in terms of parity and in terms of power, then there would be nothing to argue about. However, policy in the United States has a long history of advocating principles of racial difference where people of color, no matter how hard they to assimilate, have been treated as inferiors, unworthy to live next to whites (Adams & Sanders, 2003; Fredrickson, 1981; Lipstiz, 1998; Young, 1990).

Public policy provides society with the ground rules not only for wages, working conditions, unionization, and taxes, but also sets the boundaries for government programs like tax deductions, Medicaid, social security, food stamps, and corporate subsidies. The jobs that people get are determined by the amount of education they receive, but the amount of education students receive is determined by public policy. Those policies decide which schools will receive the resources that will enable students to take advantage of every opportunity and what teaching methods will be utilized to prepare students for positions of leadership or prepare submissive workers for the workforce (Edsall, 1984; Shea, 1989; Kincheloe, 1999). Experience in the United States shows that government demographic policies do affect economic growth and redistribution of wealth. Thus white supremacist scholars like Herrnstein and Murray, William B. Shockley, and others can argue human misery is natural and beyond human redemption, disparity is fated, and people deserve, by virtue of their innate talents, the positions they have in society. They conclude intelligence largely decides one's place in society and an individual's place within society. They believe genes influences one's job, income, marriage, and criminal activity.

They discredited President Johnson's Head Start program a part of the War on Poverty initiatives to help welfare mothers find work while their children were being cared for and educated. Herrnstein and Murray discredited other programs designed to improve the learning environment of poor children by dismissing them as an expensive waste of taxpayer money (Tucker; 2002, p. 147). They recommend that the intelligent produce more babies, that immigrants should be screened at the borders, and women with low I.Q. should not be rewarded for having children. All of these proposals are old eugenic ideas rearticulated. Conservatives have embraced eugenic ideas and argue people on welfare are lazy, immoral, prone to violence, not interested in traditional Anglo Protestant values, and have no desire for education or good work ethics (Quadagno, 1994; Stern, 1995; Chidley, 1995, Sedgwick, 1995; Vidal, 1996).

Shortly after *The Bell Curve* was published in 1994, the November 29 issue of the *Chronicle of Philanthropy* stated charitable efforts for disadvantaged people would be hampered by hereditary doctrines and things will get grimmer for poverty-stricken people. Two weeks later Murray was invited as the principal speaker at the December 1994 orientation meeting for the incoming "freshmen" class of newly elected Republican congressmen, which leaves one to wonder if public policies like the Contract with America was not influenced by eugenic rhetoric (Duster, 1995). Arguing African Americans and Hispanics have done poorly in the United States because they are inferior to whites is completely erroneous. History has proven oppressed people around the world—Eastern Europeans in New York City, the Irish in England, Koreans in Japan, Palestinians in Israel, Africans in South Africa—do not perform as well in education as the oppressor group. As one truthfully looks into the problem of disparity and oppression, one will see it is not I.Q. that determines inferior status, but inferior status is the result of oppression in society and will always lead to low standardized test scores. *The Bell Curve* was written as an explicit and powerful ideological guide for a political agenda to implement public policy against those who are deemed racially and intellectually inferior.

The belief that innate talent is fixed at birth and explains disparity in society is becoming the cornerstone of those who study psychometrics. They have spent years refining I.Q. tests so the results will correlate with the tasks needed in the job market, which means psychometricians have not been interested in the problems that comprise a test but have been concerned with ranking people. They have developed a methodology advocating that a single, quantifiable intelligence is fixed at birth or early in life. Many within the psychometric paradigm concern themselves with just innate talent and refuse to even consider other factors like persistence, will power, compassion, resourcefulness, and other characteristics that make up an individual. Herrnstein and Murray are not the first to promote these ideas. In a 1920 *Harper's* article titled "Intelligence and its Uses," Edward L. Thorndike insisted that "abler persons in the world...are the more clean, decent, just and kind." Intelligence testing in the United States and its ideological implications can be traced from the early to the middle of the twentieth century where psychometricians promoted eugenics and immigration restrictions and supported racial segregation. In an 1898 article in the *American Journal of Psychology*, by Dr. Everett Flood, a eugenicist and early proponent of I.Q. and heredity, titled "Notes on the Castration of Idiot Children," indicating that a bill was introduced to the Michigan Legislature to castrate all the inmates at the Michigan Home for the Feebleminded and epileptic, and also all persons convicted a third time for a felony. Flood also reported twenty-six children in Massachusetts were castrated because of weakness of the mind supposedly caused by epilepsy and masturbation (Kamin, 1995).

Another psychometrician, Dr. Arthur Sweeney, wrote an appendix, titled "Mental Tests for Immigrants," to the record of the hearings of the House Committee on Immigration and Naturalization in 1923, chaired by Albert Johnson, also chairman of the Eugenic Research Association. Sweeney argued that if Congress did not pass laws to prevent immigration of certain groups the United States would sink into crime and degradation. He wrote:

> We have been overrun with a horde of the unfit...We [are not opposed] to immigrants from Great Britain, Holland, Canada, Germany, Denmark, and Scandinavia...We can...however, strenuously object to immigration from Italy...Russia...Poland...Greece...Turkey...the Slavic and Latin countries...Education can be received by only those who have intelligence to receive [it]. It does not create intelligence. [We] shall degenerate to the level of the Slavic and Latin races...[into] pauperism, crime, sex offenses, and dependency...[W]e must protect ourselves against the degenerate horde....[T]his new method...will enable us to select those who are worthy and reject those who are worthless (Kamin, 1995, pp. 497–498).

The policies psychometricians proposed were not only to halt immigration but also to rank and sort people thereby justifying their discriminatory tests, allowing employers and educators to decide who will secure the available positions. Accordingly, psychometricians dismiss educational intervention as a waste of public funds because they believe intelligence is largely fixed at birth or shortly thereafter, hence those funds should be invested in gifted students, not the slow ones (Gould, 1995).

The concept of superior intelligence makes people to flourish in school, be wealthy, and stable in marriage, whereas imbecility leads to poverty, divorce, crime, and even prone to injury is the essence of Herrnstein and Murray's empirical assertion—that intelligence shapes life outcomes more strongly than does social environment. Contrary to their empirical conclusions that I.Q. dominates the socioeconomic status of people (Murray, 1995), research has shown that I.Q. is not single, unitary, and fixed as some assume. Also, if I.Q. were not a measurable variable, the socioeconomic status of people and their immense social circumstances would still strongly determine the outcomes of life, specifically the poor. The problem with some psychometricians is they refuse to look beyond I.Q. to see the obvious social influences on individuals. They fail to acknowledge recessions cause many to fall into poverty or race and class segregation tends to maintain poverty and restrict thousands of students from doing as well as others on various standardized exams (Kozol, 1991; Massy & Denton, 1993; Orfield & Chungmei, 2005; Pinkney, 1984).

Herrnstein and Murray's conclusions have influenced conservative politicians, who argue families in low income areas have a history of welfare dependency and tend to breed offspring who lack ambition, work ethics, and a sense of self-reliance, are prone to criminal behavior, and are uncommitted to assumed American values. The welfare reform Herrnstein and Murray advanced in *The Bell Curve* strikes a resemblance with the Republicans' Contract with America. Murray's contribution of *The Bell Curve* was funded by a grant from the Bradley Foundation described in *The Nation* in 1993 as the largest conservative underwriter of intellectual activity. While the Bradley Foundation is well respected in intellectual circles, its funds are allocated only to right-wing political scholars (Easterbrook, 1995).

Right-wing forces have renewed white supremacist racial myths under the umbrella of empirical science by rearticulating old social Darwinist theories and are trying to legitimize their proposals as public policy (Taylor, 1995). A very important question arises as to why the Right has rearticulated old social Darwinist theories to influence public policy.

As previously stated, after a few modest gains of the Civil Rights Movement, the state of the masses of poor African American and Hispanic people did not get any better, but deteriorated even more. When measured by indicators such as unemployment rates, numbers of families falling below the poverty line, and mortality rates the widening gap between white and black has grown immensely. In 1970 the unemployment rate was 4.9 percent and by 1979 it was 5.3 percent; in 1974, 79 percent of the public believed that inflation was more important than civil rights. By 1982, the unemployment rate had risen to 9.7 percent, which forced many to adjust to the economic dilemmas of the nation as plants closed, unemployed workers were unable to find new jobs, and the Federal Reserve Board refused to maintain inflation and keep unemployment down and promote economic growth. In 1985, the Department of Labor's Bureau of Labor Statistics reported that the African American unemployment rate was 16.3 percent compared to the overall national unemployment rate of 7.3 percent. The Center on Budget and Policy Priorities reported that the poverty rate among blacks was nearly 36 percent and that long-term unemployment among white people had increased by only 1.5 percent since 1985; however, among black people it had increased by 72 percent during the same period (Pinkney, 1984; Chomsky, 1996).

Nevertheless, the majority of white citizens were callous concerning the circumstances that blacks and other minorities lived under. A new attitude of degeneracy pervaded the United States as many white citizens believed and resented they were providing for the underprivileged. Many felt racial minorities were unfairly receiving preferential treatment in the job market and with educational opportunities. While most of the attention has been on minority preferential treatment, little attention has been given to the fact whites have received preferential treatment since the Jamestown colony and to the ways racial issues were being shaped by the Right as it explicitly revitalized and rearticulated white supremacist ideologies of the past (Lipsitz, 1998, Feagin, 2001). The use of code words (rhetoric used to disguise racial issues) was geared to mobilize the masses of the white middle class threatened by supposedly minority gains. Thus beginning with the Nixon administration neoconservatives began to reconstruct a sophisticated racial ideology and challenged the underpinning of the Civil Rights Movement's quest for social justice. They began to predict the collapse of an ambiguous "American Dream." The apolitical, perpetually prosperous, militarily invincible, and deeply self-absorbed and self-righteous mainstream American culture was being shaken to its foundation. The Right began to seek initiatives to overturn the achievements of the Civil Rights Movement by rearticulating the meaning of race and the fundamental issues arising from racial inequality. It was able to link the Civil Rights Movement, the antiwar protest against Vietnam, tied the 1968 urban riots following the assassinations of Martin Luther King Jr. and Robert Kennedy to communism, anarchy, and crime (Chambliss, 1995; Zinn, 1995). Through the use of code words, the Right reasserted white identity and reaffirmed the United States as a white man's country. While the Right blamed the government for all that was happening to the nation, it continued to cling to biological notions of race and racial purity that resembled the racism at the beginning of the century (Knapp, Kronick, Marks &Vosburgh, 1996).

The Right began to form coalitions in the 1970s to counter the Civil Rights Movement with aggressive political style: the American Conservative Union, the National Conservative Political Action Committee (NCPAC), the Conservative Caucus, the Young Americans for Freedom, and various fundamentalist Christian organizations that incorporated millions of their followers. During the 1980s new leaders emerged such as Richard A. Viguerie; Paul Weyrich and his Committee for the Survival of a Free Congress; Howard Philips and his Conservative Caucus; Rev. Jerry Falwell of the Moral Majority; and Joseph Coors, founder of the Heritage Foundation. The Right fed upon discontent, anger, insecurity, and resentment and flourished on white backlash as it collected millions of dollars from blue-collar workers and their families. While some argued the Right wanted to restore a patriarchal society, race was the crucial factor in the reaction to societal gains of the 1960s, which affected the electoral picture (Crawford, 1980; Gold, 1992; Pinkney, 1984).

Many believe the Protestant values of the seventeenth century which deeply influence the political and social culture of the United States were being threatened and this fear has turned into resentment. The fear is reflected within the political and religious rhetoric of those who are part of the dominant culture. They fear American society has lost control of the global economy and their personal security, their Protestant values will not be passed down to their children, their sacred canon is being threatened, and their allegedly virtuous homogeneous culture is being destroyed. White supremacist ideological scholars such as Herrnstein and Murray have influenced white middle class people who see themselves as law-abiding, hard-working Christian citizens, while at the same time viewing "those people"—African Americans and Hispanics—as lazy, immoral, permissive, and not conforming to the Euro-American values and way of life. They see African Americans and Hispanics as causing the nation to decline in morals and as undeserving of the policies that support compensatory educational and employment opportunities, which strain economic resources (Apple, 1996; Phillips, 1982; Rose, 1990).

During the Reagan administration, the Right used the media to create nonexistent crime waves with racial overtones. In 1978, Mark Fishman wrote an essay titled "Crime Waves as Ideology" and concluded television portrayed African American and Hispanic youth as muggers, murderers, and rapists. Researchers have shown the media portrayals of crime do not correctly depict crime in the real world. Reality-based programs tend to cast African Americans as criminals and whites as the good guys (Oliver & Armstrong, 1998). University of Southern California law professor Jody David Armor, in his book *Negrophobia and Reasonable Racism* (1997), states:

> Perhaps the gravest threat today to progress toward racial justice comes from the right-wing ideologues bent on convincing white people of good faith that negative stereotypes about blacks are justified. Trotting out discredited studies, unscientific experiments, and cooked statistics, these pundits try to prove that blacks are inherently less intelligent and more violent than whites. The unmistakable implication of these "proofs" of black inferiority is the disparities between blacks and whites in education and

employment must be blamed on blacks' own inferior genes, not on past and present discrimination (p. 12).

The Center for Media and Public Affairs released a study in March 1994 suggesting while crime reports and victimization surveys by the government showed the national crime rate had not changed since 1993, yet the major television networks had more than doubled their coverage of crime and basically nurtured the panic over crime. On March 3, 1994, the *Washington Post* published "Networks Make Crime Top Story: Survey Says Coverage Fanned Public' Fear." The article said people's fear of crime does not come from looking over their shoulders, but from prime-time television network shows. The Right put a distinct black urban face to lawlessness and crime and promoted old, nineteenth-century stereotypes of the black menace to society. It presents America with an expensive promise of more police and prisons to bring domestic tranquility, intending to continue the system of segregation, control, and widespread social assumptions associating crime with African American males.

Many neoliberals and neoconservatives within the judicial system deny or downplay racism that is so much a part of their informal conversation and life. They blame President Lyndon B. Johnson's Civil Rights Act of 1964 and his War on Poverty as the major reason for crime and yet these neoliberal and neoconservative district attorneys and judges continue to hear the cases of thousands of young African American males and are incarcerating them at an alarming rate (Davis, 2003; Mauer, 1999). The incarceration of African American males is nothing new: Charshee C. L. Mcintyre, in her work *Criminalizing a Race: Free Blacks During Slavery* (1984), shows since the sixteenth century free black males were incarcerated at an alarming rate to hide the embarrassment of white male/black women offspring, to rid society of free black people, and to alleviate the fears of white people of an alleged menace to society. Angela Davis argues that the prison industrial complex resembles the old prison lease system during Jim Crow where inmates were leased out to plantations and other enterprises as slave labor. Today, the exploitation of inmates as laborers for private corporations, prison suppliers and government agencies is becoming a billion dollar business. Therefore it is imperative for government, along with certain corporate constituents and other parts of the private sector to promote and incarcerate thousands of African, Hispanic, and Native Americans (Davis, 2003).

Charles Murray also claims white students are 2.3 times better than black students and attention should be given to the more intelligent students. One judge in Florida commented black youth are genetically more prone to violence and gangs, have difficulty competing in school, and have a tendency to molest teachers (Berry, 1994; Miller, 1995; Miller, 1996). If American society continues to close its eyes to the racist discourse and history of incarcerating young African American males, then the people of the United States will be far more susceptible to the seduction of white supremacy, eugenics, I.Q., and the policy of incarcerating people by race. Since 1933 the incarceration rate of African Americans in relation to whites has greatly increased (Davis, 2003). Murray and Herrnstein cite Robert A. Gordon, a sociologist from Johns Hopkins, also financed by the Pioneer Fund, in their book *The Bell Curve,* to the effect that there is a causal relationship between low I.Q. and African American propensity to criminality (Lane, 1995; Miller, 1995).

Television news and exploitative crime shows teeming with images of young African American males as predators have made crime a metaphor for race. Historically, welfare and crime have always been used by politicians who wish to posture on race without having to actually mention it (Gray, 1995). In 1992, David Duke, a well known white supremacist leader within Klan and neo-Nazi groups, garnered two-thirds of the white vote in Louisiana as he campaigned for a seat in the United States Senate. His campaign focused upon race-baiting through code words like welfare and crime, as he articulated the unspoken but understood idea that only white people were hard working and black women were "welfare queens," (Roberts, 1997, pp. 17–19). Klan leaders repeatedly voiced concern of white women losing the ideals of Victorian social sexual restraints and African American and Hispanic women were destroying Anglo Protestant values through illegitimate sex (Wade, 1987; Quadagno, 1994).

A false pedagogy of the "American Dream" encourages many citizens into believing everyone has access to opportunities, but the reality is the United States supports a capitalistic free market which breeds inequality (Marable, 1983; Massey & Denton, 1993). The basic dimensions of social inequality—how wealthy the rich are, how utterly impoverished the poor—and even who becomes rich or poor are the result of social and political choices. Public policies that help the poor are obvious, but policies that bring aid to the rich and middle class tend to be more invisible. While Aid to Families with Dependent Children (AFDC) is supposed to provide allowances to families in need, the welfare system in the United States is available only to those who can prove they are poor; while tax deduction policies subsidize middle class and wealthy homeowners with mansions and vacation homes. However, no politician who argues in favor of balancing the budget will tackle the issue that tax deductions utilized by middle class and wealthy homeowners cost the government four times the amount of money spent on low-income families (Grigsby, 1990). Government aid is also used to build thousands of miles of highways in the suburbs to connect with downtown urban business districts. Government subsidy policies such as federal G.I. benefits are commended because they facilitate home ownership among the rising working and middle class, but have yet to work for low-income people, especially veterans who cannot afford to enter the housing market (Quadagno, 1994).

The refusal to integrate and Negrophobia caused whites to flee from the inner city to the suburbs. As African Americans moved into formerly white dwellings, landlords, banks, mortgage companies, and others forced black people to pay a premium for homes that were already antiquated and decayed (Lipsitz, 1998; Massey & Denton, 1993; Thabit, 2003). While eleven million homes were built in the United States between 1935 and 1950, racial discrimination was public policy. Troy Duster's January 19, 1995, article in the *San Francisco Chronicle*, "The Advantages of White Males," said policies directly blocked blacks from moving into white neighborhoods. He states the Federal Housing Authority manual declared that "loans should not be given to any family that might disrupt the racial integrity of a neighborhood." The manual continued: "[I]f a neighborhood is to retain stability it is necessary that properties shall be continued to be occupied by the same social and racial classes (Franklin & Moss, 2000, p. 453). Duster continued to show how white families were able to secure mortgage loans at 3 to 5 percent, while African Americans were routinely denied such loans. With a growing suburbia and an expanding interstate highway network, jobs, malls and other promising financial endeavors have followed the white middle class (Jackson, 1985).

On the other hand, financial barriers placed again in front of urban African Americans have resulted in most blacks being trapped in the ghettoes, far from the growing industrial parks that have moved to the suburbs and bring promising employment. The contemporary concentration of poor blacks into housing projects and resulting inner city segregation is not simply a matter of the market. Along with racial discrimination, government policies have directly contributed to the widening disparity between those who were able to purchase homes and moved to the suburbs versus those who are too poor to get government aid or who were excluded from programs subsidizing suburbia (Massey & Denton, 1993; Thabit, 2003). Discriminatory ramifications are far reaching: homeownership is the best asset in the United States—homes can be used as collateral for loans and (like educational loans) they can be passed on as inheritance for future generations' growth, thereby securing the next generation's economic stability (Bullard & Lee, 1994; Grigsby, 1994).

Corporate welfare is another government subsidy that fails to get the same amount of publicity as the alleged ignorant and lazy poor. The most publicized subsidies are those utilized by farmers, where the government controls the prices of goods by paying farmers not to plant crops on some of their land. Even though this program was originally set up to assist low income farmers, large-scale farmers and agribusiness have become the beneficiaries. Utility companies purchase electricity from federally owned hydroelectric plants at rock bottom prices; the Forest Service builds roads through the nation's national parks for the timber industry; and the federal government finances research for the nuclear and fossil fuels industries that the industries can pay for themselves. These same industries also earn special exemptions and deductions written into the tax codes (Shapiro, 1995).

Thus, the disparity we see in the United States is neither natural nor inevitable, nor does it reflect the abilities of individual talent as

Herrnstein and Murray suggest in *The Bell Curve*. While people in the United States have chosen to increase equality of opportunity, we have structured many of the programs to help the well off more than those below the poverty level. This implies inequality in the United States is the result of policy decisions this nation's government has made (Zinn, 1995). The United States has chosen to reduce some of the disparity between the middle class and the wealthy, but have done very little to reduce inequality as it affects the poor, which shows disparity lies in the structure of society, not in the intellect or genes of individuals.

Public policy can also improve the cognitive skills of this nation's children and expand opportunities for all. Yet those who believe intelligence is genetically determined and fixed at birth claim nothing can be done to increase the cognitive capabilities of our children, therefore the perception is programs subsidizing our children's chances to sharpen their cognitive skills are a waste of taxpayers' money. The debate now is over whether to invest in the public school system, especially in poor urban communities where it is seen as wasteful (Kozol, 1991). Herrnstein and Murray claim African Americans and Latinos are inherently less intelligent than whites and argue vehemently the differences in intelligence explain disparity in society. What American parents and students are not told is this nation's manufacturing base has relocated to developing nations that have no unions, corporate tax base, or environmental regulations; nor are we told our educational policy has a key part in the economic prosperity of the elite (Bigelow & Peterson, 2002; Brown & Lauder, 1997; Aronowitz & DiFazio, 1997).

The globalization of industry by an elite oligarchy has had enormous consequences for the working class and poor. The failure to unite against this narrow group of powerful individuals allows them to dictate to politicians and the public their goals (Bigelow & Peterson, 2002; Chomsky, 1999; Domhoff, 1998; Kelley, 1997). This corporate oligarchy has subtly done a marvelous job in educating the public to believe the causes of this nation's economic decline lie at the door of our schools. They also have remained silent as white supremacist scholars blame inner city students for having no interest in learning, saying to educate these children is wasting tax dollars, thereby persuading the middle class to become allies with neoconservative ideology and allowing corporations to move in and privatize the schools for their benefit. Here lie the roots of the eroding status of the white middle class as they focus on blaming the poor and the tax breaks the elite takes advantage of, along with our refusal to engage in meaningful discussions about inequality. Those students who are slated as gifted and/or have access to economic and educational opportunities will be able to have mobility within the American society (Chomsky, 1996; hooks, 2000; Tumin, 1985).

On the other hand, students who have received the least amount of economic opportunities and/or education are offered employment that requires the least amount of skills. However, what Herrnstein and Murray refuse to acknowledge genetic intelligence has nothing to do with one's status in life. Patterns of disparity are produced and reproduced by the economic and social structures of a nation. Policy choices throughout the history of the United States have shaped the kind of class inequality we have and helped or hurt certain group's chances to succeed (Adams & Sanders, 2003; Zinn, 1995).

Since 1619 when the first twenty enslaved Africans were traded in Jamestown, Virginia, and for the next 246 years blacks were continually brought to this land to labor perpetually as an enslaved people, while Native Americans were basically removed from their ancestral lands or exterminated if they chose to resist removal. Since emancipation became federal law in 1863, black people have remained at the bottom of the social ladder, surviving, in spite of the racial indifference and hatred toward them, as aliens with very little protection from the law (Turner, Singleton, & Musick, 1990; Wilson, 1996). The United States historically created an image of black people as depraved, degraded deviants, licentious, immoral, and rude, and has discriminated against them, maintaining a system of racial apartheid in both the North and South. Over the course of the history of the United States, violence against black people has always been used to maintain white supremacy and hegemony through invidious violence and riots (Litwack, 1961; Tuttle 1970; Runcie, 1972; Bernstein, 1990). Black children were compelled to attend segregated schools that received very little funds and, in many urban centers today, still suffer from a segregated system that marginalizes them to the fringes of education (Litwack, 1961; Franklin & Moss, 2000; Fredrickson, 1981; Orfield & Chungmei, 2005). Even now, African American and other minority children are seen as problem ridden; test prep rallies instead of real content lessons leave them to do poorly on standardized exams and drop out of school relatively early—as a result, they often find themselves in trouble with the law (Haymes, 1995; Kozol, 1991; Orfield & Kornhaber, 2001).

Can genes explain what has happened historically to people of African descent or to the Native American population in the United States? Forced to live on the periphery of society, African American, Hispanics and Native Americans suffer the most drastic and lasting effects of subordination and economic duress, which have led to reduced performance on standardized exams. Herrnstein and Murray claim socioeconomic differences between blacks and whites do not explain the gaps in black/white test scores. However, test scores are not the beginning of an explanation for disparity but the end of the explanation; the beginning is the history of racial enslavement, apartheid, and continued discrimination. Herrnstein and Murray, along with many others, believe the legacy of racial slavery, apartheid, and racial discrimination in the United States somehow disappeared during the 1960s. However, 380 years of racial enslavement, prejudice, and apartheid in the United States cannot be erased in three decades or just because President Lyndon Johnson signed the Civil Rights Act of 1964. The caste system of racial hierarchy and apartheid the United States government instituted and upheld, a doctrine of biological inequality, has consistently played an important role in keeping blacks and other nonwhites as aliens and outsiders in the mainstream society. State laws were passed stating anyone with one "drop" of black blood was nonwhite, as white supremacist scholars used religious, and later on scientific, justifications for policies based on biological inferiority (Fredrickson, 1981; Turner, Singleton, & Musick, 1984; Smedley, 1999).

These distinctive features of racial enslavement in the United States contributed enormously to the disadvantages of the descendants of enslaved black people. The legacy of racial enslavement was not a natural event; it was a well thought out policy. Although the United States government decided in 1789 to allow slave importation until 1808 many slave traders continued to import blacks illegally until the Civil War (Spears, 1900). Congress consented to racial enslavement until the Civil War; permitted the enslavement of black people to expand across the Mississippi River and this nation still lives with the consequences of those policies (Fredrickson, 1981; Fehrenbacher, 1988). Between the Civil War in 1865 and the Civil Rights Movement of the 1960s, the federal government allowed the South to sanction physical intimidation, legal state codes of apartheid and discrimination, and social customs kept blacks in the lowest caste order. White supremacist groups like the Klu Klux Klan lynched and terrorized blacks with neither embarrassment nor restraint to sustain white supremacy. Jim Crow laws maintained a system of apartheid that denied blacks their basic civil liberties, the right to vote, education and employment opportunities—southern white landlords reduced black farmers to peonage that was one step above slavery. In the North, racial prejudice and discrimination toward blacks bypassed civil liberties; educational and employment opportunities were very limited and residential segregation was maintained (Franklin & Moss, 2000; Wilson, 1996).

After the Civil War, opportunities opened up for black children to attend school, but with the advent of Jim Crow, the majority of all the progress that had been made dwindled away. Beginning sometime around 1880, the amount of funds allocated to black schools plummeted to about one third of what was spent on white schools. For example, in 1911 there were no high schools for black students in Atlanta and by 1930 about one third of the South's counties had no high schools for black children. In 1948, Clarendon County, South Carolina, paid the cost of busing white children to school but refused to do the same for African American children even though blacks were still required to pay their taxes. The racial discrimination regarding the cutting of funds toward educating black children was devastating in the South. The supposedly "separate but equal" law in the South affirmed by the Supreme Court of the United States barred thousands of black children from receiving a decent education and from well paying jobs (Lieberson, 1980; Carson; 1987; Franklin & Moss, 2000).

Racial stratification remained the law until after civil rights activists steadily challenged the system's constitutional basis. The beginning of this challenge was the *Brown vs. Board of Education of Topeka, Kansas*, case in which the Supreme Court decided the system of "separate but equal" was, in fact, inherently unequal and when a society segregates its people based on race, it is telling the world a supposedly democratic society does not practice equality. Since then African Americans and other nonwhite ethnic groups have experienced some opportunity to level the playing field: in 1940 black workers earned 43 percent as much as white workers; by 1980 it had risen to 73 percent. This is troubling for people like Herrnstein and Murray, who argue racism has ended and blacks and other minorities will never improve, low skilled jobs are disappearing, and blacks and other minorities are not intelligent enough to compete on the open market. What they fail to acknowledge is the public policy of Jim Crow may have been eliminated, but it has only been a little over forty years and the effects of its legacy will be around much longer. While segregation has been officially terminated, segregation and racial discrimination clearly continue (Card, 1993; Meyer, 2000; Orfield & Chungmei; 2005).

Research continues to prove that racial discrimination is still practiced; for instance, a study was conducted in which black and white researchers posed as potential buyers and renters with identical credentials and sought out realtors, agents, lenders, and landlords. According to the study, discriminatory practices were used against the black researchers posing as buyers and renters. The black applicants were not shown the properties shown to the white applicants and were told that there were no available apartments left to rent or were asked to seek homes or apartments in the black neighborhoods, while the white applicants were shown apartments denied to the black applicants. The result of being turned away has dire effects: it limits or hinders black applicant's access to quality schools for his or her child, to better employment opportunities, and just the freedom to enjoy life as others do (Leonard, 1987; Massy & Denton, 1993). *The New York Times*, on December 2, 1998, published Joseph Berger's article, "Pact Will Provide Minority Housing: A Yonkers Settlement to Buy and Build Homes in White Areas," which describes how the NAACP filed and won a court case against the city of Yonkers for intentionally maintaining segregated schools by confining black and Hispanic families in the southwestern corner of the city.

While many researchers will concede black children score lower than white children on achievement tests, they do show this anomaly is not due to some inferior intelligence (Meir & Wood, 2004; Orfield & Kornhaber, 2001). Some have shown the tests are culturally biased because scoring depends on knowing the discourse and language of middle class white people. On the average, black and other minority children live under the constraints of low income, bad medical care due to government cutbacks, and inferior preparation in school than their white counterparts. Another factor is segregated schools in black neighborhoods tend not to have the cultural capital to compete with suburban wealth that is able to prepare the students for success. Black students in segregated urban schools on the same academic track as white students in suburban schools are not exposed to the advanced mathematics or science courses that prepare them for college level courses. Also low income students find the curricula they learn from leave not only them marginalized in society but does not represent them in any or little positive light (Hoffer, 1985; Noguera, 2003).

Disparity can never be explained away in terms of a person's natural intelligence or one's racial genetic trait. Understanding why some do poorly on achievement tests or why they end up on a certain level of the economic ladder has nothing to do with intelligence or genes, but with public policies that affect one's social environment. Public policy directly structures the opportunities individuals have such as family income, cultural capital, quality of education, the neighborhood one lives in, job opportunities, and other factors that promote or hinder an individual. We need to understand the lack of investment in improving skills in students or reducing programs like healthcare alters and shapes inequality in society. In February 1973, Mary Jo Bane and Christopher Jencks published an article in *Harper's* titled "Five Myths About Your I.Q.," summarizing what are well-known facts about the myth of I.Q. They concluded that I.Q. tests measure only what psychometricians want to measure, that it is only a limited part of intelligence, and psychometricians refuse to acknowledge tests show little relationship to the performance of adults in real life. Psychometricians refuse to understand or acknowledge people are not poor because they may have a low I.Q. People are poor because there are policies punishing one and rewarding another. Some people, for instance, cannot find decent paying jobs, which has very little to do with intelligence scores. Also one's socioeconomic background influence how well one performs on an I.Q. test.

Conclusion

With all the scholarship discrediting the myths of psychometricians, why do the theories of I.Q. still persist? Why are people so open minded to the idea genetics leads to poverty, crime, immorality, and laziness? The receptiveness to the theory of inferior genes is particularly blatant at this period in time because it legitimates white supremacy and endorses economic disparity. On November 9, 1995, the *New York Times* printed Susan Mayer and Christopher Jencks's article "War on Poverty: No Apologies Please." They argued the belief in innate low intelligence led to widespread impressions that efforts to meliorate disparity with antipoverty programs, affirmative action, and compensatory education have not only failed but a waste of the taxpayers' money (Schwarz, 1983; Schor & Schor, 1988). It is not big of a deal if the debate concerning I.Q. and black inferiority goes back and forth between academicians; what really matters is the debate has spilled over into the opinions of journalists, talk show hosts, politicians, and policy intelligentsia who influence the public into accepting the theory that social intervention is a failure and that inferiority is an unchanging fact of nature.

The comments made during the presidential campaigns and administrations of Ronald Reagan and George Bush in the 1980s about the lack of values among the poor were pivotal to the solidification of a conservative cultural and political hegemonic order. Reagan and Bush referred to the poor as high school dropouts, welfare recipients, drug users, violent, criminal, uncivil, and welfare cheats. Republicans promised middle class whites they would restore and protect their individual liberties by privatizing schools, stimulating corporate growth through unrestrained market forces, and ensuring a long reign of conservative authority. They seek to dismantle, through judicial appointment, public school desegregation, affirmative action, and tax support for programs such as welfare and urban revitalization (Edsall & Edsall, 1991).

While Herrnstein and Murray do not promote the draconian measures of the eugenics movement, the origins of their theories are from the same paradigms. Bearing in mind the implications of innate inferior intelligence and/or genes as demonstrated in *The Bell Curve*, there is an assumption that people can be measured, labeled, and then efficiently sorted into their supposedly appropriate schools and occupations. If people believe intelligence is an innate trait operating in a free market, then we can test and assign children to their appropriate place in the classroom. We can reconcile supposedly unintelligent children and young adults to their inevitable fate by keeping their aspirations in line with eugenic ideas, so they remain content where they are and not frustrated by too much education. We can restrict voting rights, stop wasting public funds on blacks who lack moral instincts and are prone to crime, and induce or compel birth control among the poor. This is the explicit agenda psychometricians, educators, and statisticians have whose scholarship has contributed to the study of innate differences in abilities between groups (Murray & Herrnstein, 1994).

Just as there is a pedagogical epistemology to persuade the public there are innate differences among the various races and ethnic groups, there needs to be an epistemological pedagogy that counters the movement to exclude large groups of people from fully enjoying the fruits of a true democratic society. We need to, as a nation, decide to revise these policies so that all children can have an equal chance to enhance their talents and their efforts will not be encouraged or discouraged by the advantages or disadvantages of their race, ethnicity, or social status. The question arises: Are we really willing to provide each child with qualified committed teachers, the same material advantages, the same challenging curricula that reflects a true and fair picture of history and culture? Are we willing to really challenge the contradictions of the so-called American Dream which provides for some and excludes many? How much equality do we really want in the United States? Are we willing to acknowledge disparity and hegemony breed distrust, violence, and masses of discontented people? Until we as a people are ready to promote and insure an equitable public policy for all and are told the truth that such a policy will require an extensive public investment in healthcare, education, job development and training, school breakfast and lunches, and urban development, this nation will continue to produce a small elite controlling the wealth of all and an ever-growing mass of poor people.

However, the people of the United States continue to resist the idea of real equality no matter what level of investment an individual has or has not made. Some would argue to provide everyone with an equal opportunity will undermine the economic health of the nation, disparity is the price we pay to maintain this nation's wealth. During the 1980s a pedagogical epistemology was produced to teach people equality was threatening economic growth, destroying Puritan values, promoting racial and ethnic tribalism, and attacking the heterosexual privileges white males hold—all supposed evidence of the decline of society.

With the assistance of neoconservative coalitions made up of Northern and Southern middle and working-class whites and now even some blacks (hooks, 2000) and religious fundamentalists, the Reagan and Bush administrations sanctioned the dramatic transfer of wealth to the top of the stratified social order principally through fiscal policies, corporate tax breaks, and deregulation overwhelmingly profiting corporate and wealthy interests. The desire was to replace the welfare state with an unfettered free market, increasing productivity and thus prosperity, which was supposed to trickle down to all of society. By articulating racist and homophobic fears, the state arranged it so the core elements of the new conservative coalitions hurt most by the dramatic shifts in economic wealth and social privilege remained tolerant, even patriotic, so long as they were assured their sacred rights and values were protected and the undeserving inferior "others" were no longer the protected benefactors of state-sponsored entitlements.

The discourse of race, intelligence, and the rights certain groups perceived they had over others helped consolidate politically the redistribution of wealth and privilege from the middle class to the wealthy and the claim to take away entitlements from African

Americans and other minorities, the poor, and disfranchised to conservative middle- and working-class white people (Edsall & Edsall, 1991; Phillips, 1991; Reed, 1991). Politicians and policy makers influence the implementation of subsidies which create disparity where masses of people live according to the way taxes are distributed among the various socioeconomic groups. In addition, politicians put into practice policies subsidizing homeownership, regulate business, labor unions, education, and healthcare systems, which influences who receive opportunities for the development of individual talents and upward mobility in society.

CHAPTER SEVEN

EPILOGUE

Procrastination is still the thief of time. Life often leaves us standing bare,naked and dejected with a lost opportunity.

Martin Luther King Jr., 1967

The only triumph of evil is for good men to do nothing.

Edmund Burke, 1770

In 1980, President Ronald Reagan appointed William Bradford Reynolds to head the civil rights division of the Justice Department and quickly set out to eliminate affirmative action. In 1993, President Bill Clinton nominated Lani Guinier to head the civil rights division of the Justice Department, but in the wake of white conservative backlash, Clinton gave in to right-wing propaganda and withdrew the nomination. The battle to control the White House and Congress by right wing conservatives is as old as the South's struggle to maintain the enslavement of black people. While one cannot diminish the triumphs of the Civil Rights Movement, the resurgence of some within the right wing camp for control of this nation had little to do with the triumphs of the Civil Rights Movement, but a response to the audacity of black people proclaiming that their humanity was to be respected and the right to compete for any job just like whites, the audacity to demand their children had the right to receive the same educational opportunities as white children, even if that meant black children sitting next to white children, and they had a right to participate in the United States political process.

When George Wallace decided to run for president, he gave angry whites who felt their rights as white people were being destroyed by the Civil Rights Movement hope. Wallace relied upon the racial divide of black and white to garner support not only in the South; thousands of northern whites came to hear Wallace's speeches on why whites were angry at the federal government. Most whites believed blacks and the social order of the day were destroying their American way of life, that the integration of schools was too much to ask for, and the Kerner Commission had blamed them for the problems of black people. While few presidents such as Kennedy, Johnson, Carter, and Clinton tried to court black votes, they all knew their political careers would be successful only if they maintained ties with moderate and right wing white voters. All presidential candidates understand if they want successful political careers, they better accommodate white supremacy and maintain a hegemonic control over blacks (O'Reilly, 1995; Adams & Sanders, 2003).

The Reagan and Bush era saw whites hide behind perceived reverse discrimination in the job market even though black unemployment is still twice as high as whites. They used individual rights as a shield in their renewed opposition to integrating schools and housing. They voted for politicians who advocated law and order, tougher prison sentences, and a crackdown on alleged welfare queens. While blatant racial remarks are discouraged, some white politicians resorted to code words. The new buzz phrase used by conservatives was "a color-blind society," that officially recognizes no color difference, which at the same time uses race to maintain white power over blacks and other nonwhites. In a color-blind society whites assume everyone should be like them; all others must be conformed to whiteness or be marginalized and seen as causing the race problem to still exist. Therefore, by becoming color blind, whites can avoid the race issue and continue business as usual. The use of religion to prove white America held God's favor became voguish as each president claimed to be a born-again Christian to garner the votes of the religious right. However, their racism showed its face again as born-again Christians battled against liberals and called for strict God-fearing laws that coincide with Anglo Protestant ethics. The old myth, God created America to civilize the world was used again to strengthen their bulwarks against everything they believed sought to derail the mission of Christianizing the world. Islam as the enemy of the Christian world was rearticulated as American oil interests were allegedly controlled by theoretically ungodly nations.

White supremacy appeals not only to white conservatives, but also to white liberals who felt betrayed by the Black Power Movement of the 1960s and those liberals who were not outright racists yet felt a need to move to the suburbs so their children would not have to integrate with masses of children of color, their taxes would not go to waste in urban schools, and they would not have to live with urban crime. The answer to their problems was Bill Clinton, who appealed to blacks and yet remained faithful to nominally liberal middle-class and working-class whites, who hold conservative opinions on affirmative action, crime, and the welfare state. White America agreed with the media's portrayal of African Americans and Latinos as irresponsible welfare recipients with no American values. Conservative and liberal whites began to call for a return to Anglo Protestant values which hold this nation together and want those values taught in predominately non-white schools. They support a multicultural curriculum as long as it promotes we all are bound together as immigrants in a common struggle against hardship and eventually victorious. The majority of whites are not against multiculturalism as long as it does not upset the values of the dominant points of view or show American history in a negative way, they assume everyone wants to be American with white cultural and moral values (Kincheloe & Steinberg; 1997).

Racial segregation has been the most striking political and societal expression of white supremacy in the United States. Racial public policies have regulated this nation and excluded African Americans from participating as citizens until the Civil Rights Movement. The practice of racial segregation worked to exclude African Americans alongside the political process endorsed and supported by the state and federal government of the United States way into the 1960s. Throughout this book, I have shown that public policies of white supremacy grew out of Anglo Protestant culture. The most insidious expression of white supremacy is not its ability to use force, but its set of patterns, provided carefully through public policies, laws and education, that has standardized itself as the universal culture.

When educators and the general public understand educational institutions are cultural constructs and serve as the basis for whom people are, education has provided white supremacy the structural capacity to define and defend itself socially and economically. Then we can reconstruct our society and educational institutions on a more egalitarian basis whereby no one is treated genetically inferior, excluded because of skin color or poverty the cultural, political, economic, and societal development of white supremacy has its genesis in the educational institutions of the United States. White supremacist ideology has shaped the culture of the American people. Educators, both black and white, need to realize white supremacy and its hegemonic hold on education and American society as a whole is a theoretical agenda and has swayed public opinion for too long. Educators are needed at the policy level, administrative level, and in the classroom to expose and eradicate the ideology and curricula that continue to see black children's ability to learn as inferior. White supremacy has evolved into a sophisticated ideology, has influenced and advocated public policies which included Jim Crow laws in the South, residential and educational apartheid, and others based on the belief black children cannot perform equal to white children and blacks are inherently mentally inferior, prone to laziness and crime. These ideas and beliefs are still articulated, believed in some quarters, and practiced in American society today—with new enthusiasm. Educators, who bring a critical pedagogical epistemology to the forum, must not allow historical amnesia to set in. Educators aligned with communities consistently expose and eradicate those educational approaches still perpetuating white supremacy and the belief in black inferiority. Thus a working historical knowledge of white supremacy will induce not just educators but all who are interested to play an important role in ridding our society of this disease and to seek solutions for a true emancipatory atmosphere in schools.

African Americans and other people of color need to consistently and systematically equip themselves with the necessary insight and tools to educate their children and their community as a whole. Hopefully, African American educators will awake from the drowsiness of the present drive to just raise test scores at the expense of our young children to satisfy white supremacist ideology, while our young children suffer from emotional and mental stress to please some theoretical framework that claims our kids are "at risk." This drive to force Anglo Protestant culture and standards upon our children is dehumanizing, it treats our children like robots under the disguise of the standard of critical thinking. This standardization also gives educational institutions opportunities to obtain millions of dollars to study us, asking the question: Why can't these kids learn? They never look at the statement of Kenneth Clark during the court case of *Brown v. Board of Education of Topeka, Kansas:* "I don't think we quite realize the extent of this cruelty of racism and how hard it hit." Most white and some black scholars refuse to look at the root of the problem and see that racism has cut deep and its effect can still be seen in the schools they have labeled "low performing," schools for example like Morris High School in the South Bronx or Thomas Jefferson High School in the East New York section of Brooklyn attended by predominately Hispanic and African American students.

Here is a school named after Governor Morris, whose family owned a sugar plantation and black slaves. Thomas Jefferson views on black people would shock not only blacks but also whites if the knowledge of his racist views became public. Why are these and other schools still carrying the names after men who dehumanized blacks to gain wealth? There is a need not just to examine and change the curricula, but also examine the history of the institutions we send our children to and then investigate how we can change the racial structures set up centuries ago to maintain white supremacy. We can gain new insights into how white supremacy latently continues to control our communities and schools seek to create and adopt new pedagogical possibilities that are needed to liberate our children from being continually miseducated. Hopefully we will become more adept at recognizing white supremacy even when it is hidden behind a facade of standards. We can strategize and demand Schools of Education to prepare teachers who will educate our children with the knowledge that will provide our communities with leaders who possess truly democratic ideas for society.

White supremacy created social distinctions based on physical characteristics and ancestry, enslaved untold millions of blacks, used racial segregation, used science to claim we are inferior, treated Hispanics as aliens and segregated them into barrios and sought to exterminate Native Americans, and took their lands. This ideology still underlies the socioeconomic foundation of the United States, which still benefits the dominant white population. It no longer requires overt physical force, as it did in the past, to maintain its power. Today white supremacy consolidates its power by rearticulating itself through a complex system of beliefs, ideas, and practices upon society through the academy, the media, religion, traditional myths, and the political system.

This book has explored white supremacy and its purpose through education in the United States, which is to indoctrinate children with the cultural values, blind patriotic nationalism, and the political and economic systems along with the language and religion that reflect historical Anglo Protestant norms. This "Americanization" reinforces passive obedience, the continual celebration of mythical Anglo Protestant heroes and events. The curriculum does not encourage a real sense of critical thinking that might question the dominant point of view or any sense of community among the students. Instead it indoctrinates students to compete with each other and consistently advocates individual achievement through tracking and standardized testing.

Educational institutions transmit a culture of dominance and ideological hegemony. Schools and other cultural institutions select, preserve, and distribute ideas of the dominant white elite as part of their quest to control knowledge and true reform in our society. Certain historical events and periods are marginalized in textbooks or not mentioned at all in classrooms bears witness to the fact attempts are made to control and use knowledge as an asset to the benefit of a certain social group.

The scientific debate over genetic differences between groups is now well into its second century. Unlike more traditional scientific controversies, where the argument diminishes as new knowledge is produced or as scientists with opposing views retire or die away, the bitter dispute over race and whose culture will prevail has arisen anew. It is being debated all over again today in almost exactly the same terms at the beginning of the century, but with a fervor that seems more religious than scientific. The issue of race inferiority became heated again in 1994, when Richard J. Herrnstein and Charles Murray published the most incendiary piece of social science to appear within the last fifteen years, *The Bell Curve: Intelligence and Class Structure in American Life*. Herrnstein and Murray show how racist ideology can rearticulate itself through academic protocol, without any overt racist language, even acknowledging contrary viewpoints and hiding behind so-called scientific data. While the authors hide behind thick piles of data of warnings and falsifications, the Bell Curve becomes a very explosive device. Herrnstein and Murray's book received top billings throughout the media, was featured on *Nightline,* and was sold on every bookshelf in the nation, including those of Kmart nationwide. The argument has not confined itself to academic journals and scientific conferences; the subject of racial differences is being debated from university classrooms to bars. This debate has received extensive coverage in the nation's popular culture and media.

The belief science operates synonymously with politics gave scientific authority a powerful strategy for influencing public policy. The results of this kind of scientific investigation, in which groups of people are defined as genetically inferior, has facilitated formal and informal alliances between right wing political groups, including fascists and racists who have been more than pleased to use scientific authority as a source of prestige for their own agendas. The use of science to promote race superiority and whiteness has been accomplished with the cooperation of or at the very least without protest from even those who do not support racism or eugenics.

We as Americans try to defend the hypocrisy of the men who drafted the Declaration of Independence and the United States Constitution, who violated their own words and surrendered themselves and the nation to avarice and power by endorsing the racial enslavement of Africans and their descendants. They sent this nation on a disastrous path of racial division and conflict. The United States lost its first opportunity to correct the greed and avarice of the nation; instead, the United States turned its back on its black population and ended the Reconstruction period by putting the South back into the hands of white supremacist leaders. W. E. B. Du Bois stated in *Black Reconstruction in America, 1860–1880* (1935), "The slave went free; stood a brief moment in the sun; then moved back again toward slavery" (p. 30). When President Warren G. Harding was inducted into the Klu Klux Klan and expanded racial segregation, he validated the federal government's sanction of white supremacy

(Wade, 1987). This complete retreat from racial equality by the United States federal government resulted in, as Congressman John Lewis called it in *Without Sanctuary* (2000), "atrocities and torture of an American holocaust" (p. 7) and moved thousands of ordinary people to civil disobedience during the Civil Rights Movement of the 1960s.

It lost its second opportunity during World War II to set in motion changes that would begin to rid this nation of white supremacist ideology. The audacity of the United States to fight a war against another white supremacist nation with a segregated military is oxymoronic. Thousands of blacks and other nonwhites fought the war expecting America to change its racist assumptions only to return to a more oppressive country, and the American government failed to address the white supremacist ideology within its own borders. The third failure of the United States to address white supremacist hegemonic order came about in the 1970s as neoconservatives and new right wing organizations reacted to the Civil Rights Movement by labeling the War on Poverty a failure and calling for welfare reform and for fewer affirmative action programs. They rearticulated white supremacist ideology through academic scholarship utilizing intelligence as the new tool to exclude black and other people of color from educational opportunities and from participating in the civic culture.

Finally, white supremacist academic scholars utilized eugenics to argue blacks were inherently inferior to whites genetically. *The Bell Curve* was published when poverty was on the rise and gave new fire to the already growing debate among educational scholars, policy makers, researchers, and the courts claiming blacks were unfit to live in the American society. *The Bell Curve* is particularly damaging to black children as they are finding it difficult to escape the claws of poverty. Again, America has failed to retreat from white supremacist ideology as the Republican Party embraced *The Bell Curve* and made public their Contract with America. The nation's most recent failure was President George W. Bush's decision not to attend the ninety-fifth annual NAACP convention in 2004. During his 2000 campaign, Bush had no problem giving a speech at the white supremacist Bob Jones University in South Carolina to gain support for his election.

American racial oppression has not changed much because racial oppression has always come from the upper echelons of society. With the recent rise of the Republican Party and their use of race to launch attacks on the social programs that have sought to alleviate poverty and ensure some measure of equality, white supremacy has once again caused the United States to fail to even try to eradicate its four hundred years of racial oppression.

Educators can try to turn the tide of white supremacy but the possibility of change must be firmly established in unromantic appraisals of white supremacy and assessments must be taken as to where teachers, curriculum developers, and school policy makers find themselves within this paradigm. Educators can begin to educate themselves about the many facets of white supremacy and how it operates in American society to not only oppress blacks but how it enslaves the minds and destroys the hopes of thousands of black, white, and other students of various ethnic groups. Attention must be given to analyzing and deconstructing the political economy of textbooks and their racial formations.

There can be college courses for potential teachers, educators, and curriculum developers where they can to begin to question not only the contents of the school curriculum but also the latent factors maintaining the dominant culture in schools instilling students with knowledge presenting only the Eurocentric version and does not allow for critical reflection. More importantly, there can be avenues allowing educators to perceive the pervasiveness of the curriculum as a servant of conservative capitalist interests of homogeneity and social control, rather than as a means to educate and enlighten the minds and hearts of young people.

In teaching about white supremacy in the classroom, the teacher can engage students to discuss how white supremacy has influenced them to act or react to certain conditions and topics in our society. As we freely give knowledge to students, we can teach in a way empowering students; at the same time, we can be healers, ensuring they do not walk away feeling there is no hope for change. Black students come to class angry, alienated, and understanding oppression, but restrain themselves from articulating the oppression and racism they face daily because many times they do not feel the freedom or support of the teacher in the class and believe no one has their interests in mind. White students sometimes come to class and find classroom demographics exposes their whiteness ceases to be dominant. They realize they are confronted by black students who are raising their voices to be heard or they have come face-to-face with black anger; many teachers are ill prepared when confronted with these scenarios and do not know how to facilitate the dialogue for fear of it becoming fierce. There must be courses willing to prepare teachers to deal with the racism and inequities and prepare them to openly discuss the issues all students face today.

The effects of America's brand of apartheid have left deep wounds in American society and there are no short-term solutions. Race relations have taken a downward spiral among the black and white student population. A huge racial canyon remains in the United States, and there are few signs the coming century will see this abyss closed. While the right to vote has been assured, the electorate is still controlled by the white majority. African Americans remain at the mercy of a white majority that remains racist—not in the overt sense, but with a new cleverness, denying the unmistakable fact African Americans suffer from a real disadvantage in American society and will continue to do so until radical action is taken. There are no easy solutions to the problem of white supremacy nor are there easy solutions to the issues of race and inequality. While a socialistic redistribution of the wealth is ruled out by the white majority and the most foreseeable way to lessen the gap between black and white is some form of affirmative action, white reactions are to be expected to invoke a merit criteria to prevent any rapid black advancement. Whites will claim they are better qualified in the skills needed for a highly technological society. The goal of the next Reconstruction will need to be a multiracial and multiethnic society that could be fused into a single nation on the basis of shared democratic values.

Personal Reflections

I believe we have reached a point in time where race relations will never improve unless we from all racial and ethnic backgrounds decide to dedicate our very lives and resources not just in times of prosperity, but especially in times of racial crises to openly confront the hegemonic white supremacist forces that continue to fragment society. As we expose white supremacy for what it really is, we have an opportunity to discuss race to the point where even rage can be expressed without either side walking away from the table. White people must let go of their fears of black people, of feeling like we want revenge or as if we want to inflict violence for the sake of violence. White people need to begin to honestly acknowledge how white supremacy has pathologically destroyed the lives of blacks, other people of color, and themselves. Then begin to assist in healing those wounds.

Black people must begin to stop hiding their anger and let it surface so we can move on and begin to heal the wounds of over four hundred years of oppression, rape, pillage, and death. Only then can we begin to sit down with whites and openly hold dialogue, critically investigate and study the madness of white supremacy. It is only when white people stop allowing themselves to be brainwashed and denying the existence of institutional white supremacist infrastructures in our schools and curricula then we can begin to make the change from a hegemonic school system whose values and epistemologies are those of the white elite. People of color must stop denying the anger that bell hooks, in *Killing Rage: Ending Racism* (1995), so clearly articulated that we must acknowledge—anger at having spent centuries "consenting to white power to achieve—assimilation, changing ourselves, suppressing our true feelings." Black people refuse to let this anger rise because we have tried to be accepted into white society, hoping to be treated as equals. We must stop being traumatized when it does not seem to work. When we stop trying to assimilate and look for acceptance by a society that does not value our worldview, we can begin to rid our schools of the hegemonic order plaguing our youth. Then and only then can we (black and white) begin to build a multiracial society based on justice, interracial unity, and a desire to work toward eliminating white supremacy and its agent of institutional racism.

Our reluctance to talk about race, white supremacy, and the many issues confronting this nation relating to race in any capacity has left us in a state of silence; when there is any conversation, it only touches the surface or most of the responsibility is shifted on people of color. Blacks and other people of color have historically been asked to stand down and be exemplary citizens in the face of white racial violence. Middle class whites argue regulations, taxes, and programs that benefit the poor, preferences for blacks, and funds for inner city schools are a waste, and I am finding some middle class black people are beginning to think the same way as their middle class white counterparts. This middle class fear of not attaining the "American Dream" has caused much fear among not only white but black people who believe in the Calvinist idea of the Horatio Alger myth. We have now, as in the past, placed the blame of society's woes upon the masses of poor people in this nation. Our society has allowed the mass media to subliminally convince us into thinking the poor have somehow depleted the wealth of this nation. Yet we refuse to look beyond the surface of all these issues and see how poverty and inequality are products of hegemonic white supremacist public policies.

We allow the curriculum to continually erase, deny, and silence the past to make the present visions of racial harmony and pluralism more promising. We have allowed historical knowledge to be suppressed and developed institutional amnesia, forgetting our history and culture in the quest to assimilate and partake in the superficial "American Dream." We have permitted ourselves to be indoctrinated into believing racism no longer continues to play a major role in the distribution of wealth and in living conditions. People are afraid to talk about racism because of the tension that comes with the subject and some refuse to discuss it because it disturbs their enjoyment as consumers even if they are victims of racism. Confronting the issue of race in the United States is very painful, because for black people it brings to the surface the wounds that racism cause and the anger they feel about white people and for white people it brings with it guilt or resistance to the feelings they have and a fear of black people wanting revenge for all the wrongs done. Both blacks and whites really need to understand how white supremacist attitudes and ideology started—yes, there was the enslavement of blacks, that there was hooded whites terrorizing blacks and anyone else who did not subscribe to white supremacy.

However, very few understand how white supremacy evolved, how it oppressed blacks and other people of color, how it became public policy, and how it continually rearticulates itself in the United States. White supremacy has plagued us since the first Europeans landed upon these shores, and as bell hooks (1994) says:

> It goes beyond prejudice and discrimination and even transcends bigotry, largely because it arises from outlooks and assumptions of which we are largely unaware (p. 4).

This unawareness of racial hegemonic supremacy has caused many of us to think white supremacy and racial apartheid has disappeared from our lives. Some blacks have allowed themselves to be colonized into thinking racism has been eradicated, but I wonder if we as black people realize American society is set up to conform us to white standards of acceptable behavior or face the prospect of being placed on the margins of society or being warehoused within the urban ghettos and prisons.

People were taught to believe race is biological and genetic, and these differences within humanity are obvious to us all. The reality is this concept of race involves more than just excluding a group of people; it is a discourse or structure of ideas that denigrate those being excluded. Society wants to eradicate hate and racism in the United States, but instead of dealing with it forthrightly, we continue to sweep racism under the carpet, and it just accumulates until it begins to wear through the carpet. Nor will we lift the carpet and clean up the dirt from under the carpet; we just either spread it out more evenly or move it to another area and think it will just disappear and go away. What we fail to realize is sooner or later the dirt will resurface again and again until we clean it up. We hide it from the public view and pretend it does not exist anymore. We now are taught it is only on the fringes of society, not facing the fact racism is ingrained in our society and our institutions. It will just torment us until we deal with it forthrightly and confront its roots.

We can begin to discuss and implement solutions to counter white supremacist influence upon society and education. We can discuss how to assist our students in understanding how white supremacy is constructed and how it now negotiates and conceals itself to maintain control and deny a truly egalitarian education. Students can critically examine the historical idea of white supremacy and who actually supports and upholds it. Most United States citizens have been taught and still unconsciously hold beliefs race determines one's behavior and race is the most important calculus of social identity. Whether public school teachers and college instructors are willing to admit societal interactions influence our racial identity and have been conditioned to respond automatically to the presence of certain physical features, which causes the dominate culture to feel threatened when oppressed groups begin to demand their rights and privileges. Even though science has begun to retreat from the idea there are races, white supremacy can still resort to academic scholars like J. Philippe Rushton, Daniel Vining Jr., Ralph Scott, Robert Gordon, Charles Murray, and other "professors of hate" to keep the perceived differences in race before the public (Horowitz, 1995; Miller, 1995). Therefore it becomes easy for right wing groups to support men like George Wallace, Jessie Helms, Ronald Reagan, George W. Bush, and others who advocate a return to Anglo Protestant values and traditions, and camouflaged racial rhetoric.

Those who produce curricula to instill loyalty, patriotism, and nationalism alongside the belief that certain groups are superior and others inferior will always feel the need to protect and defend Western civilization at the cost of belittling all non-Western civilizations and their histories. This ideology leads one to ponder the question: How long will we as black people continue to allow ourselves to be miseducated? How long will we allow our minds to be shaped by Eurocentric epistemologies? I wonder, how long will we allow our children to be passive learners and not challenge the textbooks that hold Eurocentric biases? When we do not, what higher purpose are we serving but that of our former slaveowners? African American children in the United States are educated to believe in the superiority of Anglo Protestant culture and compels them to become "good Negroes" and are taught to defend the very system that miseducates them. As parents we have a responsibility to encourage our children to become critical researchers and search out answers for their generation. When will we awake from our slumber and protest the fact that all of us—students, teachers, and parents alike—have been wounded and deprived by the horrible visitations of this nation's racial nightmare? When will we all move past the spaces called fear and move into the threatening spaces of alleged racial superiority and expose these hidden spaces to the light? As nurturers of the next generation of young minds, we can go forth upon the shoulders of Martin, Malcolm, Ella Baker, and others and bring our youth from the margins to the center. We can encourage them to dream ot new possibilities. We can sow seeds deep in the hearts of our youth, letting them know that they have worth, that they can create knowledge for themselves, and that they can bring about a change in our society

REFERENCES

Abzug, Robert B. (1970). The Influence of Garrisonian Abolitionists' Fear of Slave Violence on the Antislavery Argument, 1829–1840. *Journal of Negro History*, 55, 15–28.

Adams, Alice Dana (1973). *The Neglected Period of Antislavery in America, 1801–1831*. Corner House, Williamstown.

Adams, Francis D. & Sanders, Barry (2003). *Alienable Rights: The Exclusion of African Americans in a White Man's Land, 1619 2000*. HarperCollins, New York.

Alderman, Clifford Lindsey (1974). *Rum, Slaves and Molasses: TheStory of New England's Triangular Trade*. Bailey Brothers & Swinfen, Whitstable (UK).

Alexander, James W. (1854). *The Life of Archibald Alexander, D. D. the First Professor in the Theological Seminary at Princeton. New Jersey*. Charles Scribner's Sons, New York.

Allen, James; Als, Hilton; Lewis, John; & Litwack, Leon F. (2000). *Without Sanctuary: Lynching Photography in America*. Twin Palms, Santa Fe.

Allen, Theodore W. (1994). *The Invention of the White Race, Racial Oppression and Social Control*. Vol. I. Verso, New York.

Ammon, Harry (1971). *James Monroe: The Quest for National Identity*. Citadel Press, New York.

Andrews, Charles C. (1830). *History of the New York African Free Schools*. 1969 reprint, Negro University Press, New York.

Ani, Mirimba (1994). *Yurugu: An African-Centered Critique of European Cultural Thought and Behavior*. Africa World Press, Trenton.

Apple, Michael W. (1988). *Teachers and Texts: A Political Economy of Class and Gender Relations in Education*. Routledge, New York.

Apple, Michael W. (1990). *Ideology and Curriculum*. Routledge Kegan Paul, Boston.

Apple, Michael W. (1996a). Dominance and Dependency: Situating the Bell Curve Within the Conservative Restoration. Joe L. Kincheloe, Shirley R. Steinberg & Aaron D. Gresson III (Eds.) *Measured Lies: The Bell Curve Examined*. St. Martin's Press, New York, 51-69.

Apple, Michael W. (1996b). *Cultural Politics and Education*. Teachers College Press, New York.

Aptheker, Herbert (1943). *American Negro Slave Revolts*. Columbia University. 1993 reprint. Press, New York.

Aptheker, Herbert (1951). *A Documentary History of the Negro People in the United States: From the Colonial Times through the Civil War*. Vol. I. Citadel Press, New York.

Armour, Jody David (1997). *Negrophobia and Reasonable Racism*. New York University Press, New York.

Aronowitz, Stanley & DiFazio, William (1994). *The Jobless Future: Sci-tech and the Dogma of Work*. University of Minnesota Press, Minneapolis.

Aronowitz, Stanley, & DiFazio, William (1997). The New Knowledge Work. A. H. Halsey, Hugh Lauder, Phillip Brown, & Amy Stuart Wells (Eds.) *Education Culture, Economy, and Society*. Oxford University Press, New York, 193-206.

Artz, Lee, & Murphy, Bren Ortega (2000). *Cultural Hegemony in the United States*. Sage Publications, Thousand Oaks.

Asante, Molefi Kete (1987). *The Afrocentric Idea*. Temple University Press, Philadelphia.

Asante, Molefi Kete (1991). The Afrocentric Idea in Education. *Journal of Negro Education*, 60, 170-180.

Asante, Molefi Kete, & Abarry, Abu S. (Eds.) (1996). *African Intellectual Heritage, a Book of Sources*. Temple University Press, Philadelphia.

August, Eugene R. (Ed.) (1971). *Thomas Carlyle's the Nigger Question and John Stuart Mill's the Negro Problem*. Appleton Century-Crofts, New York.

Bancroft, Frederic (1959). *Slave Trading in the Old South*. Frederick Ungar, New York.

Banks, Curtis W. (1992). The Theoretical and Methodological Crisis of the Africentric Conception. *Journal of Negro Education*, 61, 262 272.

Barkan, Elazar (1990). *From Race to Ethnicity: Changing Concepts of Race in England and the United States Between the Two World Wars*. University of Michigan Press, Ann Arbor.

Barnett, S. A. (1988). *Biology and Freedom: An Essay on the Implications of Human Ethnology*. Cambridge University Press, New York.

Basler, Roy P. (Ed.). (1953). *The Collected Works of Abraham Lincoln*. Rutgers University Press, New Brunswick.

Bates, Thomas R. (1975). Gramsci and the Theory of Hegemony. Journal of History of Ideas, 36, 351–366.

Bederman, Gail (1995). *Manliness and Civilization: A Cultural History of Gender and Race in the United States, 1880–1917*. University of Chicago Press, Chicago.

Bennett, Lerone, Jr. (1969). *The Shaping of Black America: The Struggles and Triumphs of African-Americans, 1619–1990s*. Penguin Books, New York.

Bennett, William J. (1988). *Our Children and Our Country: Improving America's Schools and Affirming the Common Culture*. Simon & Schuster, New York.

Bercovitch, Sacvan (1978). *The American Jeremaid*. University of Wisconsin Press, Madison.

Bernasconi, Robert & Lott, Tommy L. (Eds.). (2000). *The Idea of Race*. Hackett Publishing Company Inc., Indianapolis.

Bernstein, Iver (1990). *The New York City Draft Riots: Their Significance for American Society and Policies in the Age of the Civil War*. Oxford University Press, Oxford.

Berry, Mary Frances (1971). *Black Resistance, White Law: A History of Constitutional Racism in America*. Penguin Press, New York.

Berwanger, Eugene H. (1967). *The Frontier against Slavery: Western Anti-Negro Prejudice and the Slavery Extension Controversy*. University of Illinois Press, Urbana.

Berwanger, Eugene H. (1972). Negrophobia in Northern Proslavery and Antislavery Thought, *Phylon*. 33, 266-275.

Bigelow, Bill (1995). Discovering Columbus: Rereading the Past. Bill Bigelow & Bob Peterson (Eds.) *Rethinking Columbus: the Next 500 Years*. Rethinking Schools, Milwaukee. 17-21.

Bigelow, Bill & Peteraon, Bob (2002). *Rethinking Globalization: Teaching for Justice in an Unjust World*. Rethinking Schools, Milwaukee.

Blacker, C. P. (1952). *Eugenics Galton and After*. Gerald Duckwoth, London, (UK).

Bluestone, Barry & Harrison, Bennett (1982). *The Deindustrialization of America: Plant Closings, Community Abandonment, and the Dismantling of Basic Industry*. Basic Books, NewYork.

Blum, William (2000). *Rogue Statbe: A Guide to the World's Only Superpower*. Common Courage Press, Monroe.

Bodo, John R. (1954). *The Protestant Clergy and Public Issues, 1812-1848*. Princeton University Press, Princeton.

Boesak, Allan (1990). *Black and Reformed: Apartheid, Liberation and the Calvinist Tradition*. Orbis Books, Maryknoll.

Bourdieu, Pierre (1977). Cultural Reproduction and Social Reproduction. JeromeKarabel & A. H. Halsey (Eds.) *Power and Ideology in Education*. Oxford University Press, New York, 487-510.

Bourdieu, Pierre (1986). The Forms of Cultural Capital. J. E. Richardson (Ed.) *Handbook of Theory of Research for the Sociology of Education*. Greenwood Press, Westport, 241-258.

Breggin, Peter, and Breggin, Ginger Ross (1998). *The War Against Children of Color: Psychiatry Targets Inner-City Youth*. Common Courage Press, Monroe.

Bremer, Francis J. (1976). *The Puritan Experiment: New England and Society from Bradford to Edward*. St. Martin's Press, New York.

Brickman, William W. (1982). *Educational Historiography: Tradition, Theory and Technique*. Emeritus, Cherry Hill.

Brodie, James Michael (1993). *Created Equal: The Lives and Ideas of Black American Innovators*. William Morrow, New York.

Brown, Phillip, & Lauder, Hugh (1997). Education, Globalization, and Economic Development." A. H. Halsey, Hugh Lauder, Phillip Brown, & Amy Stuart Wells (Eds.) *Education Culture, Economy, and Society*. Oxford University Press, New York, 172-192.

Bullard, Robert D. & Lee, Charles (1994). Racism and American Aparthied. Robert D. Bullard, J. Eugene Grigsby III, and Charles Lee (Eds.) *Residential Apartheid: The American Legacy*. Center for Afro-American Studies, University of California, Los Angeles. 1-16.

Burman, Stephen (1995). *The Black Progress Question: Explaining the African American Predicament*. Sage Publications, Thousand Oaks.

Callahan, Raymond E. (1962). *Education and the Cult of Efficiency: A Study of the Social Forces That Have Shaped the Administration of the Public Schools*. University of Chicago Press, Chicago.

Campbell, Penelope (1971). *Maryland in Africa: The Maryland State Colonization Society, 1831–1857*. University of Illinois Press, Urbana.

Card, David (1993). Trends in Relative Black-White Earnings Revisited. *AmericanEconomic Review*, 83, 85-91.

Carlson, Robert A. (1975). *The Quest for Conformity: Americanization Through Education*. John Wiley and Sons, New York.

Carruthers, Jacob H. (1994). Black Intellectuals and the Crisis in Black Education. Mwalimu J. Shujaa (Ed.) *Too Much Schooling, Too Little Education: A Paradox of Black Life in White Societies*. Africa World Press, Trenton. 37-55.

Carson, Clayborne; Garrow, David J.; Gill, Gearld; Harding, Vincent; & Hine, Darlene Clark (Eds.) (1991). *The Eyes on the Prize Civil Rights Reader: Documents, Speeches and First hand Accounts From the Black Freedom Struggle, 1954–1990*. Penguin Books, New York.

Carspecken, Phil Francis (1996). The Set Up: Crocodile Tears For the Poor. Joe L. Kincheloe, Shirley R. Steinberg, & Aaron D. Gresson III (Eds.) *Measured Lies: The Bell Curve Examined*. St. Martin's Press, New York, 109-125.

Castenell, Louis A., & Pinar, William F. (1993). *Understanding Curriculum as Racial Text: Representations of Identity and Difference in Education*. State University of New York Press, Albany.

Cell, John W. (1982). *The Highest Stage of White Supremacy: The Origins of Segregation in South Africa and the American South*. Cambridge University Press, Cambridge.

Chamblis, William (1995). Moral Panics and Racial Oppression. Darnell F. Hawkins (Ed.) *Ethnicity, Race and Crime: Perspectives Across Time and Place*. State University of New York Press, Albany.

Chidley, Joe (1995). The Heart of the Matter. Russell Jacoby & Naomi Glauberman (Eds.) *The Bell Curve Debate: History, Documents and Opinions*. Time Books, New York, 119-123.

Chomsky, Noam (1994). *Secrets, Lies and Democracy—Interviewed by David Barsamian*. Odonian Press, Tucson.

Chomsky, Noam (1996). *Class Warfare: Interviews With David Barsamian*. Common Courage Press, Monroe.

Chomsky, Noam (1999). *Profit Over People: Neoliberalism and Global Order*. Seven Stories Press, New York.

Chomsky, Noam (2000). *Chomsky on Miseducation*. Rowman & Littlefield Publishers, Inc. Lanham.

Chomsky, Noam (2002). *Understanding Power*. New Press, New York.

Cohen, William (1963). Thomas Jefferson and the Problem of Slavery. *Journal of American History*, 56, 503-526

Cole, Charles C., Jr. (1954). *The Social Ideas of Northern Evangelists*. Columbia University Press, New York.

Cone, James H. (1992). *A Black Theology of Liberation*. Orbis Books, Maryknoll.

Cooke, Jacob E. (1957). *Frederic Bancroft, Historian :The Colonization of American Negroes, 1801–1865*. University of Oklahoma Press, Norman.

Cornish, Dudley Taylor (1987). *The Sable Arm: Black Troops in the Union Army, 1861–1865*. University Press of Kansas, Lawrence.

Cralle, Richard K. (Ed.) (1855). *The Works of John C. Calhoun*. D. Appleton, New York.

Crawford, Alan (1980). *Thunder on the Right: The New Right and the Politics of Resentment*. Pantheon Books, New York.

Crook, Paul (1994). *Darwinism, War and History*. Cambridge University Press, Cambridge.

Curry, Leonard P. (1981). *Free Blacks in Urban America, 1800–1850: The Shadow of the Dream*. University of Chicago Press, Chicago.

Curti, Merle (1943). *The Growth of American Thought*. Harper & Brothers, New York.

Daniels, Roger (1990). *Coming to America: A History of Immigration and Ethnicity in American Life*. HarperCollins, New York.

Danzinger, Sheldon, and Gottschalk, Peter (Eds.) (1993). *Uneven Tides Rising: Inequality in America*. Russell Sage Foundation, New York.

Davis, Brion (1966). *The Problem of Slavery in Western Culture*. Oxford University Press, New York.

Davis, F. James (1991). *Who is Black? One Nation's Definition*. Pennsylvania State University Press, University Park.

Davis, Angela (2003). *Are Prisons Obsolete?* Seven Stories Press, New York.

Davis, Michael D. & Clark, Hunter R. (1992). *Thurgood Marshall Warrior at the Bar, Rebel on the Bench*. Birch Lane Press, New York.

Day, Beth (1974). *Sexual Life between Blacks and Whites: The Roots of Racism*. Thomas Y. Crowell, New York.

Dees, Morris (1996). *Gathering Storm—America's Militia Threat*. HarperCollins, New York.

Degler, Carl N. (1991). *In Search of Human Nature: the Decline and Revival of Darwinism in American Social Thought*. Oxford University Press, New York.

Dempsey, Van, & Noblit, George (1996). Cultural Ignorance and School Desegregation: A Community Narrative. Mwalimu J. Shujaa (Ed.) *Beyond Desegregation: The Politics of Quality in African American Schooling*. Corwin Press, Thousand Oaks, 115-137.

Dillon, Merton (1959). The Failure of American Aboloitionists. *Journal of Southern History*. 25, 159-177.

Doherty, Robert W. (1962). Status Anxiety and American Reform Some Alternatives. *American Quarterly*, 19, 329-226.

Domhoff, G. William (1998). *Who Rules America? Power and Politics in the Year 2000* Mayfield, Mountain View.

Donnan, Elizabeth (1969). *Documents Illustrative of the History of the Slave Trade*. Vol. IV. Octagon Books, New York.

Drake, St. Clair (1990). *Black Folk Here and There*, Vols. I & II. University of California Press, Los Angeles.

Drake, Thomas E. (1950). *Quakers and Slavery in America*. Yale University Press, Gloucester.

Du Bois, W. E. B. (1963). *The ABC of Color*. International Publishers, New York.

Du Bois, W. E. B. (1973). *The Education of Black People: Ten Critiques, 1906–1960*, Herbert Aptheker (Ed.) Monthly Review Press, New York.

Du Bois, W. E. b. (1997). *The Souls of Black Folks*. David Blight & Robert Gooding Williams (Eds.). Bedford Books, Boston.

Dudley, Edward, and Novak, Maximillian E. (Eds.) (1972). *The Wild Man Within: An Image in Western Thought from the Renaissance to Romanticism*. University of Pittsburgh Press, Pittsburgh.

Dumond, Dwight L. (Ed.) (1939). *Letters of James Gillespie Birney, 1831–1857*. Vol. I. D. Appleton–Century, New York.

Duster, Troy (1995). Bell Curve—Symposium. *Contemporary Sociology*, 24, 158-161.

Dyer, Thomas G. (1980). *Theodore Roosevelt and the Idea of Race*. Louisiana State University Press, Baton Rouge.

East, Edward M. (1929). *Heredity and Human Affairs*. Charles Scribner's Sons, New York.

Easterbrook, Gregg (1995). Blacktop Basketball and the Bell Curve. Russell Jacoby & Naomi Glauberman (Eds.) *The Bell Curve Debate: History, Documents and Opinions*. Time Books, New York. 30-43.

Edsall, Thomas Byrne (1984). *The New Politics of Inequality*. W. W. Norton, New York.

Edsall, Thomas Byrne & Edsall, Mary D. (1991). *Chain Reaction: The Impact of Race, Rights, and Taxes on American Politics*. W. W. Norton, New York.

Edwards, June (1998). *Opposing Censorship in the Public Schools: Religion, Morality and Literature*. Lawrence Erlbaum Associates, Mahwah.

Egerton, Douglas R. (1993). *Gabriel's Rebellion: The Virginia Slave Conspiracies of 1800–1802*. University of North Carolina Press, Chapel Hill.

Elben, Jack (1972). Growth of the Black Population in Antebellum America, 1820–1860. *Population Studies*. 26, 273-289.

Fanon, Franz (1963). *The Wretched of the Earth*. Grove Press, New York.

Feagin, Joe R. (1991). The Continuing Significance of Race: Antiblack Discrimination in Public Places. *American Sociological Review*, 56, 101-116.

Feagin, Joe R., Vera, Hernan & Imani, Nikitah (1996). *The Agony of Education: Black Students at White Universities and Colleges*. Routledge, New York.

Feagin, Joe R. (2001). *Racist America: Roots, Current Realities and Future Reparations*. Routledge, New York.

Feagin, Joe R. & O'Brien, Eileen (2003). *White Men on Race: Power, Privilege, and the Shaping of Cultural Consciousness*. Beacon Press, Boston.

Feldstein, Stanley (Ed.) (1972). *The Poisoned Tongue: A* Documentary History of American Racism and Prejudice. William Morrow, New York.

Ferguson, Ann Arnett (2000). *Bad Boys: Public Schools in the Making of Black Masculinity*. University of Michigan Press, Ann Arbor.

Fischer, David Hackett (1965). *The Revolution of American Conservatism: The Federalist Party in the Era of Jeffersonian Democracy*. Harper & Row, New York.

Foner, Eric (1965). Politics and Prejudice: The Free Soil Party and the Negro, 1849–1852, *Journal of Negro History*, 50, 239-256.

Foster, Charles I. (1953). Colonization of Free Negroes in Liberia. 1816–1835, *Journal of Negro History*, 38, 41-66.

Foster, Michele (1997). *Black Teachers on Teaching*. New Press, New York.

Fox, Early Lee (1919). *The American Colonization Society, 1817-1830*. John Hopkins University Press, Baltimore.

Franklin, John Hope (1989). *Race and History: Selected Essays, 1938–1988*. Louisiana State University Press, Baton Rouge.

Franklin, John Hope, & Moss, Alfred A., Jr. (2000). *From Slavery to Freedom: A History of Negro Americans*. 8th Edition, McGraw-Hill, New York.

Fredrickson, George M (1971). *The Black Image in the White Mind: The Debate on Afro-American Character and Destiny, 1817– 1914*. Wesleyan University Press, Hanover.

Fredrickson, George M. (1975). A Man but Not a Brother: Abraham Lincoln and Racial Equality. *Journal of Southern History*, 41, 39- 58.

Fredrickson, George M. (1981). *White Supremacy: A Comparative Study in American and South African History*. Oxford University Press, New York.

Fredrickson, George M. (1988). *The Arrogance of Race: Historical Perspectives on Slavery, Racism, and Social Inequality*. Wesleyan University Press, Hanover.

Freeden, Michael (1979). Eugenics and Progressive Thought: A Study in Ideological Affinity. *Historical Journal*, 23, 645-671.

Freehling, Allison G. (1982). *Drift toward Dissolution: The Virginia Slave Debate of 1831-1832*. Louisiana State University Press, Baton Rouge.

Frehrenbacher, Don E. (1988). Slavery, the Framers, and the Living Constitution. Robert Goldwin & Art Kaufman (Eds.) *Slavery and Its Consequences: The Constitution, Equality and Race*. American Enterprise Institute for Public Policy Research, Washington, D.C.

Freire, Paulo (1970). *Pedagogy of the Opressessed*. New Revised 20th Anniversary Edition. (1999). Continuum, New York.

Freire, Paulo (1985). *The Politics of Education: Culture Power and Liberation*. Bergin & Garvey Publishers, Inc., South Hadley.

Friedman, Lawrence J. (1970). *The White Savage: Racial Fantasies in the Postbellum South*. Prentice-Hall, Englewood Cliff.

Friedman, Lawrence J. (1975). *Inventors of the Promised Land*. Alfred A. Knopf, New York.

Gales, Joseph (1834). Annals of theCongress of the United States: The Debates and Proceedings in the Papers and Public Documents, and All the Laws of a Public Nature, with a Copious *Index*. Gales & Seaton, Washington, D.C.

Gans, Herbert J. (1995). *The War against the Poor: The Underclass and Antipoverty Policy*. Basic Books, New York.

Gold, Howard J. (1992). *Hollow Mandates, American Public Opinions and the Conservative Shift*. Westview Press, Boulder.

Gomez, Jewelle (1993). Black Women Heroes: Here's Reality, Where's the Fiction? Louis A. Castenell, Jr. & William F. Pinar (Eds.) *Understanding Curriculum as Racial Text: Representations of Identity and Difference in Education*. New York University Press, Albany.

Gossett, Thomas F. (1963). *Race, the History of an Idea in America*. Southern Methodist University Press, Dallas.

Gould, Stephen Jay, (1978). Flaws in A Victorian Veil. *Natural History*, 87, 22-23, 26.

Gould, Stephen Jay, (1981). *The Mismeasure of Man*. W. W. Norton, New York.

Grant, Madison (1916). *The Passing of the Great Race, or the Racial Basis of European History*. Charles Scribner's Sons, New York.

Grant, Madison (1933). *The Conquest of a Continent, or the Expansion of Races In America*. Charles Scribner's Sons, New York.

Grant, Madison & Davison, Stewart (Eds.) (1928). *The Founders of the Republic on Immigration, Naturalization and Aliens*. Charles Scribner's Sons, New York.

Gray, Herman (1995). *Watching Race: Television and the Struggle for "Blackness."* University of Minnesota Press, Minneapolis.

Greene, Jack P. (Ed.) (1965). *The Diary of Colonel Landon Carter of Sabine Hall, 1752-1788*. University Press of Virginia, Charlottesville.

Greene, Lorenzo Johnston (1942). *The Negro in Colonial New England, 1620-1776*. Columbia University Press, New York.

Greider, William (1992). *Who Will Tell the People: The Betrayal of American Democracy*. Simon & Schuster, New York.

Griffin, Clifford S. (1960). *Their Brother's Keeper: Moral Stewardship in the United States 1800–1865*. Rutgers University Press, New Brunswick.

Grigsby, William (1990). Housing Finance and Subsidies in the United States. *Urban Studies*, 27, 831-845.

Groves, C. P. (1948). *The Planting of Christianity in Africa,* Vol. I. Lutterworth. 1964 reprint, Press, London.

Haberman, Martin (1995). *Star Teachers of Children in Poverty*. Kappa Delta Pi, West Lafayette.

Hall, Stuart (1977). Culture, the Media and Ideological Effect. James Curran, Michael Gurevitch & Jane Woollacott (Eds.) *Mass Communication and Society*. Sage Publications, Beverly Hills.

Hall, Stuart (1997). *Representation: Cultural Representations and Signifying Practices*. Sage Publications, Thousand Oaks.

Handler, Joel F. & Hansenfeld, Yeheshel (1997). *We the Poor People: Work, Poverty, and Welfare*. Yale University Press, New Haven.

Haney Lopez, Ian F. (1996). *White by Law: The Legal Construction of Race*. New York University Press, New York.

Hannaford, Ivan (1996). *Race: The History of an Idea in the West*. John Hopkins University Press, Baltimore.

Harding, Jeremy (1993). *The Fate of Africa: Trial by Fire*. Simon & Schuster, New York.

Harding, Vincent (1981). *There Is a River: The Black Struggle for Freedom in America*. Harcourt Brace Jovanovich, San Diego.

Harding, Vincent (1990). *Hope and History: Why We Must Share the Story of the Movement*. Orbis Books, Maryknoll.

Harlow, Ralph Volney (1939). *Gerrit Smith: Philanthropist and Reformer*. Henry Holt, New York.

Harris, Cherl I. (1993). Whiteness as Property. *Harvard Law Review*, 106, 1710-1791.

Hasian, Marouf A., Jr. (1996). *The Rhetoric of Eugenics in Anglo- American Thought*. University of Georgia Press, Athens.

Hawkins, Mike (1997). *Social Darwinism in European and American Thought: Nature as Model and Nature as Threat*. Cambridge University Press, Cambridge.

Haymes, Stephen Nathan (1995). *Race, Culture and the City: A Pedagogy for Black Urban Struggle*. State University of New York Press, New York.

Hennessy, James Pope (1968). *Sins of the Fathers: A Study of the Atlantic Slave Traders, 1441–1807*. Alfred A. Knopf, New York.

Henry, William Writ (1891). *Patrick Henry: Life Correspondence and Speeches*. Vol. I. Charles Scribner's Sons, New York.

Herman, Edward & Chomsky, Noam (1988). *Manufacturing Consent: The Politica Economy of the Mass Media*. Pantheon Books, New York.

Higginbotham, Leon, Jr. (1978*).* *In the Matter of Color, Race and the American Legal Process: The Colonial Period*. Oxford University Press, New York.

Higginbotham, Leon, Jr. (1996). *Shades of Freedom: Racial Politics* and Presumptions of the American Legal Process. Oxford University Press, New York.

Hirsch, E. D. (1988). *Cultural Literacy: What Every American Needs to Know*.Vintage Books, New York.

Hoare, Quintin & Smith, Geoffrey Nowell (Eds.) (1971). *Selections* From the Prison Notebooks of Antonio Gramsci. International Publishers, New York.

Hoffer, Thomas Greeley, Andrew & Colman, James S. (1985). Achievement Growth in Public and Catholic Schools. *Sociology of Education*, 58, 74-97.

Hofstadter, Richard (1944). *Social Darwinism in American Thought.* 1992 reprint, Beacon Press, Boston.

Hood, Robert E. (1994). *Begrimed and Black. Christian Traditions on Blacks and Blackness.* Fortress Press, Minneapolis.

hooks, bell (1994). *Teaching to Transgress: Education as the Practice of Freedom.* Routledge, New York.

hooks, bell (2000). *Where We Stand: Class Matters.* Routledge, New York.

Horseman, Reginald (1981). *Race and Manifest Destiny: The Origins of American Racial Anglo-Saxonism.* Harvard University Press, Cambridge.

Howard, Gary R. (1999). *We Can't Teach What We Don't Know: White Teachers, Multiracial Schools.* Teachers College Press. Columbia University, New York.

Hurd, John Codman (1858). *The Law of Freedom and Bondage in the United States,* Vols. I & II. Little, Brown & Company, Boston.

Ingle, Dwight J. (1973). *Who Should Have Children? An Environmental and Genetic Approach.* Bobbs-Merrill, Indianapolis.

Jackson, Kenneth (1985). *The Crabgrass Frontier: The Suburbanization of the United States.* Oxford University Press, New York.

Jacobs, Donald (1993). *Courage and Conscience: Black and White Abolitionists in Boston.* Indiana University Press, Bloomington.

Jarvis, Edward (1844). Insanity Among the Coloured Population of the Free States. *American Journal of the Medical Sciences*, 7, No. 13, 71-83.

Jefferson, Thomas (1787). *Notes on the State of Virginia.*William Peden. (Ed.) 1992 University of North Carolina Press, Chapel Hill.

Jennings, Francis (1975). *The Invasion of America: Indians, Colonialism, and the Cant of Conquest.* W. W. Norton, New York.

Jewell, Sue K. (1993). *From Mammie to Miss America and Beyond Cultural Images and the Shaping of U.S. Policy.* Routledge, New York.

Johnson, Tammy, Boydon, Jennifer Emiko, & Pittz, William J. (Eds.) (2001). *Racial Profiling and Punishment in U.S. Public Schools: How Zero Tolerance Policies and High Stakes Testing Subvert Academic Excellence and Racial Equity.* 5-25. Oakland, California, Bridging the Gap Between Analysis and Action Applied Research Center.

Johnson, Thomas H. & Miller, Perry (1938). *The Puritans.* American Book Company, New York.

Johnston, James Hugo (1970). *Race Relations in Virginia and Miscegenation in the South, 1776–1860.* University of Massachusetts Press, Amherst.

Jordan, Winthrop D. (1968). *White Over Black: American Attitudes Towards the Negro, 1550–1812.* W. W. Norton, New York.

Joshi, S. I. (Ed.) (1999). *Documents of American Prejudice: An Anthology of Writings on Race from Thomas Jefferson to David Duke.* Basic Books, New York.

Kamin. Leon J. (1995). The Pioneers of I.O. Testing. Russell Jacoby & Naomi Glauberman (Eds.) *The Bell Curve Debate: History, Documents and Opinions.* Time Books, New York. 476-509.

Karoly, Lynn A. & Burtless, Gary (1995). Demographic Change, Rising Earnings, Inequality and the Distribution of Personal Well-Being, 1959–1989. *Demography*, 32, 379-405.

Kates, Don B. (1968). Abolition, Deportation, Integration: Attitudes Toward Slavery in the Early Republic. *Journal of Negro History*, 53, 33-47

Katz, Michael (1971). *School Reform: Past and Present*. Little, Brown & Company, Boston.

Keddie, Nell (1971). Classroom Knowledge. Michael F. D. Young (Ed.) *Knowledge and Control: New Directions For the Sociology of Education*. Collier-Macmillan, London.

Kelley, Robin D. G. (1997). *Yo' Mama's Disfunktional: Fighting the Culture Wars in Urban America*. Beacon Press, Boston.

Kerber, Linda (1967) Abolitionists and Amalgamators: The New York City Race Riots of 1834, *New York History*, 48, 28-39.

Kincheloe, Joe L. (1993). The Politics of Race, History, and Curriculum. Louis A. Castenell, Jr. & William F. Pinar (Eds.). *Understanding Curriculum as Racial Text: Representations of Identity and Difference in Education*. New York University Press, Albany.

Kincheloe, Joe L. (1995). *Toil and Trouble: Good Work, Smart Workers, and the Integration of Academic and Vocational Education*. Peter Lang, New York.

Kincheloe, Joe L. & Steinberg, Shirley R. (1996). Who Said It Can't Happen Here. Joe L. Kincheloe, Shirley R. Steinberg & Aaron D. Gresson III (Eds.) *Measured Lies. The Bell Curve Examined*. St. Martin's Press, New York. 3-47.

Kincheloe, Joe L. & Steinberg, Shirley R. (1997). *Changing Multiculturalism*. Temple University Press, Philadelphia.

Kincheloe, Joe L. (1999). *The Stigma of Genius: Einstein, Consciousness, and Education*. Peter Lang, New York.

King, Joyce E. (1996). Bad Luck, Bad Blood, Bad Faith: Ideological Hegemony and theOppressive Language of Hoodoo Science. Joe L. Kincheloe, Shirley R. Steinberg and Aaron D. Gresson III (Eds.) *Measured Lies: The Bell Curve Examined*. St. Martin's Press, New York, 177-192.

Kliebard, Herbert (1986). *The Struggle for the American Curriculum, 1893–1958*. Routledge & Kegan Paul, Boston.

Knapp, Peter; Kronick, Jane C. & Marks, R. Williams (1996). *The Assault on Equality*. Praeger, Westport.

Kohn, Hans (1957). *American Nationalism: An Interpretative Essay*. Macmillan, New York.

Kozol, Jonathan (1991). *Savage Inequalities, Children in America's Schools*. Harper Perennial, New York.

Labaree, Leonard W. (Ed.) (1961). *The Papers of Benjamin Franklin*, Vol. IV. Yale University Press, New Haven.

Lacy, Dan (1972). *The White Use of Blacks in America*. Atheneum, New York.

Ladson-Billings, Gloria (1994). *The Dreammakers: Successful Teachers of African American Children*. Jossey-Bass, San Francisco.

Lane, Charles (1995). Tainted Sources. Russell Jacoby & Namoi Glauberman (Eds.) *The Bell Curve Debate: History, Documents and Opinions*. Times Books, New York. 125-139.

Larson, Edward J. (1991). Belated Progress: The Enactment of Eugenic Legislation in Georgia. *Journal of the History of Medicine and Allied Science*, 46, 44-64.

Larson, Edward J. (1995). *Sex, Race, and Science: Eugenics in the Deep South*. Johns Hopkins University Press, Baltimore.

Lawsen, Ellen Nickenzie & Merrill, Marlene D. (1984). *The Three Sarahs: Documents of Antebellum College Women*. Edwin Mellen Press, New York.

Lee, Carol D.; Lomotey, Kofi & Shujaa, Mwalimu J. (1990). How Shall We Sing Our Scared Song in a Strange Land? The Delimma of Double Consciousness and the Complexities of an African- Centered Pedagogy. *Journal of Education*, 172, 45–61.

Leonard, Jonathan S. (1987). The Interaction of Residential Segregation and Employment Discrimination. *Journal of Urban Economics*, 21, 323-346.

Levy, Frank (1987). *Dollars and Dreams: The Changing American Income Distribution*. Russell Sage Foundation for the National Committee for Research on the 1980 Census, New York.

Lewontin, R. C. (1991). *Biology as Ideology: the Doctrine of DNA*. Harper Perennial, New York.

Lifton, Robert J. (1986). *The Nazi Doctors: Medical Killing and the Psychology of Genocide*. Basic Books, New York.

Lipsitz, George (1998). *The Possessive Investment in Whiteness: How White People Profit From Identity Politics*. Temple University Press, Philadelphia.

Litwack, Leon F. (1958). The Federal Government and the Free Negro, 1790–1860. *Journal of Negro History*, 43, 261-278

Litwack, Leon F. (1961). *North of Slavery: The Negro in the Free States, 1790–1860*. University of Chicago Press, Chicago.

Litwack, Leon F. (1980). *Been in the Storm so Long: The Aftermath of Slavery*. Vintage Books, New York.

Loewen, James W. (1995). *Lies My Teacher Told Me: Everything Your American History Textbook Got Wrong*. New Press, New York.

Logan, Rayford W. (1943). Some New Interpretations of the Colonization Movement. *Phylon*. 4, 328-334.

Logan, Rayford W. (1954). *The Betrayal of the Negro: From Rutherford B. Hayes to Woodrow Wilson*. 1997 reprint, Da Capo Press, New York.

Lovejoy, Arthur (1966). *The Great Chain of Being*. Harvard University Press, Cambridge.

Lugg, Catherine (1996). Attacking Affirmative Action: Social Darwinism as Public Policy. Joe L. Kincheloe, Shirley R. Steinberg & Aaron D. Gresson III (Eds.), *Measured Lies: The Bell Curve Examined*. St. Martin's Press, New York. 367-378.

Mabee, Carlton (1979). *Black Education in New York State from Colonial to Modern Times*. Syracuse University Press, Syracuse.

Macedo, Donaldo (1994). *Literacies of Power: What Americans Are Not Allowed to Know*. Westview Press, Boulder.

Macedo, Donaldo & Bartolome, Lilia I. (1999). *Dancing With Bigotry: Beyond the Politics of Tolerance*. St. Martin's Press, New York.

Marable, Manning (1978). Thoughts on the Political Economy of the New South Since the Civil Rights Movement. *Radical America*. 12, 9-21.

Marable, Manning (1983). *How Capitalism Underdeveloped Black America*. South End Press, Boston.

Martin, Don T. (1989). A Critique of the Concept of Work and Education in the School Reform Reports. Christine M. Shea; Ernest Kahane, & Peter Sola (Eds.) *The New Servants of Power: A Critique of the 1980s School Reform Movement*. Greenwood Press, New York.

Marty, Martin E. (1970). *The Righteous Empire: The Protestant Experience in America*. Dial Press, New York.

Massy, Douglass & Denton, Nancy A. (1993). *American Apartheid: Segregation and the Making of the Underclass*. Harvard University Press, Cambridge.

Mathews, Donald G. (1965). Methodist Mission to the Slaves, 1829- 1844. *Journal of American History*, 51, 615-631.

Mattern, David B. (Ed.) (1991). *The Papers of James Madison, Vol. XVII, 1778–1798*. University of Virginia Press, Charlottesville.

Mazrui, Ali A. (1986). *The Africans*. Little, Brown & Company, Boston.

Mauer, Marc (1999). *Race to Incarcerate: The Sentencing Project*. New Press, New York.

McCarthy, Cameron (1993). Multicultural Approaches to Racial Inequality in the United States. Louis A. Castenell, Jr. & William F. Pinar (Eds.). *Understanding Curriculum as Racial Text: Representations of Identity and Differences in Education*. State University of New York Press, Albany.

McIntyre, Charshee C. L. (1984). Criminalizing a Race: Free Blacks During Slavery. Kayode Publications, Ltd., New York

McManus, Edgar J. (1966). *A History of Negro Slavery in New York*. Syracuse University Press, Syracuse.

McNeil, Linda M. (2000). *Contradictions of School Reform: Educational Costs of Standardized Testing*. Routledge, New York.

McNeil, Linda & Valenzuela, Angela (2001). The Harmful Impact of the TAAS System of Testing in Texas: Beneath the Accountability Rhetoric. Gary Orfield & Mindy L. Kornhaber (Eds.). *Raising Standards or Raising Barriers: Inequality and High-Stakes Testing in Public Education*. A Century Foundation Book, New York

Mclaren, Peter (1994). *Life in Schools: An Introduction to Critical Pedagogy in the Foundations of Education*. Longman, New York.

Mclintyre, Charshee C. L. (1984). *Criminalizing a Race: Free Blacks during Slavery*. Kayode Publications, New York.

McMillen, Neil R. (1990). *Dark Joubrney: Black Mississippians in the Age of Jim Crow*. University of Illinois Press, Urbana.

McPherson, James (1965). *The Negro's Civil War: How American Blacks Felt and Acted During the War for the Union*. 1991 reprint, Ballantine Books, New York.

McPherson, James, & Katz, William L. (Eds.) (1969). *The Anti- Slavery Crusade in America*. Arno Press, New York.

Memmi, Albert (1991). *The Colonizer and the Colonized*. Beacon Press, Boston.

Meir, Deborah & Wood, George (2004). *How the no Child Left Behind Act is Damaging Our Children and Our Schools*. Beacon Press, Boston.

Meyer, Stephen Grant (2000). *As Long as They Don't Move Next Door: Segregation and the Racial Conflict in American*. Neighborhoods. Rowman & Littlefield, Lanham.

Miller, Adam (1995). Professors of Hate. Russell Jacoby and Naomi Glauberman (Eds.) *The Bell Curve Debate: History, Documents and Opinions*. Times Books, New York. 162-178.

Miller, Hay (1993). *This Little Light of Mine: Fannie Lou Hamer*. Dutton Books, New York.

Miller, Jerome G. (1996). *Search and Destroy: African American Males in the Criminal Justice System*. Cambridge University Press, New York.

Mills, C. Wright (1956). *The Power Elite*. Oxford University Press, New York.

Mohl, Raymond A. (1970). Education as Social Control in New York City, 1784-1825 *New York History*, 51, 219-237.

Moore, Barrington (1966). *Social Origins of Dictatorship and Democracy: Order and Peasant in the Making of the Modern World*. Beacon Press, Boston.

Moore, Steven & Stansel, Dean (1995). *Ending Corporate Welfare as We Know It*. Cato Institute, draft report, March 6.

Morgan, Edmund S. (1975). *American Slavery, American Freedom: The Ordeal of Colonial Virginia*. W. W. Norton, New York.

Morias, Herbert M. (1967). *History of the Negro in Medicine*. Publishers Co., New York.

Morris, Aldon (1993). Centuries of Black Protest: Its Significance for America and the World. Herbert Hill & James E. Jones, Jr. (Eds.) *Race in America: the Struggle for Equality*. University of Wisconsin Press, Madison. 19-69.

Moses, Wilson Jeremiah (1989). *Alexander Crummell: A Study o Civilization and Discontent*. University of Massachusetts Amherst.

Mudimbe, V. Y. (1988). *The Invention of Africa: Gnosis, bPhilosophy, and the Order of Knowledge*. Indiana University Press, Bloomington.

Mullane, Deridre (Ed.) (1993). *Crossing Danger Water: Three Hundred Years of African American Writing*. Anchor Books, New York.

Munford, Clarence J. (1996). *Race and Reparations: A Black Perspective for the 21st Century*. Africa World Press, Trenton.

Murray, Andrew E. (1966). *Presbyterians and the Negro: A History*. Presbyterian Historical Society, Philadelphia.

Murray, Charles (1995). The Bell Curve and Its Critics. *Commentary*, 99, 23-30.

Murray, Charles & Herrnstein, Richard (1994). Race, Genes, and I.Q.—An Apologia. *The New Republic*, 211, 9-37.

Nagel, Paul (1971). *This Scared Trust: American Nationality, 1798- 1898*. Oxford University Press, New York.

Nash, Gary B. (1992). *Red, White and Black: The Peoples of Early North America*. Prentice Hall, Englewood Cliffs.

Nicolay, John G. & Hay, John (Eds.) (1894). *Abraham Linco;ln —Complete Works*, Vol. I. Century Company, New York.

Noguera, Pedro (2003). *City Schools and the American Dream: Reclaiming the Promise of Public Education*. Teachers College Press, New York.

Norton, Mary Beth (1991). *A People and a Nation: a History of the United States*. Houghton Mifflin, Boston.

Nye, Russel B. (1966). *This Almost Chosen People: Essays in the History of American Ideas*. Michigan State University Press, East Lansing.

Ohanian, Susan (1999). *One Size Fits Few: The Folly of Educational Standards*. Heineann, Portsmouth.

Oliver, Mary Beth & Armstrong, G. Blake (1998). The Color of Crime: Perceptions of Caucasians and African Americans' Involvement in Crime. Mark Fishman and Gray Cavender (Eds.) *Entertaining Crime: Television Reality Programs*. Aldine De Gruyter, New York.

Omi, Michael & Winant, Howard (1983). By the Rivers of Babylon: Race in the United States. *Socialist Review*. 13, 31-65.

Omi, Michael, & Winant, Howard (1994). *Racial Formation in the United States from the 1960 to the 1990s*. Routledge, New York.

Orfield, Gary (1993). School Desegregation After Two Generations: Race, Schools, and Opportunity in Urban Society. Herbert Hill & James E. Jones (Eds.) *Race in America: the Struggle for Equality*. University of Wisconsin Press, Madison. 234-262.

Orfield, Gary & Eaton, Susan E. (Eds.). (1996a). *Dismantling Desegregation: the Quiet Reversal of Brown v. Board of Education*. The New Press, New York.

Orfield, Gary & Kornhaber, Mindy L. (Eds.) (2001). *Raising Standards or Raising Barriers? Inequality and High-Stakes Testing in Public Education*. The Century Foundation Press, New York.

Orfield, Gary & Lee, Chungmei (2005). *Why Segregation Matters: Poverty and Educational Inequality*. Harvard University, The Civil Rights Project.

O'Reilly, Kenneth (1995). *Nixon's Piano: Presidents and Racial Politics from Washington to Clinton*. Free Press, New York.

Oshinsky, David M. (1996). *Worse Than Slavery: Parchman Farm and the Ordeal of Jim Crow Justice*. Free Press, New York.

Osofsky, Gilbert (1967). *The Burden of Race: A Documentary History of Negro-White Relations in America*. Harper & Row, New York.

Pagano, Jo Anne (1996). Speculation Based on Speculation: The Problem of the Bell Curve and the Question of Schooling. Joe L. Kincheloe, Shirley R. Steinberg & Aaron D. Gresson III (Eds.) *Measured Lies: The Bell Curve Examined*. St. Martin's Press, New York, 193–202.

Pakenham, Thomas (1991). *The Scramble for Africa: The White Man's Conquest of the Dark Continent from 1876 to 1912*. Random House, New York,

Parenti, Christian (1999). *Lockdown America: Police and Prisons in the Age of Crisis*. Verso Press, London.

Paterson, Orlando (1996). *Rituals of Blood: Consequences of Slavery in Two American Centuries*. Basic Civitas Books, New York.

Paul, Diane (1984). Eugenics and the Left. *Journal of the History of Ideas*, 45, 567–590.

Pease, Jane & Pease, William (1974). *They Who Would Be Free: Black's Search for Freedom, 1830–1861*. Atheneum, New Yotk.

Perlmutter, Philip (1992). *Divided We Fall: A History of Ethnic, Religious, and Racial Prejudice in America*. Iowa State University Press, Ames.

Phillips, Kevin P. (1982). *Post-Conservative America: People, Politics and Ideology in a Time of Crisis*. Random House, New York.

Phillips, Kevin P. (1990). *The Politics of Rich and Poor: Wealth and the American Electorate in the Reagan Aftermath*. Random House, New York.

Pieterse, Jan Nederveen (1992). *White on Black: Images of Africa and Blacks in Western Popular Culture*. Yale University Press, New Haven.

Pinar, William F. (1995). The Curriculum: What Are the Basics and Are We Teaching Them. Joe L. Kincheloe and Shirley Steinberg (Eds.), *Thirteen Questions: Reframing Education's Conversation*. Peter Lang, New York.

Pinar, William F.; Reynolds, William M.; Slattery, Patrick & Taubman, Peter M. (1995). *Understanding Curriculum*. Peter Lang, New York.

Pinar, William F. (2001). *The Gender of Racial Politics and Violence in America*. Peter Lang, New York.

Pinkney, Alphonso (1984). *The Myth of Black Progress*. Cambridge University Press, Cambridge.

Plimmer, Charlotte & Plimmer, Denis (1973). *Slavery: Anglo- American Involvement*. Harper & Row, New York.

Popenoe, Paul, & Johnson, Roswell H. (1935). *Applied Eugenics*. Macmillan, New York.

Powell, Thomas (1992). *The Persistence of Racism in America*. Rowman & Littlefield Publishers, Inc., Boston.

Quadagno, Jill (1994). *The Color of Welfare: How Racism Undermined the War on Poverty*. Oxford University Press, New York.

Ratner, Lorman (1968). *Powder Keg: Northern Opposition to the Anti-Slavery Movement, 1831-1840*. Basic Books, New York.

Reed, Alfred C. (1913). Immigration and the Public Health. *Popular Science Monthly*, 83, 313–338.

Reed, James (1978). *The Birth Control Movement in American Society: From Private Vice to Public Virtue*. Princeton University Press, Princeton.

Reilly, Philip R. (1991). *The Surgical Solution: A History of Involuntary Sterilization in the United States*. John Hopkins University Press, Baltimore.

Ratteray, Joan Davis (1994). The Search for Access and Content in the Education of African Americans. Mwalimu J. Shujaa (Ed.) *Too Much Schooling Too Little Education: A Paradox of Black Life in' White Societies*. Africa World Press, Trenton, 123–141.

Reich, Robert B. (1992). *The Work of Nations: Preparing Ourselves for 21st-Century Capitalism*. Vintage Books, New York.

Rieder, Jonathan 1985. *The Jews and Italians Against Liberalism*. New York, Columbia University Press.

Richards, Leonard L. (1970. *Gentleman of Property and Standing: Anti-Abolitionist Mobs in Jacksonian America*. Oxford University Press, New York

Ripley, C. Peter (1991). *The Black Abolitionist Papers*, Vols. III & IV. University of North Carolina Press, Chapel Hill.

Ripley, C. Peter (1993). *Witness for Freedom: African American Voices on Race, Slavery, and Emancipation*. University of North Carolina Press, Chapel Hill.

Robert, Joseph Clarke (1941). *The Road From Monticello: A Study of the Virginia Slavery Debate of 1832*. Duke University Press, Durham.

Roberts, Dorothy (1997). *Killing the Black Body: Race, Reproduction, and the Meaning of Liberty*. Pantheon Books, New York.

Robinson, Henry S. (1969). Some Aspects of the Free Negro Population of Washington D.C., 1800–1862. *Maryland Historical Magazine*, 64, 43–64.

Robinson, Randall (2000). *The Debt: What America Owes to Blacks*. Plume Books, New York.

Rodney, Walter (1972). *How Europe Underdeveloped Africa*. Howard University Press, Washington, D.C.

Roediger, David R. (1991). The Wages of Whiteness: Race and the Making of the American Working Class. Verso Press, London, UK.

Rogers, Joel Augustus (1967). *Sex and Race: Negro-Caucasian Mixing in All Ages and All Lands*, Vol. I. Helga M. Rodgers Publications, New York.

Rose, Peter I. (1964). *They and We: Racial and Ethnic Relations in the United States.* McGraw-Hill, New York.

Rosen, Bruce (1972). Abolition and Colonization: The Years of Conflict, 1820–1834. *Phylon*, 33, 177–192.

Rothman, David J. (1971). *The Discovery of the Asylum: Social Order And Disorder in the New Republic.* Little, Brown & Company, Boston.

Rowan, Carl (1996). *The Coming Race War in America: A Wake Up Call.* Little, Brown & Company, Boston.

Ruchames, Louis (Ed.) (1969). *Racial Thought in America: From the Puritans to Abraham Lincoln: A Documentary History,* Vol. I. University of Massachusetts Press, Amherst.

Runcie, John (1972). Hunting the Nigs in Philadelphia: The Race Riot of August 1834. *Pennsylvania History*, 39, 187–218.

Schor, Elisbeth B. & Schor, Daniel (1988). *Within Our Reach: Breaking the Cycle of Disadvantage.* Anchor/Doubleday, New York.

Schor, Julit B. (1991). *The Overworked American: The Unexpected Decline of Leisure.* Basic Books, New York.

Sedgwick, John (1995). Inside the Pioneer Fund. Russell Jacoby & Naomi Glauberman (Eds.) *The Bell Curve Debate: History, Documents and Opinions.* Time Books, New York, 144-161.

Schwartz, John E. (1983). *America's Hidden Success: A Reassessment of Twenty Years of Public Policy.* W. W. Norton, New York.

Scott, James C. (1990). *Domination and the Art of Resistance: Hidden Transcripts.* Yale University Press, New Haven.

Segal, Charles M. & Stineback, David C. (1977). *Puritans, Indians and Manifest Destiny.* G. P. Putnam's Sons, New York.

Selden, Steven (1999). *Inheriting Shame: The Story of Eugenics and Racism in America.* Teachers College, Columbia University, New York.

Semali, Ladislaus (1996). In the Name of Science and of Genetics and of the Bell Curve: White Supremacy in American Schools. Joe L. Kincheloe, Shirley R. Steinberg & Aaron D. Gresson III (Eds.) *Measured Lies: The Bell Curve Examined.* St. Martin's Press, New York, 161–175.

Shea, Christine M. (1989). Pentagon vs. Multinational Capitalism: The Political Economy of the 1980s School Reform Movement.

Christine M. Shea, Ernest Kahane & Peter Sola (Eds.) *The New Servants of Power: A Critique of the 1980s School Reform Movement.* Greenwood Press, New York.

Shujaa, Mwalimu J. (1994). Education and Schooling: You Can Have One Without the Other. Mwalimu J. Shujaa, (Ed.) *Too Muc Schooling Too Little Education: A Paradox of Black Life in White Societies.* Africa World Press, Trenton, 13–36.

Sleeter, Christine E. (1993). How White Teachers Construct Race. Cameron McCarthy & Warren Crichlow (Eds.) *Race Identity and Representation in Education.* Routledge, New York. 157-171.

Smedley, Audrey (1999). *Race in North America: Origin and Evolution of a Worldview* Westview Press, Boulder.

Smith, J. David (1993). *The Eugenic Assault on America: Scenes in Red, White and Black*. George Mason University Press, Fairfax.

Smith, John David (Ed.) (1993a). *Anti-Black Thought, 1863–1925*, Vol. III, *Van Evrie's White Supremacy and Negro Subordination: The New Proslavery Argument*, Part I. Garland Publishing, New York.

Smith, John David (Ed.) (1993b). *Anti-Black Thought, 1863–1925*, Vol. VIII, *Racial Determinism and the Fear of Miscegenation Post–1900*. Garland Publishing, New York.

Smith, John David (Ed.) (1993c). *Anti-Black Thought, 1863–1925*, Vol. IX, *Disfranchisement Proposals and the Klu Klux Klan: Solutions to the Negro Problem*, Part I. Garland Publishing, New York.

Smith, John David (ed.) (1993d). *Anti-Black Thought, 1863–1925*, Vol. X, *The American Colonization Society and Emigration: Solutions to the Negro Problem*, Part II. Garland Publishing, New York.

Smith, Linda Tuhiwai (1999). *Decolonizing Methodologies: Research and Indigenous Peoples*. Zed Books, London.

Smith, Roger M. (1995). *Civic Ideas: Conflicting Visions of Citizenship in U.S. History*. Yale University Press, New Haven.

Spears, John R. (1900). *The American Slave Trade: An Account of Its Origin, Growth and Suppression*. Corner House, Williamstown.

Spengler, Oswald (1928). *The Decline of the West*. Alfred. A. Knopf, New York.

Spivey, Donald (1978). *Schooling for the New Slavery: Black Industrial Education, 1868–1915*. Greenwood Press, Westport.

Spring, Joel (1994). *Deculturalization and the Struggle for Equality: A Brief History of the Education of Dominated Cultures in the United States*. McGraw-Hill, New York.

Spring, Joel (1997). *The American School, 1642–1996*. McGraw-Hill, New York.

Spring, Joel (2004). *The Intersection of Cultures:Multicultural Education in the United States and the Global Economy* McGraw-Hill, New York.

Spring, Joel (2005). *Conflict of Interests: the Politics of American Education*.McGraw-Hill, New York.

Stanfield, John H. (1985). *Philanthropy and Jim Crow in American Social Science*. Greenwood Press, Westport.

Staudenraus, P. J. (1961). *The African Colonization Movement, 1816- 1865*. Columbia University Press, New York.

Steinberg, Stephen (1995). *Turning Back: The Retreat from Racial* Justice in American Thought and Policy. Beacon Press, Boston.

Stern, Michael (1995). A Dystopian Fable. Russell Jacoby & Naomi Glauberman (Eds.) *The Bell Curve Debate: History, Documents and Opinions*. Time Books, New York, 115–118.

Stockwell, John (1978). *In Search of Enemies: A CIA Story*. W. W. Norton, New York.

Stoddard, Lothrop (1920). *The Rising Tide of Color Against White World-Supremacy*. Blue Ribbon Books, New York.

Stotsky, Sandra (1999). *Losing Our Language: How Multicultural Classroom Instruction is Undermining Our Children's Ability Read, Write, and Reason*. The Free Press, New York.

Sutch, Richard (1972). The Breeding of Slaves for Sale and the Westward Expansion of Slavery, 1850–1860. *Institute of Business and Economic Research*. University of California, Berkley, California.

Takaki, Ronald (1979). *Iron Cages: Race and Culture in 19th-Century America*. Oxford University Press, New York.

Thabit, Walter (2003). *How East New York Became a Ghetto*. New York University Press, New York.

Taylor, Howard F. (1995). The Bell Curve Symposium, *Contemporary Sociology*. 24, 153–158.

Thorndike, Edward L. (1927). *The Measurement of Intelligence*. Teacher's College, Columbia University, New York.

Thorndike, Edward L. (1940). *Human Nature and the Social Order*. Macmillan Company, New York.

Tice, Larry E. (1987). *Proslavery: A History of the Defense of Slavery in America, 1701–1840*. University of Georgia Press, Athens.

Tingling, Marion (1977). *The Correspondence of the Three William Byrds of Westover Virginia, 1684–1776*, Vol. II. University of Virginia Press, Charlottesville.

Tucker, William H. (1994). *The Science and Politics of Racial Research*. University of Illinois Press, Urbana.

Tumin, Melvin M. (1985). *Social Stratification: The Forms and Functions of Inequality*. Prentice-Hall, Englewood Cliffs.

Turner, Jonathan H.; Singleton, Royce, Jr.; & Musick, David (1984). *Oppression: A Socio-History of Black-White Relations in America*. Nelson-Hall, Chicago.

Tuttle, William, Jr. (1970). *Race Riot: Chicago in the Red Summer of 1919*. Atheneum, New York.

Van Deusen, Glyndon Garlock (1937). *The Life of Henry Clay*. Little, Brown & Company, Boston.

Van Evire, John H. (1863). *Negroes and Negro Slavery: the First an Inferior Race: the Latter its Normal Condition*. Van Evire, Horton & Company, New York.

Van Evire, John H. (1868). *White Supremacy and Negro Subordination: or Negroes a Subordinate Race and Slavery its Normal Condition*. Van Evire, Horton & Company, New York.

Vaughan, Alden T. (1996). *Roots of American Racism: Essays on the Colonial Experience*. Oxford University Press, New York.

Vidal, Maria R. (1996). Genetic Rationalizations and Public Policy: Herrnstein and Murray on Intelligence and Welfare Dependency. Joe L. Kincheloe, Shirley R. Steinberg & Aaron D. Gresson III (Eds.), *Measured Lies: The Bell Curve Examined*. St. Martin's Press, New York, 219–226.

Wade, Wyn Craig (1987). *The Fiery Cross: The Ku Klux Klan in America*. Simon & Schuster, New York.

Walker, David (1829). *David Walker's Appeal to the Coloured Citizens of the World, but in particular, and very expressly, to those of the United States of America*. 1993 reprint. Introduction by James Turner. Black Classic Press, Baltimore.

Ward, Robert De C. (1920). The Immigration Problem Today. *Journal of Heredity*, 11, 323-328.

Washington, Joseph R., Jr. (1967). *The Politics of God*. Beacon Press, Boston.

Washington, Joseph R., Jr. (1984). *Anti-Blackness in English Religion, 1500–1800*. Edwin Mellen Press, Lewiston.

Washington, Joseph R., Jr. (1988). *Race and Religion in Early Nineteenth Century America, 1800–1850: Constitution, Conscience, and Calvinist Compromise*, Vol. I. Edwin Mellen Press, Lewiston.

Watkins, William H. (2001). *White Architects of Black Education: Ideology and Power in America, 1865–1954*. Teachers College Press, New York.

Weindling, Paul (1985). Weimar Eugenics: The Kaiser Wilhelm Insitiute for Anthropology, Human Heredity and Eugenics in Social Context. *Annals of Science*, 42, 303–318.

Well-Barnett, Ida B. (1969). *On Lynching*. Arno Press, New York.

West, Cornel (1994). *Race Matters*. Vintage Books, New York.

Westergaard, John (1979). Power, Class and the Media. James Curran, Michael Gurevitch & Janet Woollacott (Eds.) *Mass Communication and Society*. Sage Publications, Beverly Hills, 95- 115.

White, Charles (1799). An Account of the Regular Graduation in Man and in Different Animals, and Vegetables, and From the Former to the Latter. Robert Bernasconi (Ed.) (2001). *Concepts of Race in the 18th Century*, Vol. VIII. Thoemmes Press, Bristol, England.

Wilhelm, Ronald (1994). Exploring the Practice-Rhetoric Gap: Current Curriculum for African-American History Month in Some Texas Elementary Schools, *Journal of Curriculum and Supervision*, 9, 217–233.

Wilkins, Roger (1984). Smiling Racism. The Nation. November, 437.

Wilmore, Gayraud S. (1996). Black Religion and Black Radicalism: An Interpretation of the Religious History of Afro-*American People*. Oribis Books, Maryknoll.

Wilmore, Gayraud S., and Cone, James H. (1979). *Black Theology: A Documentary History, 1966–1979*. Oribis Books, Maryknoll.

Wilmore, Gayraud S., and Cone, James H. (1993). *Black Theology: A Documentary History*, Vol. II, *1980–1992*. Oribis Books, Maryknoll.

Wilson, Carter A. (1996). *Racism: From Slavery to Capitalism*. Sage Publications, Thousand Oaks.

Wood, Forrest G. (1970). *Black Scare: The Racist Response to Emancipation and Reconstruction*. University of California Press, Berkeley.

Wood, Forrest G. (1990). *The Arrogance of Faith: Christianity and Race in America from the Colonial Era to the Twentieth Century*. Alfred A. Knopf, New York.

Wuthenau, Alexander von (1992). Unexpected African Faces in Pre- Columbian America. Ivan Van Sertima (ed.), *African Presence in Early America*. Transaction Publishers, New Brunswick, 82-101.

Yeo, Frederick L. (1997). *Inner-City Schools, Multiculturalism, and Teacher Education*. Garland Publishing, New York.

Young, Iris Marion (1990). *Justice and the Politics of Difference*. Princeton University Press, Princeton.

Zinn, Howard (1995). *A People's History of the United States, 1492- Present*, revised and updated edition. Harper Perennial, New York.

Zweigenhaft, Richard L., & Domhoff, William G. (1991). *Blacks in the White Establishment? A Study of Race and Class in America*. Yale University Press, New Haven.

Studies in the Postmodern Theory of Education

General Editors
Joe L. Kincheloe & Shirley R. Steinberg

Counterpoints publishes the most compelling and imaginative books being written in education today. Grounded on the theoretical advances in criticalism, feminism, and postmodernism in the last two decades of the twentieth century, Counterpoints engages the meaning of these innovations in various forms of educational expression. Committed to the proposition that theoretical literature should be accessible to a variety of audiences, the series insists that its authors avoid esoteric and jargonistic languages that transform educational scholarship into an elite discourse for the initiated. Scholarly work matters only to the degree it affects consciousness and practice at multiple sites. Counterpoints' editorial policy is based on these principles and the ability of scholars to break new ground, to open new conversations, to go where educators have never gone before.

For additional information about this series or for the submission of manuscripts, please contact:

Joe L. Kincheloe & Shirley R. Steinberg
c/o Peter Lang Publishing, Inc.
275 Seventh Avenue, 28th floor
New York, New York 10001

To order other books in this series, please contact our Customer Service Department:

(800) 770-LANG (within the U.S.)
(212) 647-7706 (outside the U.S.)
(212) 647-7707 FAX

Or browse online by series:

www.peterlangusa.com